THE POLITICS OF SACRED SPACE

F SACRED SPACE

The Old City of Jerusalem
in the Middle East Conflict

Michael Dumper

LYNNE
RIENNER
PUBLISHERS

BOULDER
LONDON

Published in the United States of America in 2002 by
Lynne Rienner Publishers, Inc.
1800 30th Street, Boulder, Colorado 80301
www.rienner.com

and in the United Kingdom by
Lynne Rienner Publishers, Inc.
3 Henrietta Street, Covent Garden, London WC2E 8LU

Library of Congress Cataloging-in-Publication Data
Dumper, Michael.
    The politics of sacred space : the old city of Jerusalem in the Middle East conflict /
Michael Dumper.
        p. cm.
    Includes bibliographical references (p.)
    ISBN 1-58826-016-X (alk. paper)
    1. Jerusalem—Politics and government—20th century.   2. Jerusalem—Ethnic
relations.   3. Jerusalem—International status.   4. Arab-Israeli conflict—1993—Peace.
I. Title.

DS109.94.D87   2002
956.94'4205—dc21

                                                                          2001041793

British Cataloguing in Publication Data
A Cataloguing in Publication record for this book
is available from the British Library.

Printed and bound in the United States of America

⊗   The paper used in this publication meets the requirements
    of the American National Standard for Permanence of
    Paper for Printed Library Materials Z39.48-1984.

5   4   3   2   1

For Rowan

Contents

Illustrations

Maps

Tables

Acknowledgments

Research for this book has spanned more than a decade, during which time I met, had long discussions with, and formally interviewed scores of people. It is not possible to list all those who helped and guided me. However, I must single out a handful of people who were always extremely generous with their time and encouragement of my work: Adnan Husseini, Yusuf Natshe, Nazmi Ju'beh, Kevork Hintlian, and Yitzhak Reiter. To them, many many thanks. Nevertheless, as much as I may have been influenced by our discussions together, all the views expressed in this work are my own.

I must also thank my head of department, Iain Hampsher-Monk, for continuing to support some research expenses even after it was clear that this book would not meet the deadline for the 2001 Research Assessment Exercise in the UK. For his moral and material support in this way, I am very grateful. I would like to thank Alexandra Malm-Howarth for her assistance in collecting some of the data and preparing the manuscript. She worked uncomplainingly and conscientiously in trying to meet ridiculous deadlines at very short notice.

Finally, I need to thank Ann for keeping my feet on the ground, providing the perfect environment in which to work, and accepting my frequent absences with grace and humor despite the additional burden it placed on her.

—*M. D.*

1

Introduction:
Studying the Old City of Jerusalem

The Old City of Jerusalem is a study of political tectonics. It straddles the cusp of two climatic regions, where the Mediterranean climate of the coastal plain climbs the mountainous Judean ridges to meet the desert heat of the Arabian hinterland. It lies directly on the border running through Arab East Jerusalem and Israeli West Jerusalem, drawn up following the war of 1948 between Israelis and Palestinians and the Arab states (see Map 1.1). It is where the Orient meets the Occident, where not one but two peoples have declared it the capital of their state, and where not two but three world religions meet, share, and compete over access to holy sites and their interpretation of the divine (see Map 1.2). Parts of the Old City are reminiscent of monasteries and villages in the highlands of mainland Greece. In certain parts you can be forgiven in thinking yourself in Cairo or Damascus, and in other parts you have no doubt that you are witnessing a resurgent Judaism and that you are in modern-day Israel.

Given this heterogeneity and this multiplicity of interfaces, it is hardly surprising that the Old City is also the crucible of conflict and animosity. A number of images will help set the scene. Walking through the Muslim quarters at dusk, while the Maghreb prayer is being conducted, you will see the silver dome of al-Aqsa Mosque being lit up, and hear the little prayer rooms squeezed between the shutting shops hum with muttered invocations. If you are observant you can also see small knots of Israeli schoolchildren moving purposefully and quickly. They do not stop to play, to point out curiosities to each other, or to buy from the sweet shops and peddlers. Their heads are down and their conversations muted. You will also notice that there are at least two armed escorts with them wearing yarmulkes, whispering into their walkie-talkies and keeping a vigilant eye on the atmosphere of the street around them. Later on, around midnight, you will see the same young men on the streets and alleyways, still armed but more relaxed, joking and chatting to each other, aware that the danger

1

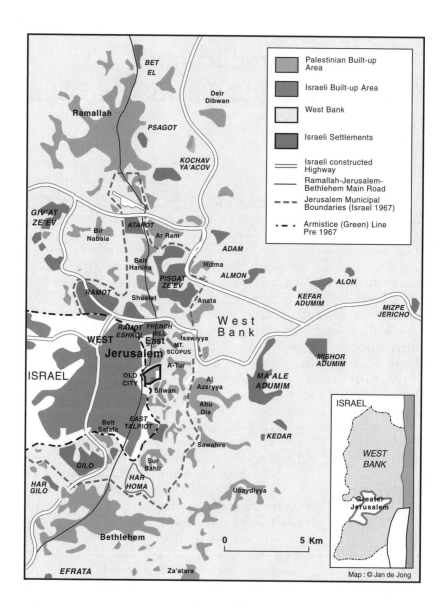

Map 1.1   Jerusalem Today

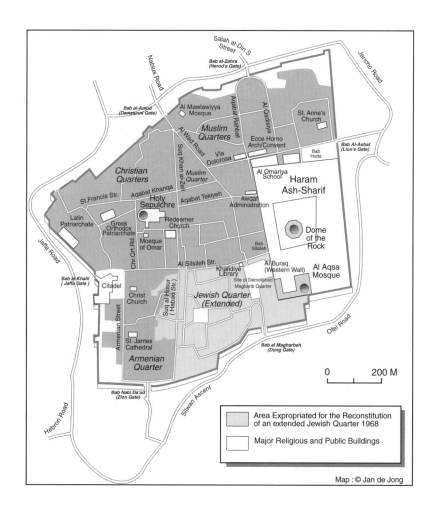

Map 1.2   The Old City of Jerusalem

of the day has passed (at night very few Palestinians venture outside their courtyard houses). These are the Israeli settlers in the Old City, escorting children from their residences in the Muslim quarters to schools in the Jewish Quarter by day, roaming the streets by night to assert their presence. Their movements are electronically monitored and directed from a command room in the heart of a Palestinian area that they would most like to acquire.

A second image is from within the Christian quarters. A procession is taking place from a monastery in one corner of the Old City to the Church of the Holy Sepulchre, perhaps half a mile away. The black-robed monks lead the procession, followed by members of the lay community singing hymns and chants. Sundry passers-by and tourists attach themselves to this colorful and solemn movement. Suddenly, thirty young men from a smaller Christian denomination confront the procession. There is pushing. Sticks and bars are brandished, accompanied by shouts and hisses. The monks remain impassive, but their followers hurl abuse and accusations of collaboration with the Israeli government at their opponents. The Israeli police are nowhere to be seen. A fight is just about to ensue when the leader of the monks is able to persuade the leaders of the opposing group that a meeting with their bishop has been arranged, and the dispute over precedence in the Holy Sepulchre will be resolved. The crowd gradually and reluctantly dissolves. The monks, more subdued now, proceed on their way, but the tension in the quarter remains.

A third image is set in the offices of the principal Islamic institution in the Old City, the Islamic Trust, also known as the Awqaf Administration. Climbing up its rust-colored wide stone steps, polished from a hundred years of use, and through the green marble portals, you enter a high and long antechamber from which dozens of rooms can be reached. The acoustics are appalling. Conversations emanating from the clusters of men in *kafiya*s (head scarves) seated along the wall reverberate and amplify, deafening any new arrivals. Inside the chief engineer's office, there is a furious argument ensuing.

The Awqaf Administration's architects and archaeologists have been restoring a former Mamluk palace to its formal glory. Cleaning the facade to reveal its black and white joggling and carved friezes, removing later concrete accretions, retiling the inner courtyard, and tidying up and concealing the ugly tangle of electricity and telephone lines and water and waste piping has been expensive and time-consuming. In all this, by dint of patient consultation and negotiation, they have received the cooperation of several large families who have squeezed into the former palace rooms. But the residents have unanimously and categorically refused to allow the removal of the concrete breeze-block washroom in the corner of the inner courtyard, thereby destroying the aesthetically pleasing view of the inner courtyard and obscuring the beautifully restored *mihrab* (prayer niche).

The Awqaf Administration's team is despairing. In their view, the whole purpose of the restoration project is compromised and the funds wasted. To the residents, never normally agreeing among themselves to anything, the convenience of the courtyard washroom is paramount. Aesthetic considerations appear nowhere close to the top of their concerns. In any case, which family is going to sacrifice its own space for communal ablutions? They threaten to make trouble by appealing to the project funders, the Jordanian Ministry of Waqfs in Amman, or by asking the Fatah (the reverse acronym for Harakat al-Tahrir al-Filastin) faction of the Palestine Liberation Organization (PLO) to intercede, or by calling upon the Planning Department of the Israeli Jerusalem Municipality to block the washroom's removal. The chief engineer has been asked to mediate, and amid the rising crescendo of threats and angry voices swirling around him, he is thinking deeply. Finally, a decision is made. In the interests of the long-term continuation of the restoration program, the cooperation of the residents of the Muslim quarters is essential. Because the palace has been already restored for posterity, the washroom can stay. For the time being.

What these three images are intended to convey is the complexity of relations in the Old City. It is a complexity born of the long history of the place with countless inter- as well as intracommunal disputes over the ages. In addition, the complexity stems from the central role the city has played in the Palestine-Israel conflict, with national, regional, and international political forces all playing their part. Most observers of the conflict will agree on the centrality of Jerusalem in the current Middle East peace negotiations. A quick review of diplomatic developments will clearly show this. From the Madrid Peace Conference in 1991, when Palestinians and Israelis first sat down for face-to-face talks, through to the Oslo Accords in 1993, and on to the current impasse, the issue of Jerusalem has both been the major obstacle and the key to progress in an agreement.

It was the Israeli Likud Party's aversion to including Jerusalem on the negotiating agenda during the Washington talks following the Madrid conference that led to the collapse of the Israeli National Unity government in 1992. Secret negotiations culminated in the Oslo Accords between Israel and the PLO in September 1993. It was partly through the Palestinian concession to keep Jerusalem out of the proposed interim phase and the Israeli concession to accept its inclusion on the agenda of the permanent status talks that the Oslo Accords were concluded. Finally, even since the Oslo Accords, Jerusalem has proved the issue over which the peace process is put in jeopardy. The Israeli intention to construct a completely new settlement on the outskirts of Jerusalem (Jabal al-Ghaneim, or Har Homa) followed hard on the opening of the Hasmonean Tunnel in 1996 close to the Islamic holy place of Haram ash-Sharif. The Palestinians perceived both these steps as a deliberate attempt to alter the status quo prior to permanent status talks and directly caused the breakdown in the negotiations between the two sides.

In July 2000, a summit was held between U.S president Bill Clinton, Israeli prime minister Ehud Barak, and Palestinian president Yasser Arafat at Camp David. It lasted for an unprecedented marathon of thirteen days before collapsing. All observers agree that though there were no dramatic breakthroughs on the other Permanent Status Issues, it was the Jerusalem issue, together with that of refugees, that proved to be the most difficult and ultimately the most defeating of issues. Finally, in September 2000, a heavily armed visit to the Islamic shrine of the Haram ash-Sharif compound— site of the Dome of the Rock and al-Aqsa—by the Likud Party leader, Ariel Sharon, provoked a violent clash, leaving six Palestinians dead. It led to a renewed intifada (uprising) with weeks of rioting throughout the West Bank, Gaza Strip, and in Israel itself, with the loss of 600 lives and more than 5,000 injured, and was dubbed the "al-Aqsa Intifada." The intifada, in turn, led to the collapse of the Barak premiership and his replacement by Sharon himself.

Since the Oslo Accords, there has been a spate of new publications on Jerusalem, reflecting a recognition of its centrality in the peace negotiations; but despite this fact, there are three main reasons for writing yet another book, which I will discuss next.

First, while not denying the centrality of Jerusalem as a whole, it is the underlying contention of this book that the imperfect implementation of the Oslo Accords has changed the issues that need to be researched. It is the Old City of Jerusalem that should now be the focus of greater study. It is becoming increasingly clear what the rough contours of a settlement over Jerusalem will look like. Palestinian aspirations for the future of the city will be heavily circumscribed by Israel's perceived security needs, which in turn are supported by the U.S. government, the principal enforcer behind the Oslo process.

To restate this more concretely, Palestinian hopes for a complete Israeli withdrawal to the 1967 borders of Jerusalem have become increasingly unlikely since the interim phase. Immediately following an agreement, the most they may be able to secure is a significant foothold in the eastern part of the city within a framework of shared or devolved municipal functions. An agreement may also include the cession of Israeli sovereignty over predominantly Jewish areas, but these will be phased in over a long period of time and are likely to be contingent on other issues.

As can be seen by the precedents set in the West Bank, particularly in Hebron and the Gaza Strip, in the current balance of power, Israel is most likely to retain overall security and access controls in Jerusalem. However, the Palestinian architects of the Oslo process intended that there be a more equitable outcome; the lack of leverage on the part of the Palestinian, Arab, and Islamic side has meant that Israeli concerns have taken priority. As a result, the focus of debate has shifted to the intractable part of the issue of Jerusalem, that is, of the Old City and the holy sites within it. For it is here that the scenario of Palestinian sovereignty within a framework of Israeli security priorities outlined above is the most difficult to apply.

Most of the more promising proposals for the future of the city have alluded to the Old City and the administration of the holy sites being accorded some sort of special status or regime. These have ranged from internationalization to extraterritorialization to a shared administration by a religious council and are discussed in greater detail in Chapter 6. In this book, I argue that these regimes are no longer feasible. First, as a result of the activities of the Israeli settlers in the Old City, the opportunity for a special regime that would recognize the religious, ethnic, and national-residential patterns in the Old City has almost passed. It would take enormous political will on the part of an Israeli government to reverse the gains made by the settlers in taking over properties throughout the Old City. The precedent set by the handling of the settlers in Hebron by past and present Israeli governments attests to this view. Also, the lack of cooperation between the religious leaderships both within their own communities and across sectarian boundaries does not indicate that a shared administrative framework is viable.

In redirecting the focus of study in this way, I clearly run the risk of affirming and contributing, at least intellectually, to the trend that runs against Palestinian interests and may be accused of providing support to an Israeli perspective for a solution. This is certainly not my intention here. Rather, I am aware, from many years of research and teaching of the Jerusalem issue and participation in several study groups and workshops with Israelis and Palestinians, how much research is still required, at least on the Palestinian side, to provide the basic data for negotiations.[1] The projected shift of political and diplomatic focus to the Old City will require a complementary shift in academic research. If the prognosis outlined above is correct, extensive and intensive discussion will center on questions of shared administration of certain holy sites, of pilgrim quotas, property ownership and use, rights of access, and reparation. In the absence of a special regime, there will also be a need to discuss, unfortunately, the partition of the Old City in ways that satisfy both national and sectarian concerns. Focusing entirely on the Old City, my attempt in this book is to point to the hitherto unrecognized difficulties that lay ahead and to outline some of the issues that need to be resolved in the Old City before a negotiated solution can be achieved.

Irrespective of this change in the perceived crux of the Jerusalem issue, the second reason for my writing this book is the absence of studies on the Old City itself. Since 1993, there have been several new political studies on the Jerusalem issue, but the focus of these has been mainly on the metropolitan area of Jerusalem under which the Old City is generally subsumed. There have also been numerous publications on particular aspects of Jerusalem. These include histories of specific religious communities, architectural surveys, sociological and anthropological studies, and in-depth site descriptions for the serious traveler.[2] There have also been a number of polemic and journalistic accounts. Yet there is not a single study in the English language that analyzes the sectarian dynamics of the Old City in terms that relate it to the politics of the Palestinian-Israeli conflict and the peace negotiations. This is partly due to the complexity of the subject. Although the Old City constitutes a smaller geographical area than the whole of municipal and metropolitan Jerusalem, it nevertheless presents a formidable subject for serious research.

Furthermore, there is the problem of access to documents and personalities. The ethnic, national, and religious background of a scholar may open doors to one or possibly two of the religious communities, but it will be a fortunate and exceptional scholar who can overcome the caution or suspicion of all three. Gaining access to relevant documents and people of even one community is difficult enough. One needs introductions to key people and a track record of scholarly professionalism. The prospect of obtaining only a partial picture, due to the lack of access to all the parties across the political and religious divide, is a great dissuader to in-depth research. I have labored under such disadvantages. However, as a one-time resident of the city and a frequent visitor for more than fifteen years, together with a record of research on both religious and political aspects of Jerusalem, it seemed that I was adequately placed to attempt to carry out such a project.

In addition to both the political trends that indicate the growing importance of the Old City as a subject of study and the absence of any available literature, there is yet a third, more academic reason why the Old City merits a study in its own right. The Old City comprises a series of overlapping quasi-autonomous religious administrations that distinguish it from the rest of Jerusalem. Its "holiness" suggests a special kind of political and geographical entity. The Old City also plays a distinctive role in the mythology and ideology of the parties involved in the Arab-Israeli conflict and is a unique legal enclave in the Israeli polity. These features suggest that both within Jerusalem itself and between Jerusalem and the Israeli and Palestinian state apparatuses, an unusual relationship exists that requires special and more detailed attention.

This aspect of the study touches upon a wider academic issue, namely, that of the relationship between holy cities and the modern state in general. The relationship between holy cities and central and local government is both a theoretically underdeveloped and underresearched area. While there can be little dispute that holy cities exist, such as Varanasi, Lourdes, Rome, Mecca, Medina, Qom, and Najaf, a consistent definition is elusive, and there have been no attempts to construct a taxonomy. Is the mere quantity of holy sites—such as places of worship, mausoleums, shrines, tombs, seminaries, monasteries, and convents—an adequate indication of a holy city? If not, how does one measure "holiness"? By the number of pilgrims, citations in religious texts, wealth derived from religious activity, the number of persons employed by religious administrations? In addition, how does one define the space between the holy sites themselves? Holy cities are sacred spaces whose holiness is derived from more than the mere accumulation of sites, that is, the holiness of a city is greater than the sum of its holy parts.

Despite these difficulties, one can, nevertheless, distinguish holy cities by four main elements. First, they support an institutional religious hierarchy often graced by the presence of leading clerics who have considerable political influence, locally, nationally, and regionally. Second, holy cities have an administrative apparatus controlling large swathes of property as well as religious, welfare, and educational services that provide the clerics and senior functionaries with an important local constituency and undergird a communal identity. Third, they have an independent financial base in the form of endowments and donations. This allows holy cities to absorb external funds independent of the strength or weakness of the local economy, which, in turn, allows them to finance religious personnel and projects relatively free from state intervention. Finally, they can point to an important network of diasporic and international contacts built up through pilgrimage and educational activities. Such contacts and interactions offer a degree of protection to the clergy and their administrations and can strengthen their immunity from state intervention. Taking all these aspects together, one can see how the sovereignty of a state is to a considerable extent circumscribed in a holy city.

Thus, a comparative study of Jerusalem and Rome, for example, would yield some useful insights into the limits of state sovereignty over the local and municipal governance of those cities as a result of the presence of holy sites.[3] However, such a study is beyond the scope of this book but is intended to be the subject of another research project of mine. Nevertheless, this book will recognize that the special features of a holy city outlined above do present themselves in Jerusalem and contribute significantly to the dynamics within the Old City. For example, an examination of the preeminent Muslim institution in the Old City of Jerusalem, the Awqaf Administration, along the lines of those four factors cited above, would reveal the following:

1. There is a clerical hierarchy including a mufti whose influence for Muslims extends beyond the confines of Jerusalem to the whole of historic Palestine and to some extent into the Mashrik region, the East Mediterranean littoral.
2. There is an administrative structure responsible for the greater pro-portion of property in the Old City and large stretches outside.
3. There is some internally generated income derived from rents, fees, and endowments in the form of *waqf*s, as well as from external donations and subventions.
4. There is an international network that places a protective cloak over the Islamic land and properties.

The political implications of this are plain: Since the Israeli occupation of the Old City in 1967, the holiness of Jerusalem and the Old City has played a direct and crucial role in preserving an Islamic and Palestinian presence in the Old City in the face of persistent Israeli attempts at colo-nization and absorption. The particular fascination of Jerusalem as a holy city, however, is its uniqueness as the locus of holiness for *three* religions, not just one, all of which share those elements of holiness described above.

This struggle over the Old City and between the three religious com-munities can be studied in several ways. For example, it can be studied in hegemonic terms in that the struggle can be seen as both territorial and cul-tural or ideological. It is territorial in the sense of a struggle over access to specific sites and over control over property and land. Whose rights have precedence over shared holy sites? Whose legal authority determines the interactions between religious landlord and tenant? Yet it is cultural and ideological because the struggle is also over the character and meaning of the Old City. Is its ambience Jewish, Christian, or Muslim? Whose reli-gious festivals receive precedence? Is it an Arab-Islamic city or an exotic religious enclave within a modern Israeli city? What place does it hold in the life of the international religious communities that form its spiritual hinterland?

The Old City can also be studied in terms of its political economy. Here is a unique district of a burgeoning modern city, coveted by powerful religious groups and political entities. Real estate values, rents, fees, and retail revenues would all be reflecting supply and demand factors. A study in the political economy of the Old City would trace the distortion of mar-ket forces by political exigencies and a skewed legal framework. Despite the rhetoric of ownership and belonging, the uncertainty of the future of the

Old City casts a huge economic blight over it. As a result, private enterprise lacked sufficient guarantees for a decent return on investment. Therefore, any major investment was direct government aid, municipal investment, or the subsidy of quasi-public bodies such as religious institutions. In the early 1980s, an ideologically directed Israeli settler movement seeking to capitalize on a supportive legal system and low property values was able to mobilize sufficient funds to acquire properties throughout the Old City. Their activities coincided with and perhaps precipitated the increase in subventions to the Awqaf Administration for its extensive restoration program. Together they altered the blighted nature of the Old City. This line of argument would seek to demonstrate that what we are witnessing today in the Old City is, in effect, the marshaling of economic forces along ethnonationalistic lines to secure territorial control over the sacred space.

A final example is that it can be studied in terms of levels of interaction. The first level is the lower level of struggle and competition that reflects the internal fragmentation and division of the main religious communities into denominations, factions, and sects. An example of this is the suspicion and jockeying for position between the three leading Christian patriarchates over their preeminence vis-à-vis the practice of certain rituals in the Holy Sepulchre or vis-à-vis the secular authorities (see Chapter 5). Similar rivalries can also be found within the Jewish and Muslim communities, notably the intense competition between different Hassidic sects over control of the rituals around the Western (Wailing) Wall, and the attempts by the Palestinian wing of the Muslim Brotherhood, Hamas, and the Hizb al-Tahrir (Party of Liberation, also known as the Tahriris) to infiltrate and influence the activities of the Awqaf Administration.

The level most clearly visible to the general public is the second, or middle, level of rivalry and competition between the three main religious communities—Jewish, Christian, and Muslim. This level, seen through much media and political attention, focuses mainly on the territorial, that is, the access to and the administration and ownership of particular sites. These projects include the tunneling work under the Muslim quarters carried out by the Israeli Ministry of Religious Affairs, unilateral restoration work carried out by the Islamic Endowments Administration (Awqaf Administration), and the construction of apartments in one of the monasteries in the Christian quarters.

A higher level of contest and struggle is the third level. It encompasses the interests of neighboring states, other regional powers, and international players. Historically there has been great concern by outside parties in any significant shifts in the balance of religious power and control over the Christian Holy Places. The Crimean War (1853–1866) and the subsequent Capitulation Treaties that ceded powers of protection to European states and to Russia over the Christian communities in Palestine are the most obvious examples of this osmotic relationship between the external and internal politics of Jerusalem and the region. More recently, one can point to the huge support given to their respective communities in the city by the Islamic Conference Organization and the World Zionist Organization. The existence of these three levels of contest and struggle make it very difficult for an outside researcher to follow all the twists and turns over the past three decades of Israeli rule in the Old City. Furthermore, from time to time the dynamics of other levels impinge on each other. For example, the signing of the Memorandum of Understanding between Israel and the Holy See (the Vatican) in 1994 is an example of a higher-level interaction. But it impinged on the lowest level in that it caused considerable anger and resentment in the other Christian sects, as it was seen as an attempt by the Catholic community to improve its position at the expense of the other communities (see Chapter 5).

In this book, I study the struggle over the Old City using as my main focus the middle level of interaction. Although the Palestinian-Israeli conflict is primarily an ethnonationalistic conflict with some confessional overtones, in the struggle over the Old City confessional issues are more prominent. It is my contention that by focusing on the relationships between the three main religious communities within the Old City, the underlying political dynamics that have impeded the peace negotiations can be fully revealed. In addition, an analysis based on the middle level of interactions puts the researcher in a better position to examine the impact on both the higher and lower levels.

Three main actors are examined in this study, one from each of the religious communities: the Israeli settler groups, the Awqaf Administration, and the Christian patriarchates. These actors have been selected for two reasons. First, they are indicative of the main activities of that community in the Old City; and second, they are in the forefront of the interface between the three communities—not only institutionally but also on a day-to-day level. Clearly, other actors such as the Israeli and Jordanian states and the PLO and the Palestinian National Authority (PNA), among others, have played an important part. Reference and some analysis will be given to their respective roles. But the focus of this study is the political interaction in the Old City of religious forces and their component parts. Each of the main actors will be dealt with in a separate chapter, Chapters 3, 4, and 5, allowing an in-depth analysis of their activities and role in the Old City. Prior to these chapters, Chapter 2 discusses the political context in which the main actors operate. Finally, Chapter 6 brings together all the material and links it to the evolution and future of the peace negotiations.

The period under review is from the Israeli occupation of the Old City in 1967 to the present. The main features of this period for the purposes of this study are the gradual transition from Israeli Labour Party dominance and the heyday of the Israeli mayor, Teddy Kollek, to a period of Likud Party dominance and the rise of the Israeli settler groups in the Old City. In addition, a major change took place during the mid-1980s, which saw a Palestinian renaissance, particularly after the intifada and the establishment of the PNA following the Oslo Accords.

The area under study is the Old City within the walls. It, therefore, excludes Israeli West Jerusalem, Palestinian East Jerusalem, and Israeli settlements in East Jerusalem. This has the advantage of a clearly defined geographic area. However, there are drawbacks. Much of what goes on in the rest of Jerusalem and its hinterland affects the Old City. The closure of Jerusalem to West Bank and Gaza Strip Palestinians has a direct impact upon the economy and the political and religious life of the Old City. Similarly, one cannot fully grasp the extent of the activities of the Israeli settlers unless one is aware of their objectives in relation to the government-built settlements in East Jerusalem or of their acquisition program in areas abutting the Old City, such as Silwan, Sheikh Jarrah, and Ras al-Amud. In the same way, the demographic realities in the Old City need to be understood in relation to the wider patterns in the city. Thus, while the focus will firmly remain on the Old City, certain relevant broader issues will also be discussed.

Additionally, it is important to make clear that the current delineation of the Old City into four confessional quarters—Jewish Quarter, Muslim quarters, Christian quarters, and Armenian Quarter—is a recent twentieth-century development (see Table 1.1).

The boundaries and nomenclature were instituted by the British during the mandate era (1922–1948) to maintain an equilibrium between the populations of those communities centered on their holy sites. Communal solidarities stretched across geographical and confessional borders, and interactions in the Old City were fluid and unconstrained by administrative

Table 1.1 Area of the Old City

Quarter	Area (*dunams*)	Percentage
Muslim quarters, including the		
Haram ash-Sharif compound	438	50.3
Jewish Quarter	130	14.9
Armenian Quarter	123	14.1
Christian quarters	180	20.7
Total	871	100.0

Source: Taken from the Welfare Association, *Jerusalem Old City Revitalisation Plan, Interim Summary Report,* 1999, 17.

Note: Four *dunams* is roughly equal to 1 acre.

demarcations. One striking example of this was the construction of *mikvaot*, or Jewish ritual baths, within the Muslim-owned *hammam*, or public baths.[4] Furthermore, the officially designated quarters did not match the spatial geography of the much smaller and more cohesive networks of family alliances that constituted the social and political life of the Old City. As Salim Tamari has written in his commentary on a recently unearthed diary on the social mores of the mandate period:

> There was no delineation between neighbourhood and religion; we see a substantial intermixing of religious groups in each quarter. The boundaries of habitat, furthermore, were the *mahallat*, the neighbourhood network of social demarcations within which a substantial amount of communal solidarity is exhibited.[5]

Participation in each other's religious festivities and ceremonies, including weddings and funerals, were ways in which these solidarities were expressed. Yet in discussing the post-1967 situation, the problem of terminology remains. The demarcation of the Jewish Quarter by the Israeli state is not simply the Jewish Quarter as it existed prior to 1948 but twice the area including the Hara al-Magharib, which was razed immediately following the 1967 war. This expansion was achieved by administrative fiat and has not been accepted by those Palestinians and Armenians who lost their properties. For the purposes of this book, this area is referred to as the "enlarged Jewish Quarter" to reflect the contentious and changing nature of the area in question (see Map 1.2).

The officially labeled Muslim and Christian quarters also require some qualification. In these quarters, the pattern of residence presents a mixed picture. Most Christians—Palestinian, Arab, or otherwise—in the Old City live in the so-called Christian quarters, but so do many Muslims.[6] Indeed, most of the retail properties are rented or owned by Muslims. Likewise, the so-called Muslim quarters are predominantly inhabited by Muslims, but this would be to overlook the significant collection of churches, convents, and hostels located there and, more important, the Via Dolorosa, which wends its way through the Muslim areas. In addition, these two quarters comprise many smaller quarters or *hara* (Arabic for quarter), such as Bab al-Hutta or Bab al-Wad, which make up the daily discourse in referring to geographical areas in the Old City. In light of these considerations, references to these areas will be to the Christian quarter*s* and Muslim quarter*s* (lower case and in the plural) to indicate the subordinate units within them and their lack of homogeneity. The label Armenian Quarter is less problematic. It includes the Monastery of St. James and the property it owns surrounding the monastery. Although the Armenian Quarter is much more homogeneous than the Christian and Muslim quarters, it must be remembered that many Armenian properties adjacent to the traditional Jewish Quarter were expropriated by the Israeli government when it was enlarged in 1968.

Following this brief overview, it should be evident that the Old City is a site of enormous religious, political, and academic complexity. A closer study of its internal dynamics and their impact upon the negotiations between Israelis and Palestinians will without doubt provide some valuable insights into the negotiations themselves and, it is hoped, will help to clarify some of the underlying issues. Before turning to the three key actors in the politics of the Old City identified above, let us explore in more detail the legal and political developments that provide the overarching context to the conflict.

Notes

1. The Israeli side has made great efforts through a number of institutions to collect the required data to discuss options in detail. Chief among these is the Jerusalem Institute for Israel Studies. Over the past decade a team of researchers selected from academia, the government, and the Israeli Jerusalem Municipality have been working on different aspects, from municipal frameworks to cultural and religious issues. The Truman Institute of the Hebrew University of Jerusalem and the Jaffee Centre in Tel Aviv University have also sponsored useful studies and seminars. In contrast, the lack of preparation and expertise is a major contributing factor to the minimal gains obtained by the Palestinian side. The chief danger in this lack of preparation is that unnecessary concessions may be made or positions become entrenched around issues that are not of lasting importance. Indeed, the lack of information and analysis of long-term issues may lead to a retreat into rhetoric and ultimately to further confrontation. More recently, a number of Palestinian think-tanks, researchers, and research centers in Jerusalem have started to produce their own work. Most of these studies recycle existing material and are short on specifics. For example, the work of Jerusalem Media and Communications Centre, Palestinian Academic Society for the Study of International Affairs, and LAW tend to focus on Israeli transgressions and less on alternative futures. But more recently there have been some notable exceptions. The International Peace and Co-operation Centre has produced the most useful evidence-based work, but unfortunately many of its studies are not yet publicly available. In 2001, Orient House, the Arab Studies Society, and the Legal Support Unit of the Negotiations Department have begun drafting important documentation to support a number of different negotiating positions.

2. See, for example, K. Al-'Asali, ed., *Jerusalem in History* (London: Scorpion, 1989); V. Azarya, *The Armenian Quarter of Jerusalem* (Berkeley and London: University of California Press, 1984); Y. Ben Arieh, *Jerusalem in the 19th Century: Emergence of the New City* (New York: St. Martin's Press, 1989); Y. Ben Arieh, *Jerusalem in the 19th Century: The Old City* (New York: St. Martin's Press, 1984); M. Burgoyne, *Mamluk Jerusalem: An Architectural Study* (London: World of Islam Trust, 1987); Y. Reiter, *Islamic Institutions in Jerusalem: Palestinian Muslim Organization Under Jordanian and Israeli Rule* (The Hague: Kluwer Law

International, 1997); and D. Tsimhoni, *Christian Communities in Jerusalem and the West Bank Since 1948: An Historical, Social, and Political Study* (Westport, Conn.: Praeger, 1993).

3. See the useful and pathbreaking comparative study by F. E. Peters, *Jerusalem and Mecca: A Typology of Holy City in the Near East* (New York: New York University Press, 1986).

4. An example of this phenomenon is in the Hammam al-'Ayn, a *waqf* of the Khalidi family, in the Tariq al-Wad.

5. S. Tamari, "Jerusalem's Ottoman Modernity: The Times and Lives of Wasif Jawhariyyeh," *Jerusalem Quarterly File*, no. 9 (summer 2000): 8.

6. See Table 2.2 in Chapter 2.

2

The Background to the Struggle

On 7 June 1967, Israeli armed forces captured Jerusalem. In a broadcast on the same day, the Israeli chief of staff, General Moshe Dayan, announced:

> We have united Jerusalem, the divided capital of Israel. We have returned to the most sacred of our Holy Places, never to part from it again. To our Arab neighbours we stretch out, again at this hour—and with added emphasis—the hand of peace. And to our Christian and Moslem fellow-citizens we solemnly promise religious freedom and rights. We came to Jerusalem not to possess ourselves of the Holy Places of others, or to interfere with the members of other faiths, but to safeguard the City's integrity and to live in it with others in unity.[1]

Thus began the long period of Israeli rule over Palestinian East Jerusalem. It was a period that saw the transformation of the eastern sector of the city from an almost completely Palestinian and Arab city to one that, by the end of the twentieth century, had equal numbers of Palestinians and Israelis. It was also a period that in Israeli and some Christian circles began with much hope for a new era of religious cooperation. Whatever the outcome of the current conflict and negotiation over Jerusalem, it is clear that the Israeli era of domination is over and that new arrangements and accommodations have to be put in place.

In this chapter, I outline the main developments that both transformed the city and brought to a close the Israeli era. The chapter is divided into two parts. The first part deals with the holy sites, in particular. It begins with a brief discussion of the principal legislative actions affecting the holy sites in Jerusalem and the Old City. This is followed by a discussion on the lack of clarity in the usage of terms such as *holy places* and *Status Quo*, both in the legislation and in the subsequent practice. Another section examines the administration of the holy places under Israeli rule. The second part of the chapter outlines the wider social and political developments

17

that impinge on the holy sites and their supporting religious communities. It describes a number of demographic, planning, and social policy issues that affect the life of the communities in the Old City before going on to look at the political changes brought about by the beginning of the peace negotiations after the Madrid conference in 1991.

Holy Sites

Legal Framework

On 27 June 1991, the Knesset enacted three laws that were to affect the juridical status of Jerusalem and the holy sites located within its confines: the Law and Administrative Ordinance (Amendment) Law, the Municipal Corporations Ordinance (Amendment) Law, and the Protection of the Holy Places Law.[2] The first law extended Israeli legal jurisdiction and administration to the whole of Jerusalem and additional areas stretching from Qalandia Airport in the north to Sur Bahir in the south. The rest of the West Bank and the Gaza Strip remained under military rule.

The second law incorporated the above areas into the Israeli Jerusalem Municipality. One result of this law was that on 29 June, the Palestinian Arab mayor of East Jerusalem was given an order to dissolve the Arab Municipal Council in East Jerusalem and terminate its activities. This decision was strongly opposed by the Palestinian political leadership with the result that Mayor Ruhi al-Khatib was deported to Jordan.

Although the Israeli government denied it, these two laws, nevertheless, amounted to the de facto annexation, or incorporation, of East Jerusalem, including the Old City and adjacent areas in the West Bank, into Israel. The Israel view was that, in the words of Abba Eban, the Israeli ambassador to the United Nations at the time, the process was simply "an integration of services."[3] In this context it is important to note Ian Lustick's view that annexation never actually took place. His argument is based on the fact that the term is not used in any of the legal documentation pertaining and that none of the normal criteria for annexation, such as the imposition of citizenship, have taken place. He contrasts Israel's treatment of Jerusalem with those areas in Galilee not allocated to the Jewish state by UN Resolution 181 (the Partition Plan of 1947) and the area known as the Triangle ceded by Jordan in the Rhodes Agreement in 1949. In the latter cases, the term *annexation* was used and citizenship imposed.[4] In addition, the application of Israeli law on Arab East Jerusalem was always only partial. Exemptions were made in many crucial areas such as the registration of companies, the definition of "absentee" property, the introduction of the

Israeli curriculum, and the administration of the Muslim Shari'a court system.[5]

Whatever the technical definition of Israeli legislation in 1967, the Israeli government did not regard its occupation of East Jerusalem and the Old City in the same way as it is held in international law. It was not, in the government's view, "the belligerent occupier" of enemy territory. It was, instead, a legitimate extension of Israeli civil law over territory brought under its control as laid down by the Law and Administration Ordinance announced by the Israel provisional government in 1948. There could be no belligerent occupation or annexation of a *terra nullus*, that is, of territory without a sovereign controlling body. The position of Jordan could be discounted because its annexation of Jerusalem in 1950 had not been recognized by the international community.[6]

Furthermore, the Israeli government contested the view that it was obliged to respect international legal agreements enshrined in the Hague and Geneva conventions, for in the government's eyes the agreements could not apply to Jerusalem.[7] While not recognizing the applicability of the conventions to Jerusalem, the Israeli government did to some extent try to work within its ambit. On 27 June 1967, in accordance with Article 27 of the Geneva Convention, the Israeli Knesset passed the third of the three laws mentioned: the Protection of Holy Places Law. This law, clearly, was to have great relevance to the focus of our study on the Old City. It stated:

1. The Holy Places shall be protected from desecration and any other violation and from anything likely to violate the freedom of access of the members of the different religions to the places sacred to them or their feelings with regard to those places.
   a. Whosoever desecrates or otherwise violates a Holy Place shall be liable to imprisonment for a term of seven years.
   b. Any person who does anything likely to impair freedom of access to a Holy Place or to hurt the feelings of anyone to whom a place is sacred, shall be liable to imprisonment for a term of five years.
2. This law shall add to and derogate from any other law.
3. The Minister of Religious Affairs is charged with the implementation of the Law, and he may, after consultation with, or upon the proposal of, representatives of the religions concerned and with the consent of the Minister of Justice, make regulations as to any matter relating to such implementation.[8]

Because the majority of religious sites in Jerusalem are located inside the Old City, the Holy Places Law is of particular interest to our study of the interactions between the different communities who hold them sacred. Of most significance, the Protection of Holy Places Law did not contain any explicit reference to the maintenance of the long-standing "Status Quo" arrangements. Indeed the law failed to define either what a holy place or the Status Quo was. To avoid confusion in this study, therefore, a short review of these terms is required before taking the discussion any further.

Definition of Holy Places and Status Quo

The definition of the term *holy place* is of great importance. Its misuse has led to confusion and acrimony. Over the centuries, a holy place in Jerusalem has accrued a special status, exempting it from civil legislation and issues such as taxation and health and safety regulations. The Ottomans, British, Jordanians, and Israelis have all been obliged to recognize limits on their jurisdiction and administrative authority in dealing with them. Thus, the designation of a particular site as a holy place is of some legal, political, and economic significance.

In the literature on Jerusalem, however, it is important to recognize that the term *holy places* has a technical as well as a popular usage. Historically, the term does not encompass all the holy sites in the city belonging to the three religions. Initially, it was used by scholars and jurists as referring strictly to the *Christian* holy places listed in a number of Ottoman edicts, in particular the firmans of 1757 and 1852, which laid down a series of ritualistic arrangements known as the Status Quo.[9] The sites mentioned are:

- The Church of the Holy Sepulchre and its dependencies (Old City)
- The Convent of Dayr al-Sultan (Old City)
- The Sanctuary of the Ascension (on the Mount of Olives)
- The Tomb of the Virgin Mary (near Gethsemane)
- The Church of the Nativity (in Bethlehem)
- The Milk Grotto (in Bethlehem)
- The Shepherd's Field (near Bethlehem)

Note that only the first two on this list are in the Old City. This definition of *holy place* was to continue until the British Mandate period, during which the mandatory authorities extended the list to also include the Western (or Wailing) Wall (Old City), Rachel's Tomb (between Jerusalem and Bethlehem), and the Cenacle on Mount Zion. What this British list did was to introduce non-Christian sites into the collective term *holy places*. What had previously contained a specific Christian reference with procedural arrangements laid down by the Ottoman firmans now included a shared Muslim and Jewish site.

The introduction of additional sites into the term was to continue. Following the United Nations General Assembly adoption of Resolution 181 proposing the partition of Palestine and the establishment of a *corpus separatum* for Jerusalem, a much extended list of holy places also came into use. The UN list compiled by the Conciliation Committee on Palestine in 1949 added the following sites to the ones already listed:

- Muslim: Dome of the Rock (Old City); Al-Aqsa Mosque (Old City); Mosque of the Ascension; Tomb of David
- Christian: Church of St. Anne (Old City); Church of St. James (Old City); Church of St. Mark (Old City); House of Caiaphas; Pool of Bethesda
- Jewish: Tomb of Absalom synagogues (some in the Old City, e.g., Hurva synagogue); Bath of Rabbi Ishmael; Pool of Siloam; Cemetery of Mt. Olives; Tomb of Zachariah

This extended UN list of holy places provides a taxonomy that more truly reflected the political realities of the twentieth century. Furthermore, it is the last list on which there is some international consensus and that, therefore, has the support of international law. But it greatly dilutes the use of the term *holy places*, originally reflecting those places to which the Status Quo arrangements applied. In addition, and more important, one should note that there is a much greater number of Christian and Jewish holy sites on the list and relatively few Islamic ones. This is a reflection of the dominance of the UN at that time by Christian powers and supporters of Zionism. To that extent, the UN list should be treated with some caution as a final defining list (see Map 2.1).

Thus, the problem that remains is that many documents and agreements refer to holy places without specifying which list is being referred to. For example, during the Camp David meetings in July 2000, there were frequent references to the holy places but without specifying which ones. It is possible that this lack of clarity contributed to the failure of the summit. However, to compile a list that reflects current popular perceptions would carry further dangers. Such a list would degenerate into a generalized taxonomy of holy sites incorporating many contentious sites that do not meet the agreement of the parties concerned. Once a site is elevated to a list, certain rights and obligations will flow to that site and eventually lead to nationalistic claims. For example, the inclusion of the sites such as the Islamic Mamilla cemetery in West Jerusalem, or of the Jewish shrine of Shimon Hatzadik in Arab East Jerusalem, or of the ruins of the Justinian church in the Jewish Quarter onto a new list would be problematic. It would, in the highly polarized situation of Jerusalem, help establish ethnic and national claims to those sites located in areas beyond the current areas of residence and jurisdiction.

For the purposes of this study and despite the reservations mentioned above, the term *holy places* is used to refer to the UN list. When referring

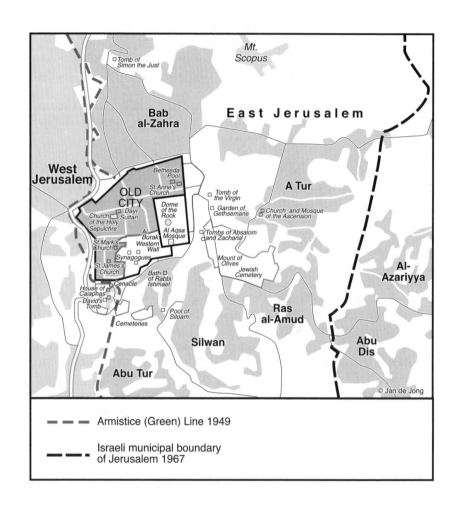

Tomb of
Simon the Just

Mt.
Scopus

Bab
al-Zahra

East Jerusalem

West
Jerusalem

A Tur

OLD
CITY

Bethesda
Pool

St.Anne's
Church

Tomb of
the Virgin

Church
of the Holy
Sepulchre

Dayr
Sultan

Dome
of the
Rock

Garden of
Gethsemane

Church and Mosque
of the Ascension

Al
Burak
Western
Wall

Al Aqsa
Mosque

Tombs of Absalom
and Zacharia

St.Mark's
Church

Synagogues

Mount of
Olives

Al-
Azariyya

St.James's
Church

Bath
of Rabbi
Ishmael

Jewish
Cemetery

House of
Caiaphas

Cenacle

David's
Tomb

Pool of
Siloam

Ras
al-Amud

Cemeteries

Silwan

Abu
Dis

Abu Tur

© Jan de Jong

- - - - Armistice (Green) Line 1949

——— Israeli municipal boundary
of Jerusalem 1967

Map 2.1   UN List of Holy Places in Jerusalem

to those holy sites mentioned in the Ottoman firmans, *Christian Holy Places* will be used. Other holy or religious sites will be referred to as holy sites.

The term *status quo* with reference to the holy places also needs clarification, as it, too, has undergone a similar genesis and transmutation. *Status Quo*, in upper-case letters, originally referred to those rights and powers of the various Christian denominations within the Christian Holy Places listed in the Ottoman firman. These were agreed upon both in writing and, in a great many cases, tacitly by custom or by oral agreement. They covered procedures to be followed in the maintenance, restoration, cleaning, and ritual use of the Christian Holy Places, and dealt with issues concerning precedence on shared festivals and holy days.[10]

The mandatory government attempted to codify these agreements as specified by Article 14 in the mandate charter and in 1922 proposed a Holy Places Commission. However, disputes between the Christian denominations and their Western-state supporters over the composition and presidency meant that no commission was ever formed and the powers of adjudication remained with the British High Commission.[11] After the withdrawal of the British in 1948, the term was used to refer to the modus operandi that evolved during the mandate period. This could be defined as the preservation of existing rights in all holy places and sites the guarantee of freedom of access and worship subject to the requirements of public order and decorum, and finally, the removal of all matters pertaining to the holy places and sites from the jurisdiction of the civil courts and their handing over to the British high commissioner. These latter powers were appropriated by the successor states of Jordan and Israel in 1949.

Since 1967, the term *status quo* is often used in Israeli academic and political circles to denote the modus operandi with regard to all the holy sites of all the religious communities, and not just the Christian Holy Places or the holy places (UN list) in general. This form of usage implies both a continuation of the arrangements set up by the Ottomans and the British and a measure of consent by the religious communities in the post-1967 situation, which is manifestly lacking. The demolition of the mosques in the Magharib quarter and the installation of an Israeli police station in the Haram ash-Sharif that was imposed by the Israeli government were neither a continuation of previous arrangements nor did these steps receive the consent of the Muslim leadership. Therefore, the use of the term *status quo* in the lower case will not be used in this study when referring to the post-1967 religious situation. Instead it will be replaced by the term *modus vivendi* to signify the relative stability of the relationships between and within the different communities brought about by the presence of the Israeli occupation and control over the Old City. The term *Status Quo*, in upper-case letters, will refer as it traditionally has done so, to the Christian Holy Places.

Israeli Administration of the Holy Places

The absence of a definition of *holy place* or of a reference to the Christian Status Quo and the former modus operandi in the 1967 Protection of the Holy Places Law is not without significance. To have accepted the arrangements prevailing in 1967 would have placed Israel and the Jewish community in the straitjacket imposed by the Ottoman and British regimes concerning these matters. To have accepted the inherited definitions would have also placed restrictions upon Jewish access to the Jewish holy sites in the Old City, such as the Western Wall. Yet to have tampered with them unilaterally through civil legislation ran the risk of incurring the dismay and opposition of Israel's Western and Christian supporters.

The Israeli government, therefore, was faced with a dilemma. The climate of Israeli public opinion immediately after the 1967 war was particularly assertive over these matters. Israeli soldiers had placed an Israeli flag over the Dome of the Rock, which had to be removed at the express order of the Israeli defense minister, General Moshe Dayan. The chief rabbi of the Israeli Army, Rabbi Shlomo Goren, later chief Ashkenazi rabbi of Israel, went immediately to pray in the Haram ash-Sharif, prostrating in the direction of the supposed Holy of Holies of Soloman's Temple.[12] As Professors Roger Friedland and Richard Hecht conclude:

> The rabbi's actions were not just the acknowledgement of the providence of God in delivering the city, the Temple Mount, and the Western Wall to the Jews nor devout ritual actions in the return to the most sacred of places. They were also political acts announcing that for him the Status Quo (sic) was no longer the ruling paradigm for the governing of sacred space in Jerusalem.[13]

Similarly, the Israeli minister of religious affairs, Zerah Warhaftig, declared that the Temple Mount, or Haram ash-Sharif, "was acquired by our forefathers. King David not only conquered the Mount but also bought it with good money from the Jebusite. There is not the slightest doubt that the Mount belongs to the Jewish people."[14] The minister acknowledged that the government had no intention of replacing the mosques there with a synagogue. Yet such utterances in the light of the destruction of the Magharib quarter and the demolition of its mosques and the absence of a reference to the modus operandi in the Holy Places Law signaled the ambiguity the Israeli government had toward the modus operandi, the holy places, and holy sites in general.

Another important legal implication of the protection of the Holy Places Law and the occupation in general was the extension of the jurisdiction of the Israeli Ministry of Religious Affairs over East Jerusalem, including the Old City and the adjacent parts of the West Bank. During the early months of the occupation, government policy toward the Muslim and Christian communities and their respective hierarchies had been confused. It was faced with the practicalities of disentangling those parts of the bureaucracy that dealt with the West Bank from those that dealt primarily with Jerusalem and the adjacent areas now incorporated into the new Israeli municipal boundaries. In the face of clerical resistance, the separation of the incorporated parts from the West Bank was difficult to achieve without greater and direct government intervention.[15]

In the first few weeks of occupation, the Israeli Ministry of Defense was placed in charge of dealings with the Muslim religious establishment and Muslim holy sites. Following the passing of the Israeli legislation that incorporated East Jerusalem and parts of the West Bank into Israel, the government transferred responsibility to the Ministry of Religious Affairs. The ministry, controlled by members of the orthodox Jewish National Religious Party, embarked upon the aggressive application of Israeli law to these areas. This meant that a number of extremely controversial changes would have had to be introduced. For example the *qadi*s (religious judges) of East Jerusalem would not be allowed to adjudicate on Shari'a matters unless they renounced their Jordanian citizenship and swore allegiance to the state of Israel. In addition, if they accepted these conditions, they would have to accept the amendments in Shari'a law enacted by the Knesset and adopted by the Israeli *qadi*s.[16] Furthermore, all the holy sites that were *waqf*, namely, the vast majority of them, would be covered by the Israeli Absentee Property Law of 1950 and be placed under the jurisdiction of the Custodian of Absentee Property. Finally, the ministry would also have the right to censor the Friday sermon delivered in all Old City mosques, including the revered al-Aqsa Mosque.[17] These conditions were not acceptable to the Muslim leadership in Jerusalem, and a campaign of resistance threatened to destabilize the relatively smooth introduction of the Israeli military government in the occupied Palestinian territories. In January 1968, responsibility for Muslim affairs was transferred back to the Ministry of Defense. The administrative framework established by the Jordanian government remained in operation and provided a relatively advanced degree of autonomy. This will be explained in greater detail in Chapter 4.

For the Christian communities, the accommodation to the Israeli occupation was not quite so highly charged. Between 1948 and 1967, Israel had officially recognized more than twelve different Christian denominations inside Israel. These communities were given freedom to appoint their own clergy, to retain an independent administration over church property (save for a number of long-running disputes), the freedom to run their own schools, and to have matters of personal status be dealt with by their own religious courts.

Prior to 1967, the armistice lines of 1949 separated ecclesiastical superiors based in Jerusalem from their subordinates, congregations, institutions, and communal assets. They had been able to coordinate, however, activities with their co-religionists in Israel by frequent visits across the lines. In 1967, the removal of the frontier made their life much easier. Christian concern over the Israeli occupation of Jerusalem was primarily exercised by fears that the new Israeli administration would alter the Christian Status Quo arrangements at their expense in some way. Government pronouncements on religious matters were, thus, closely scrutinized for clues of any impending changes. Even before the end of the 1967 war, the Israeli government was aware of the need to assuage Christian anxieties on this issue.

On 7 June 1967, the Israeli prime minister, Levi Eshkol, announced that the Ministry of Religious Affairs had instructions to establish a "council of religious clergymen" to make "arrangements" in the holy places.[18] The next day the Israeli minister of religious affairs, Zerah Wahrhaftig, informed the different religious communities that regulations concerning the holy places would be drawn up. It was never made clear who would establish the council and what its composition would be. In fact, it was never set up, echoing somewhat the difficulties the British Mandate authorities had experienced. Nor, indeed, were the regulations ever published. (These regulations should not be confused with the "code of behavior" regulations one often sees at holy places issued by the Ministry of Religious Affairs.)[19] As a result, the Christian leadership in Jerusalem was unable to secure an unequivocal commitment from the Israeli government to maintain the Christian Status Quo arrangements and not intervene either in favor of one or another of the Christian sects or in the internal affairs of the sects. This provided the Israeli government with an important instrument for leverage over the Christian communities and meant that their relations with the Israeli state was continually subject to pressures and piecemeal agreements.[20]

The changes brought about by the Israeli occupation of the Old City for the Jewish community were considerable. The extensive enlargement and reconstruction of the Jewish Quarter is discussed in the next chapter. The main point to note in this chapter is the untrammeled extension of Israeli law to the Jewish Quarter, the control over the Western Wall, or Kotel, and the jurisdiction of the Ministry of Religious Affairs. There is a rabbi of the Old City and a rabbi of the Western Wall who coordinate rituals and supervise the maintenance of the Western Wall. During most of the period under review, the Ministry of Religious Affairs has been a virtual fiefdom of the National Religious Party, a hawkish largely Ashkenazi party of Jewish orthodoxy. In the 1980s and 1990s, it came under the influence of Gush Emunim, the militant settler movement. Due to the vicissitudes of Israeli coalition politics, the ministry has been able to secure considerable autonomy over its activities in the Western Wall area, including the long-term project of tunneling along the wall to the north under Palestinian residences, causing some of them to collapse. This has brought it into conflict not only with the Palestinian residents, the Awqaf Administration, and the United Nations Education, Scientific, and Cultural Organization, but also with the Israeli Department of Antiquities.[21] In addition, disagreements over the best use to make of the razed Magharib quarter have led to the paralysis of plans for its developments as a Jewish holy place, with the result that it remains an open plaza with only security and toilet facilities installed.[22]

The dilemma the government faced over the administration of the holy places and the preservation of the Christian Status Quo arrangements was resolved by both compromise and coercion. On the one hand, Christian Holy Places and the Status Quo arrangements were left largely untouched, and the internal administration and maintenance of the Haram ash-Sharif was left to the Awqaf Administration. On the other hand, the Israeli army took control over the points of access and policing responsibilities in the Haram compound. In addition, the Western Wall and adjacent area was removed entirely from Muslim jurisdiction and handed over to the Israeli Ministry of Religious Affairs.

Wider Political Developments
Affecting the Old City and Holy Places

As has been made clear in Chapter 1, the focus of this study is the Old City. Nevertheless, wider political developments of two main types have had a serious impact upon the internal dynamics of the Old City. The first kind is the impact of Israeli government policies applied incrementally over the whole period under review. It is not the intention of this book to cover all of these. Instead, a number of the most significant are selected to illustrate the interaction between the wider context of Jerusalem and the specificities of the Old City. These include such issues as changes in demography as well as the pursuit of planning, settlement, and residential policies designed to isolate Jerusalem from the West Bank hinterland or to impede institutional development. The second type of wider political developments that have had an impact upon the Old City are the series of international and bilateral agreements and diplomatic understandings. These range from the Jordanian act of legal separation from the West Bank in 1988 through to the Oslo Accords and the Vatican agreements with Israel and the PLO.

Demography, Settlement, Access, and Residency

The population figures for Jerusalem are much disputed. The figures presented by the official Statistical Abstract of Jerusalem have been accused of both overcounting and undercounting the Palestinian population. The over-counting critics point to the fact that while there is an agreed amount of Palestinians with Jerusalem Identity Cards, a large proportion of them, possibly as many as 40,000, do not actually live in the municipality, preferring to settle on the periphery where housing conditions are much better. This is especially the case of official residents of the Old City. However, there is also evidence to suggest that the result of this movement outward is another movement inward of illegal residents who let the vacated premises and further sublet them so that the actual number is greater than those who have left. In the absence of a more accurate census, the official figures will be cited, with the proviso that they are only rough indications. A study of demographic changes in Jerusalem since 1948 reveals two main trends: (1) the complete dominance of the Jewish population in the Israeli West Jerusalem and (2) since 1967 the gradual and increasing dominance of the Jewish population in Palestinian East Jerusalem.[23] Table 2.1 indicates the overall population balance since 1967.

This has meant that the Christian and Muslim holy sites in Israeli West Jerusalem have lost their population hinterland and that a similar pattern is occurring in the Palestinian East Jerusalem. This loss of hinterland impacts the amount of religious personnel that are appointed and can be supported, as well as the revenue that such institutions and sites might generate. As a result, the maintenance and use to which they are put can suffer. The Israeli policy of closing Jerusalem to residents of the West Bank and Gaza Strip exacerbates this problem. Of greater importance to this study is the population breakdown in the Old City. Table 2.2 shows how the non-Israeli Jewish population has continued to retain its dominance.

Table 2.1   Residents of Jerusalem According to Population Groups in Selected Years, 1967–1998

| Year | Number of Residents (thousands) | | | Percentage | |
	Palestinians	Israelis	Total	Palestinians	Israelis
1967	68.6	197.7	266.3	25.8	74.2
1970	76.2	215.5	291.7	26.1	73.9
1975	96.1	259.4	355.5	27.0	73.0
1980	114.8	292.3	407.1	28.4	71.6
1985	130.0	327.7	457.7	28.4	71.6
1990	146.3	378.2	524.5	27.9	72.1
1995	174.4	417.0	591.4	29.5	70.5
1998	200.1	433.6	633.7	31.6	68.4

Source: M. Choshen and N. Shahar, eds., *Statistical Yearbook of Jerusalem* (Jerusalem: Jerusalem Institute for Israel Studies, 1999), 46.

Table 2.2   Population of the Old City by Religious Group

Religious Group/Quarters	Jews	Muslims	Christians	Total
Christian quarters	107	1,025	3,900	5,032
Armenian Quarter	592	510	1,193	2,295
Jewish Quarter	1,723	480	17	2,230
Muslim quarters	380	20,799	1,460	22,639
Total	2,802	22,894	6,570	32,186

Source: Welfare Association, *Jerusalem Old City Revitalisation Plan: Interim Summary Report,* Jerusalem, January 1999, 19.

Note: Data is based on a private survey commissioned by the Welfare Association in 1998. Two hundred and ten families were surveyed, totaling 1,334 individuals distributed in thirty representative clusters in the Old City. Males formed 48.1 percent of the sample and females 51.9 percent. This ratio is comparable to the West Bank.

Another incremental policy has been the construction of Israeli settlements in and around Palestinian East Jerusalem. The growth of these settlements and the political and legal issues surrounding them are well documented and need not be repeated here.[24] The most important point to note, however, is that the rapid expansion of Israeli settlements led to population change in Palestinian East Jerusalem in favor of Israeli Jews. From the early 1990s onward, there have been more Israeli Jews living in the eastern part of the city than Palestinians. In this way, two objectives were achieved. First, as the settlements spread and became more established, Palestinian areas, particularly the Old City, became enclaves within a modern Israeli city. Second, the enclaves themselves became increasingly cut off from the West Bank hinterland. The ebb and flow of social exchange, the dissemination of sounds, smells, the casual encounters, and the natural expansion into other areas all became circumscribed by a growing wall of settlements in and around East Jerusalem.

The effects of these settlement policies are exacerbated by two supplementary polices. The first is the closure of Jerusalem to West Bank and Gaza Strip Palestinians. Roadblocks ring the city, and Palestinians without a Jerusalem residency permit have to obtain special permission to enter it. This has dramatically contributed to the loss of a population hinterland described above, disrupting economic, cultural, religious, and political activities in East Jerusalem and the Old City. Furthermore, it can be seen as a violation of the freedom of access to holy places and of worship. As such, it is a transgression not only of UN resolutions and charters but also of Israel's own undertaking and guarantees and of its own laws, such as the Holy Places Law.

The second policy is the withdrawal of residency permits and the confiscation of a Jerusalem Identity Card from those Palestinians who cannot prove that Jerusalem is their center of life. As indicated earlier, many Palestinian Jerusalemites, perhaps as many as 40,000, have moved out of the city to seek better housing conditions, as the prospect of receiving a building permit in East Jerusalem was virtually nil. At the same time, they retained their residency permit and the ownership or tenancy of their property in East Jerusalem or the Old City. The main reason for this is that as Jerusalem residents, they are entitled to Israeli National Insurance benefits such as child allowances. However, in 1996, the government of Benjamin Netanyahu, in conjunction with the more anti-Palestinian mayor of Jerusalem, Ehud Olmert, began a policy of withdrawing residency permits from individuals who had moved outside the municipal borders for whatever reason. By September 1999, 2,812 residency permits had been withdrawn.[25]

This general loss of a population hinterland and the process of creating enclaves is also supported by restrictive planning policies and building regulations. holy places and their support apparatus (maintenance workers, administrators, accountants, guards, guides, cleaning, fundraising activities, etc.) require the opportunity to change the use of buildings, to expand, renovate, and reconstruct—otherwise, they stagnate and decline. Planning permission is frequently denied to Christian and Muslim institutions that wish to develop their activities. Examples of this are the refusal to allow the opening of the Islamic Cultural Centre in Shaykh Jarrah and the attempts by the Armenian Patriarchate to build a church on part of its cemetery on Mt. Zion.[26]

Another set of policies that establish Israeli control over travel and tourism also have an impact on the Old City. Israeli control over the main points of entry to the city is reinforced by the Israeli private sector domination of the international tourist trade to Jerusalem. This encourages visits and participation in religious rituals to be determined by Israeli institutions and through Israeli perspectives. In turn, government support for projects that enhance the Jewish presence in the city at the expense of other religious communities also contributes to the decline of non-Jewish holy places. An example can be seen in contrasting Israeli government support for the Cardo shopping area in the Jewish Old City with the lack of support for the Suq al-Qattanin in the Muslim quarters of the Old City.

Finally, other policies also impinge upon the functioning of the religious institutions in the Old City. Holy places require not only appropriately trained and experienced personnel to staff their administration but also individuals with standing and respect in their community. The deportation of such persons, the denial of their entry, or the refusal to regularize their residence hampers the operations of that administration. Examples include the deportation of Shaykh Abdel Hamid al-Sa'ih in 1967 and the refusal to renew the visa of the Armenian sacristan Karecki Kazanjian in 1981.[27]

International and Bilateral Agreements

There are a great number of international and bilateral agreements and other external political developments that have impinged on the life of the Old City. Because the main focus of this book is the interaction between the peace negotiations and the struggle in the Old City, only those that have taken place either following the Madrid Peace Conference in 1991 or immediately prior to it will be discussed.

The first significant action leading up to new dynamics in the Old City in the 1990s was the legal separation of the West Bank from the Hashemite Kingdom of Jordan in 1988. This had great significance for the administration of the holy places in the Old City. This step was taken during the height of the first Palestinian uprising, or intifada (1987–1992/3), against Israeli occupation when King Hussein of Jordan realized that his support among Palestinians had irrecoverably dwindled. It was also an attempt to force the PLO to take responsibility for the overall economic and political development of the West Bank and to signal to the Israelis that it was the PLO they had to deal with to solve the problems of the uprising. In the act of legal separation, Jordan recognized the role of the PLO in the West Bank, but it retained its administrative jurisdiction over the *waqf* and Shari'a courts in Jerusalem and thus the Muslim holy places. This meant that the Muslim holy places continued to be supported by Jordan and were still able to function in the highly charged and fast-moving period. It also meant that following the creation of the PNA in 1993, set up by the PLO as part of the interim phase of the Oslo Accords, the operations of the Muslim holy places were not jeopardized. The PNA was unable to generate sufficient income to meet its running costs or to operate openly in Jerusalem, so continued Jordanian involvement was vital. The Christian Holy Places were not affected in the same way because their funding was independent of Jordan. However, the legal separation did imply a certain loss of protection from the Jordanian state and contributed to the radicalization of the churches and their movement toward an overtly Palestinian position. This will be discussed further in Chapter 5.

The second important and wider political development was the Oslo Accords. This comprised two components: first, the mutual recognition of Israel and the PLO, and second, the introduction of an "interim phase." The interim phase consisted of the Israeli withdrawal from most of the Gaza Strip and a small percentage of the West Bank. Areas were designated Area A, B, or C. Area A was to be handed over to the PNA to administer fully, including all security and policing issues. Area B was to be under the civil jurisdiction of the PNA, but military and policing responsibilities were retained by the Israelis or jointly with the PNA. Area C was to be fully controlled by the Israelis. Jerusalem was not included in the interim phase withdrawal. The future of Jerusalem was to be discussed by May 1999 together with five other issues: borders, security, water, settlements, and refugees. These were to be the "permanent," or "final status," talks.

The interim phase of the Oslo Accords included two aspects that are relevant to the holy places. The first is the acceptance by Israel of the Holst letters. These were a correspondence between Israeli foreign minister Shimon Peres and Norwegian foreign minister Johan Jørgen Holst in which Israel agreed that "all Palestinian institutions of East Jerusalem, including the economic, social, educational, and cultural, and the holy Christian and Muslim places, are performing an essential task for the Palestinian population and that the government of Israel undertakes not to hamper their activities."[28] For the Palestinians, this was an essential recognition of their rights in Jerusalem during the interim period. On the one hand, it provided them with an agreement with which they could resist Israeli encroachments upon their institutional base in the city. On the other hand, it offered them some international protection in maximizing their position in Jerusalem during the interim phase in preparation for the permanent status negotiations. Both of these were utilized to promote the functions and role of religious institutions and their holy sites. The second aspect is the full withdrawal of Israeli political and military control from territories designated as Area A, and the partial withdrawal from areas designated Area B. Under these withdrawals, Rachel's Tomb, a shared Muslim and Jewish holy place along the road to Bethlehem, is in Area B. However, the Israeli government has ignored this and full Israeli control remains.

The overall impact of the interim phase, nevertheless, is that the PNA has now both control over the holy places and holy sites in Bethlehem and other parts of the Jerusalem region and is in the close vicinity to those in Jerusalem. In fact, the interim agreement also permitted Palestinian Jerusalemites to vote in the elections to the Palestine Legislative Council. Both these factors have an important psychological impact and causes the officials and administrators of the holy places, and the Israeli authorities in the city, to act strategically. Developing and consolidating, on the one hand, and restricting, on the other, Palestinian institutions in the city have been a game of cat and mouse for Palestinians and Israelis since 1967. The interim phase can be seen as a series of moves similar to the actions of opposing armies who have agreed to a cease-fire at a certain time and are trying to either outflank or seize strategic heights prior to the deadline in order to negotiate from a position of strength. The Palestinianization of religious institutions in the Old City and the growing overt support for the PNA expressed by the Christian church hierarchies have been major aspects of this maneuvering.

Stemming from this, a very significant event occurred during the disturbances known as the "al-Aqsa Intifada" of October 2000. At the height of the conflict and in an attempt to calm the tensions on a Friday prayer day, Israel not only withdrew its police and security forces from the Haram compound but also allowed Palestinian security officers to control the access to the Haram.[29] Although merely a temporary arrangement, the precedent was only possible as a result of the gradual establishment of a Palestinian institutional presence in and on the borders of Jerusalem over the preceding years.

Another important agreement affecting the Old City has been the Vatican-Israel Fundamental Agreement of 1994. The significance of this agreement for the Christian Holy Places lies more in its potential than any concrete changes to the position of the Vatican. The Memorandum of Understanding cleared the way for full diplomatic recognition of Israel by the Vatican, but no substantial changes were made in any practice concerning the administration of the Christian Holy Places. Contentious issues such as the applicability of Israeli taxation on religious property were given to committees for further discussion. The main impact lay in the perception by the other churches that in coming to a formal agreement with Israel the Vatican was attempting to create a more advantageous relationship with it at the expense of the other major Christian communities. This would, in turn, have repercussions on the procedures, protocols, and responsibilities in the Christian Holy Places themselves.

The Vatican-Israel agreement was followed in 2000 by a Vatican-PLO Basic Agreement. As with Israel, the Vatican-PLO agreement will not have a practical effect on the administration of the Christian Holy Places in the Old City. But it did go some way to reassure Palestinian opinion and the other churches that the Vatican was not attempting to overturn the Christian Status Quo by its relationship with Israel. Indeed, the Vatican-PLO agreement showed the extent to which the PLO had enlisted the Vatican's support for its position on Jerusalem (see Chapter 5).

The final piece in the jigsaw of agreements, which have had an impact on the Old City and its future status, is the Washington Declaration and the subsequent Jordan-Israel Peace Treaty of 1994. The Washington Declaration is a very important landmark in the political developments surrounding the Muslim holy places. The relevant clause states:

> Israel respects the present special role of the Hashemite Kingdom of Jordan in Muslim Holy shrines in Jerusalem. When negotiations on the permanent status will take place, Israel will give high priority to the Jordanian historic role in these shrines. In addition the two sides have agreed to act together to promote interfaith relations among the three monotheistic religions.[30]

This was the first time that Israel formally recognized Jordan's special status in regard to the Muslim holy places and confers a de facto legitimacy to the Awqaf Administration as the executive arm of the Jordanian government. Furthermore, the declaration also suggests that Israel has also relinquished any claim to realize political sovereignty over the Muslim holy places, in particular, the Haram ash-Sharif. In effect, these diplomatic moves were designed to squeeze out the PLO and to undermine its claim on Jerusalem and the Old City. By bringing in the Jordanians on the religious level, Israel hoped to affirm its control over the city on the political level. As Menachem Klein observes:

> In return for Jordan's agreement to separate political and religious questions regarding Jerusalem, [Prime Minister] Rabin was willing to endorse Jordan's special religious status over the Islamic Holy Places in Jerusalem. In effect Jordan received a foothold in the Islamic Holy Places by excluding Israel from them, while Israel strengthened its position that the existence of the Islamic Holy Places in East Jerusalem does not in itself eviscerate Israel's political sovereignty over the City. . . . This Declaration embodied Jordanian-Israeli cooperation, which clearly would weaken the Palestinian position in their struggle to establish eastern Jerusalem as their capital.[31]

Clearly, these moves were not acceptable to the PLO, which claimed they were a major impediment to the Palestinian attempt to achieve sovereignty over East Jerusalem. It tried to redress the balance by seeking the support of other Arab and Islamic states and persuaded the Islamic Conference Organization (ICO) at its Casablanca meeting in December 1994 to support its position. The conference was a diplomatic defeat for King Hussein, who left before the end. Its final communiqué recognized Jerusalem as the capital of Palestine and committed itself to supporting its return to Palestinian sovereignty.[32] In addition, the ICO convened its Jerusalem Committee, which comprised the PLO, Morocco, Saudi Arabia, and Egypt but not Jordan, to examine ways in which its support could be operationalized. Strengthened by these actions, the PLO was then able to conclude an Agreement for Cooperation and Coordination with Jordan. Nothing in the agreement confirmed Jordan's special status over the Islamic holy places. Indeed, it specifically commits Jordan to supporting the Palestinian attempt to establish its national institutions. The agreement, thus, signaled a retreat from the treaty concluded with Israel. One result of these political maneuverings was that both Jordan and the PNA claimed the right to appoint the mufti of Jerusalem. Following the death of Sulayman al-Jabari in October 1994, Jordan appointed Shaykh 'Abd al-Qadir 'Abidin as mufti while the Palestinian Authority chose the former imam of the al-Aqsa Mosque, Shaykh Ikrima al-Sabri, as its mufti.[33]

One danger in writing a book on contemporary political issues is that the author always runs the risk of being overtaken by current events. A violent confrontation between Palestinian worshippers and Israeli paramilitary police on the Haram ash-Sharif in 1996, controversy over access to the Holy Sepulchre in 1999, and the detailed discussion over the sovereignty in the Old City at the Camp David in 2000 all are part of the evolving legal and political context of the discussion in this book. They are dealt with in more detail in the following chapters.

To conclude, it is possible to argue that political developments in Jerusalem have been pulling in opposite directions. Israeli policies since 1967 have contained Palestinian demographic and institutional development in Jerusalem and particularly in the Old City. In addition, the enforced isolation of the eastern part of the city from its West Bank hinterland has led to economic decline and lack of investment. At the same time, there have also been a number of important advances in the political sphere that, in the short term, have strengthened the Palestinian position in the Old City. Since the first Palestinian intifada of 1987, Israel has accepted the PLO as a negotiating partner but, simultaneously, hopes to promote Jordan as the key actor in the Muslim holy sites. Diplomatic relations have been established between the Vatican and Israel and a Fundamental Agreement exists between the PLO and the Vatican. The majority of the Arab and Islamic states has confirmed the status of the PLO in Jerusalem. On many fronts, doors have been opened and communications established. However, there have been few actual changes to either the administration of the holy places and other religious sites or to the Old City itself. The political framework consisting of words and treaties has not yet translated into institutional structures. The result is a highly transitional situation and an uneasy dynamic where all the relevant parties are attempting to strengthen their positions prior to the start of the permanent status negotiations.

The following chapters will turn to events on the ground in the Old City. They will trace the changes and interactions both within communities and across them to show the main changes since 1967. The data presented and the overall picture drawn will allow us to speculate more accurately as to how these changes will affect the peace negotiations and the final configurations of a settlement. To reemphasize, the main argument of the book is that the real configuration of positions in the Old City is not amenable to the various schema suggested in numerous peace proposals, including those presented at Camp David. The attempt by the Israeli government to emphasize the Jewish presence in the Old City through its activities in the expanded Jewish Quarter and through the settlers in the other quarters of the Old City has to some extent succeeded. At the same time, the jockeying for influence between the PLO and the Jordanian government and, indeed, the fragmented nature of the Christian communities are very likely to frustrate a formula that does not take their concerns into account. Any attempt to extraterritorialize the Old City, for example, in the peace negotiations will run into the realities on the ground. In sum, there is a new balance of power between the religious communities comprising an increasingly interpenetrated pattern of residence that would make the drawing of lines through the Old City almost impossible. Certainly any lines reflecting political and ethnic divisions would not make sense in terms of municipal provision. These issues will be discussed further in Chapter 6 after the events affecting the three religious communities in the Old City are more fully explored.

Notes

1. Cited in W. Zander, *Israel and the Holy Places of Christendom* (London: Weidenfield and Nicolson, 1971), 98.
2. *Laws of the State of Israel,* vol. 21, 1966–1967, 75.
3. Cited in M. Benvenisti, *Jerusalem: The Torn City* (Minneapolis: Israel Typeset, Ltd., and the University of Minneapolis, 1976), 122.
4. I. Lustick, "Has Israel Annexed Jerusalem?" *Middle East Policy* 5, no. 1 (January 1997).
5. See M. Dumper, *The Politics of Jerusalem Since 1967* (New York: Columbia University Press, 1997), 42–46; see a fuller discussion of this theme in L. T. Rempel, "The Significance of Israel's Partial Annexation of East Jerusalem," *Middle East Journal* 51, no. 4 (autumn 1977).
6. R. Shehadi, *The West Bank and the Rule of Law* (New York: International Commission of Jurists and Law in the Service of Man, 1980), 10; A. Gershon, *Israel, the West Bank, and International Law* (London: Frank Cass, 1978), 78–82.
7. Article 56 of the "Protection of Cultural Property in Time of War or Military Occupation" was annexed to both the 1899 Hague Convention II and the 1907 Hague Convention IV as regulations. This article treats all religious and charitable institutions as private property. Destruction and willful damage to such property is therefore forbidden. The 1954 Hague Convention for the "Protection of Cultural Property in the Event of Armed Conflict" covers both religious buildings and *waqf* land and property on the West Bank. Jordan and Israel have signed and ratified this convention. Israel has not signed two other relevant statutes in international law: Article 53 of the 1977 Geneva Protocol I ("Protection of Cultural Objects and Places of Worship") prohibits any act of hostility against cultural property. Article 16 of the 1977 Geneva Protocol II ("Protection of Cultural Objects and Places of Worship") prohibits any act of hostility against cultural property or its use in any military effort or as an object of reprisal.
8. *Laws of the State of Israel,* 76.
9. For further details, see Zander, *Israel and the Holy Places of Christendom,* 47–54. See also A. O'Mahoney, "Church, State, and the Christian Communities and the Holy Places of Palestine," in *Christians in the Holy Land,* eds. M. Prior and W. Taylor (London: World of Islam Festival Trust, 1994).
10. See Chapter 5 for a more in-depth discussion of this issue.
11. The classic study on this issue is by Zander, chapter 3. See also O'Mahoney, 23–25.
12. Moments after the Israeli soldiers took over the Haram ash-Sharif, Rabbi

Goren also tried to persuade General Uzi Narkis, the commander of Israeli forces who captured the Old City, to detonate the Dome of the Rock. See G. Gorenberg, "Warning! Millennium Ahead," *Jerusalem Report*, 19 February 1998, 17.

13. R. Friedland and R. Hecht, "The Politics of Sacred Place: Jerusalem's Temple Mount/*al-Haram al-Sharif*," in *Sacred Places and Profane Spaces: Essays in the Geographics of Judaism, Christianity, and Islam*, eds. J. Scott and P. Simpson-Housley (New York: Greenwood Press, 1991), 39.

14. *Ha'aretz*, July 1967; cited in E. Offenbacher, "Prayer on the Temple Mount," *Jerusalem Quarterly File*, no. 36 (summer 1985): 132.

15. This issue is discussed in detail in chapter 5 of M. Dumper, *Islam and Israel: Muslim Religious Endowments and the Jewish State* (Washington D.C.: Institute for Palestine Studies, 1994).

16. See the discussion in A. Layish, "Qadis and the Shari'a Law in Israel," *Asian and African Studies* (Journal of the Israel Oriental Society) 7 (1977): 237–272.

17. For further examples, see Dumper, *Islam and Israel*, 77–78.

18. Benvenisti, *Jerusalem: The Torn City*, 267.

19. Ibid., 267.

20. See Dumper, *The Politics of Jerusalem*, 194.

21. Dumper, *Islam and Israel*, 113.

22. See the discussion in M. Safdie, *The Harvard Jerusalem Studio: Urban Designs for the Holy City* (London: Massachusetts Institute of Technology Press, 1986).

23. See the discussion on population figures in Dumper, *The Politics of Jerusalem*, 80–82.

24. See the monitoring organ of the Foundation for Middle East Peace, *Settlement Report*, published quarterly, Washington, D.C.

25. Figures provided by Badil Resource Centre and published in *Kul Al Arab*, 24 September 1999.

26. Adnan Husseini, director-general, Awqaf Administration. Interview by author, Jerusalem, 6 February 1999; G. Usher, "Fifteen Centuries and Still Counting: The Old City Armenians," *Jerusalem Quarterly File*, no. 9 (summer 2000): 37.

27. For the expulsion of Sa'ih, see I. Daqqaq, "Back to Square One": A Study in the Re-emergence of the Palestinian Identity in the West Bank, 1967–1980," in A. Scholch, ed., *Palestinians over the Green Line* (London: Ithaca Press, 1983), 72; for that of Kazanjian, see D. Tsimhoni, *Christian Communities in Jerusalem and the West Bank Since 1948: An Historical, Social, and Political Study* (Westport, Conn.: Praeger, 1993), 70.

28. G. R. Watson, *The Oslo Accords: International Law and the Israeli-Palestinian Agreements* (Oxford: Oxford University Press, 2000), 242.

29. *Ha'aretz*, 8 October 2000. The Israeli withdrawal on 6 October only lasted a few hours, as continued rioting in the streets of the Old City resulted in the Israeli army reoccupying the site.

30. Cited in M. Klein, "The Islamic Holy Places as a Political Bargaining Card (1993–95)," *Catholic University Law Review* 45, no. 3 (spring 1996): 747.

31. Ibid., 749–750.

32. Ibid., 755. The communiqué stated that the ICO "must assist the PLO in its future negotiations, until all authority and sovereignty in the occupied territories— including Honourable Jerusalem [Al-Quds al-Sharif]—will be transferred to the hands of the Palestinian [National] Authority, and to ensure the return of Jerusalem

to Palestinian authority . . . as Honorable Jerusalem [al-Quds al-Sharif] is an inseparable part of the territories occupied by Israel in 1967 and [is] subject to the same laws as the other occupied territories. Jerusalem must be returned to Palestinian sovereignty as it is the capital of Palestine."

33. S. Musallem, *The Struggle for Jerusalem* (Jerusalem: PASSIA, 1996), 109–110.

3

The Jewish Community:
The Role of Israeli Settler Groups

Negotiating an agreement over the future of the Old City will be much more complex than it might initially appear. The complexity of interactions not only between religious communities but also within them will make cooperation between the religious leadership very difficult to achieve. Furthermore, social, political, and property ownership changes in the Old City since 1967 make a return to the previous state of affairs extremely unlikely and thus diminish the prospect of an agreed solution in the short and medium terms. In this chapter, I argue that one of the main reasons for this is the expansion of the role and presence of the Jewish community in the Old City. While looking at events such as the enlargement of the Jewish Quarter, we will focus on the activities of the Israeli settler movement and its supporters. The chapter attempts to ascertain the extent of the Israeli settlers' physical penetration into the other quarters of the Old City and discusses the extent of state support they have received. The final part of the chapter briefly highlights the implications of their activities on the discussions on the future of the Old City in the peace process.

Historical Background

The Jewish community in the Old City is both a newcomer and a veteran. It is a newcomer in that it arrived following the Israeli takeover in 1967 and, like any other victorious group, immediately set about establishing itself in the Old City through demolitions and expropriations of property of the existing inhabitants and through grand reconstruction. It is also a veteran in the sense that these actions were taken on a basis of a long genealogy of belonging and presence there.

Prior to the mid-1850s, the Jewish community of Jerusalem was largely Sephardi in origin and was concentrated in what became known as the

39

Jewish Quarter of the Old City. It was not until the latter part of the Ottoman period in the nineteenth century that it received official recognition. Its leader, the *rishon le-zion*, also known as *hakham bashi* or First in Zion, was recognized by the Ottoman authorities as responsible for the liaison between themselves and the Jewish community. Despite being a "people of the book" and, thus, under the Ottoman millet system, entitled to some distinct communal organization, the small numbers of Jews meant that their affairs were subject to the Shari'a courts.

The arrival of Ashkenazi Jews in the late nineteenth century brought about changes to the equilibrium that had been established. Initially, the new arrivals accepted the authority and leadership of the *rishon le-zion,* but following disputes some groups broke away to set up independent communities under the authority of their own rabbis. The main cause of dispute between the Sephardi leadership and the new Ashkenazi arrivals was over the allocation of *halukka* funds. These funds were collected in the Diaspora for the purpose of maintaining a Jewish presence in Palestine. Donations to "our brethren" in Palestine were part of ritualistic giving in Diaspora Jewish communities. All Jews residing in Palestine were entitled to a proportion of these funds, and their allocation was in the hands of the Sephardi *rishon le-zion*.[1] Because many of the new arrivals were impoverished, this acted as a powerful form of religious, political, and social control and gave the *rishon le-zion*, and, thus, the Sephardic community, great power. Not only did its leadership have the official access to the Ottoman authorities, it also was the controller of the wealth of the community.

Following their breakaway, the Ashkenazi groups sought to compensate for the loss of protection and the lack of Ottoman recognition by accepting the protection and mediating offices of foreign consuls.[2] However, during the course of the century, they formed a General Committee to coordinate their activities and to liaise, albeit unofficially, with the Ottoman authorities. By the turn of the twentieth century, the Ashkenazi chief rabbi appointed by the General Committee was regarded as having the same status as the Sephardi *rishon le-zion*. Although the Sephardi-Ashkenazi split has been regarded as the most important in the history of the reestablishment of a Jewish presence in Jerusalem, the fragmentation of the community encompassed serious disputes between the Sephardi leadership and the growing Moroccan Jewish community, or Ma'aravim, also over the distribution of *halukka* funds. The result, after much violence, was a compromise in which the Ma'aravim set up a separate communal committee.[3]

The main point of drawing attention to these divisions is to highlight the heterogeneity and fragmentation of the Jewish community in Jerusalem. The common perception of it acting as a monolithic bloc needs to be dispelled. Although there may be an overall strategic objective of establishing a Jewish preponderance in the Old City, disputes over style, finance, timing, and the nature of the relationships to be established with both the Palestinian Muslim and Christian populations prevail in much the same way as during the Ottoman era.

The main features of Jewish community life were centered on the *kollelim*. This was a community dedicated to learning under the guidance of a rabbi and usually comprised a library and dormitory accommodation. A small *kolel* comprised a synagogue and some residential units; the larger ones would also boast a library and some teaching and studying areas. In the 1860s, for example, Rabbi Fischel Lapin purchased two courtyards in the Muslim quarters whereas in 1871 the Kolel Reissin was set up with funds donated from Sa'adia ben Yehezkel Shorr. Some of the larger *kolel* also established synagogues and seminaries, usually renting premises off Arab and Turkish landlords.

This focus on study and prayer rendered the majority of the community unproductive and, thus, reliant upon the *halukka* funds.[4] In 1876, little more than 10 percent of the Jewish population was economically productive.[5] This lack of internally generated wealth and the growing size of the community competing over a relatively static pool of external funds led to its impoverishment. By the late nineteenth century, some estimates place the Jewish population at approximately half of the total population of the Old City, though it was crammed into one-sixth of the area.

The quarter became so densely populated that some of the new immigrants were compelled to move to an area just north of the Jewish Quarter along the Aqabat Khalidi and Aqabat Saraya. By the 1880s so many of them had moved that this area became known as the Hebron market area, for many of the inhabitants came from Hebron. Another area, known to the Jews of this time as the Bab al-Huta area, which lies between the northern wall of the Haram and Herod's Gate (Bab al-Zahra), received much less attention. A small community was established just south of Herod's Gate, known as Bet Warsawa; closer to Damascus Gate, Rabbi Moses Wittenburg bought a house and founded a synagogue. Some of the more nationalistic Jewish historians have pointed out that although this area did not have a large Jewish population in the late nineteenth century, it was known as the Jewish Quarter in the tenth century.

At the same time, the first attempts were also made to establish neighborhoods outside the city walls. The success of these ventures led to further initiatives and the easing of conditions in the Jewish Quarter. The new neighborhoods not only provided additional space for the influx of new arrivals, mostly Ashkenazis from Russia and Central Europe fleeing pogroms, but also reflected an injection of Western capital from both philanthropists and mutual aid societies.[6]

Under the period of the British Mandate, the trend to settle outside the city walls accelerated. This was largely due to the huge numbers of Ashkenazi Jews arriving as a result of British support for a Jewish national home in Palestine. During the early part of the twentieth century, the expansion of the New City in the west and north of the Old City walls eased the flow of Jews wishing to settle in the Muslim quarters. In 1929, intercommunal rioting led to the start of a gradual emigration of Jews in the Muslim quarters to the New City. The tensions and rioting of the 1930s accentuated this movement until finally in 1936 the last Jewish family left the Muslim quarters. Properties that had been bought by Jewish individuals or institutions were either leased or sold to Palestinian Arabs or abandoned.

As was described in Chapter 2, following the war between Israel and the Palestinian and Arab states in 1948, Jerusalem was divided into an Israeli-held western sector and a Jordanian-held eastern sector. The Old City was located in the eastern sector. Some of the empty former Jewish properties were squatted in by Palestinian refugees from West Jerusalem and other parts of Palestine. In 1950 these and other leased properties were placed under the management of the Jordanian government's Guardian of Enemy Property whose duty was to continue to collect the rents and maintain them until a peace treaty had been signed. After the 1967 war, the functions of the Guardian were transferred to the Israeli Custodian of Absentee Property.

Expansion of the Jewish Presence in the Old City

Prior to the activities of the settler groups under discussion in this book, the Israeli government took two major steps in the Old City. First, they destroyed the Magharib, or Moroccan, quarter, to clear a plaza in front of the Western Wall, or Kotel. (This is discussed in greater detail in Chapter 4.) The area is now dedicated entirely to Jewish devotions associated with the Kotel, a favored site for bar mitzvah celebrations and Israeli military parades and ceremonies. Second, they expanded and reconstructed the former Jewish Quarter. In April 1968, the Ministry of Finance published an expropriation order that extended the traditional Jewish Quarter to more than twice its size. It was applied to the whole area between the walls in the southeast to the Tariq Bab al-Silsilah in the west, and from the Kotel in the north to the Armenian Quarter in the south. Approximately 700 buildings were expropriated, of which only 105 had been owned by Jews before 1948. More than one-quarter of the Palestinian buildings were endowed as *waqf*, both public and private.[7] The expropriated area was subsumed under the name the Jewish Quarter even though it included the former Magharib quarter and many other smaller and famous quarters, such the Harat Abu Sa'ud, redolent with Palestinian and Arab history. In addition, the expropriated area, the expropriation of which had been carried out purportedly for the public good, was intended for Jews only. This became clear following the celebrated Israeli Supreme Court judgment known as the Burkan Case, where a Palestinian sought by legal means to reoccupy his renovated property only to find he was prevented from doing so because he was not a Jew.[8]

The task of reconstruction was handed to an Israeli government-backed company known as the Company for the Reconstruction and Development of the Jewish Quarter. With the backing of the Israeli legal system, the company proceeded to introduce a policy of residential apartheid in the expropriated area. Palestinian inhabitants were evicted over a period of ten years, some by inducements, and some by harassment and coercion. However, despite these instruments at the government's disposal, the pace of evictions was slow. Accordingly, in 1973, the government amended the Absentee Property Law of 1950 so that the ownership of properties whose tenants had accepted compensation would pass to the company, irrespective of the wishes of the original owner. The result was that some 6,000 Palestinians were evicted and more than 700 workers lost their means of employment.[9]

For a time, it seemed that these two steps satisfied Israeli government intentions for the Old City. While the Israeli Labour Party, the party of government during the late 1960s and early 1970s, may have been active in introducing settlers into the West Bank and Gaza Strip, it was concerned not to create unnecessary conflict in Jerusalem. Yet following the election of the more hawkish Likud Party and its allies in 1977, a new phase was opened and militant Israeli nationalists sought opportunities to assert Israeli control over the other quarters of the Old City through settlement and the eviction of Palestinians.

In the early 1970s, a number of individuals became interested in former Jewish properties in the Muslim quarters and sought to reactivate a Jewish presence there. A bookshop, the Ben Arza, was opened close to the underground passage leading to the Western Wall plaza. In view of the wholesale eviction of Palestinian families still taking place in the enlarged Jewish Quarter at that time, the political sensitivity of such a development was illustrated by the fact that the Ben Arza bookshop became the subject of an arson attack in February 1974.[10] The late 1970s saw the establishment of a yeshiva on the second floor of the Yeshiva Torat Hayyim premises in Tariq al-Wad and the start of some Sephardi Jewish attempts to occupy the Bet Ma'aravim complex, a former hostel for North African Jews on the Aqabat Khalidi. These were sporadic and uncoordinated initiatives that attracted little attention compared to the activities of Israeli settlers in Hebron and other parts of the occupied territories.

Another more concerted effort began in the late 1970s when groups interested in the building of a Jewish temple in the Haram ash-Sharif area, mainly from a theological and ritualistic perspective, appeared. As such, their threat to the physical presence of Palestinians in the Old City was not great. The more politically aggressive groups and parties such as the radical Israeli settler movement Gush Emunim and the right-wing nationalist political party Tehiya were more active in the occupied Palestinian territories, concentrating on their encirclement of Nablus and Hebron.[11] There was, in addition, a perception that with the stagnation of the Israeli economy at that time and the need to make stringent budgetary cuts, the settlement movement in the occupied Palestinian territories had peaked.

Certainly there had been a high level of debate among the settler groups concerning future strategies in a less favorable climate. It is quite probable that there was also a redirecting of energies to issues closer to home. While perhaps disagreeing on the next steps for settlement in the occupied Palestinian territories, the settler groups could all agree on the question of Jerusalem and the need to make and keep it Jewish. In their eyes, Jordanian sovereignty of the Haram area and a large Palestinian population in the Old City was a particular affront. The attempts to blow up the Dome of the Rock and al-Aqsa Mosque in 1983 by a Jewish terrorist underground, which drew most of its members from the leaders of the settlers in the occupied territories, was a confirmation of this trend.[12]

The 1980s, however, were marked by the surfacing of a number of ultranationalistic and religious groups—inspired and composed of Gush Emunim members—which were committed to large-scale Jewish settlement in the Muslim quarters. This commitment was in line with their messianic vision of replacing the Dome of the Rock and the al-Aqsa Mosque with a Jewish temple. The groups are Ateret Cohanim, Torat Cohanim, the Young Israel Movement, and Yeshiva Birkat Avraham.

The main form in which Israeli Jewish settlement has taken place has been through the establishment of yeshivas (singular, yeshiva), some numbering up to 100 students, and their attached residential dormitories. A striking feature of these yeshivas is, despite their presence in the heart of the Muslim and Christian quarters, their extreme hostility to the continued presence of their Palestinian neighbors. The attitudes range from having rabidly anti-Arab, or anti-gentile, views to mere resentment of a non-Jewish presence in Jerusalem. They are united, though, in their common purpose of building up a strong Jewish presence in the Muslim quarters that will lead, they hope, to the reconstruction of Solomon's Temple on the site of the Dome of the Rock and the al-Aqsa Mosque.

Municipal statistics do not reveal the extent of the settlement by Israelis in the Muslim quarters. Figures taken from the 1981 census state that there were thirty-nine Israelis in the Muslim quarters. Since then the numbers have grown considerably. A 1998 survey carried out by the Welfare Association, one of the largest Palestinian nongovernmental organizations working in Jerusalem, concluded that there were at least 487 Israeli Jews living in the Muslim and Christian quarters.[13] Much greater numbers attend the synagogues and Judaic seminaries, or yeshivas, on a daily basis (see Map 3.1).

Taxonomy of Settler Groups

The activities of the main settler groups operating in Jerusalem and specifically in the Old City have been well documented in the writings of *Ha'aretz* journalist Nadav Shragai. The following taxonomy is not intended to be comprehensive but merely to indicate the nature and scope of the settlers' activities and how these have had and will continue to have an impact upon the negotiations over the future of Jerusalem. There are three categories of groups. The first category is the main Israeli Jewish groups that are active in attempts to settle in the Muslim quarters: Ateret Cohanim, Torat Cohanim, and the Young Israel Movement. Although a fourth group, the Yeshiva Birkat Avraham, or Shuvu Banim, does not have a coherent ideological commitment to settlement in the Muslim quarters in the same way as the other groups, they have been included here because of their physical presence there. The second category of settler groups has been dubbed the "front organizations" for the main settler groups. The first three of the settler groups mentioned founded a real estate and renovation nonprofit organization known as Atara L'yoshna and initially cooperated in its management. In the early 1990s, another two companies were established: Even Rush and Mordot Moriah. A third category, known as the Temple Mount groups, are not active in settlement activities as such but support the messianic vision of reconstructing the Jewish temple on the Haram ash-Sharif. These are the Faithful of the Temple Mount, the Temple Mount Society, and the Temple Mount Foundation.

The Main Settler Groups

Ateret Cohanim. Ateret Cohanim was founded in 1978 following a series of seminars held in Jerusalem on the subject of temple lore. It was organized by an Orthodox Jewish army veteran named Mattiyahu Ha-Cohen, a settler in the Golan, who was encouraged enough by the response to the seminars to start a separate yeshiva on the subject. Its members have been led by Rabbi Shlomo Chaim Ha-Cohen Aviner, the former rabbi of the Golani settlement of Keshet. Ateret Cohanim is described as an elite Gush Emunim yeshiva, dedicated to the Talmudic study of the priestly rites that took place in Solomon's Temple, and it follows the teachings of the famous rabbinical scholar Hafetz Chaim. The students believe that when Solomon's

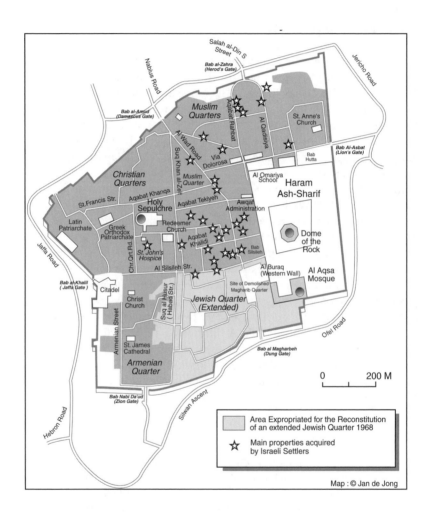

Map 3.1   Israeli Settlement in the Old City

Temple is "rebuilt," it will be necessary to have a temple priest, or *cohen* (plural, *cohanim*), ready to offer animal sacrifices and conduct services according to traditional law. Ateret Cohanim, or "priestly crown," is preparing for that eventuality. Rabbi Shlomo Aviner is reported to have said, "We should not forget that the supreme purpose of the ingathering of the exiles, and the establishment of our state is the building of the Temple. The Temple is the very top of the pyramid."[14]

In 1983 the *Jerusalem Post* estimated that the yeshiva numbered nearly fifty students. By the end of the 1990s, it is probable that their number was closer to eighty or ninety students and up to perhaps thirty families. Where possible, the students are housed in small dormitory rooms in different parts of the Muslim quarters, notably in Kolel Galicia, and the upper floor of a building called the Jerusalem and Temple College by the settlers. Ateret Cohanim students also use an apartment near Herod's Gate as a dormitory. Some of the students are still living in the Jewish Quarter or outside the city walls. Their main center for study and teaching appears to be in the former Yeshiva Torat Hayyim premises.

By the mid-1980s, Ateret Cohanim began to obtain considerable government financial and logistical support. Providing courses under the aegis of the Ministry of Education, it receives student subsidies and obtained a pledge of U.S.$250,000 from the Ministry of Religious Affairs. David Levy, the minister of housing, and his director, Asher Vener, have openly supported Ateret Cohanim, granting it U.S.$40,000 to offset some of its debt that, according to a *Jerusalem Post* report, runs into "hundreds and thousands of dollars."[15] The money was expressly given to enable the yeshiva to continue to buy flats in the Muslim quarters. The debt can be partly explained by recent purchases in the Aqabat Khalidi area, possibly in the courtyard of the Yeshiva Hayyi Olam, which totaled U.S.$160,000.

Despite its success both in the educational activities and in its settlement activities, Ateret Cohanim has tried to keep a low profile in the Old City. It has eschewed the public posturing against Muslim sovereignty of the Haram area, which is espoused by the Temple Mount groups (discussed below), and it attempted to maintain cordial relations with Palestinian neighbors at the same time as it pressed ahead with its attempts to find new properties to settle. The director of the Ateret Cohanim College is reported to have said, "We want to raise the public's spirituality. If the public wants the Temple to be it will be."[16] In the same way, although Rabbi Aviner has disavowed the terrorist methods of other members in Gush Emunim to remove the Dome of the Rock and replace it with a Jewish temple, he has not denied that Ateret Cohanim will be ready to conduct the services when it is built.

Since 1990, Ateret Cohanim has operated in the Old City in a more overt manner. This is partly due to the outcry precipitated by its occupation of the St. John's Hospice in the Christian quarters, which is discussed in detail in Chapter 5. The publicity that the incident generated made the "softly-softly" approach redundant: Most people with any interest in Jerusalem were subsequently aware of the work of Ateret Cohanim. It is also partly due to the explicit support it and its property-owning arm, Atara L'yoshna, began to receive from the Likud-led government of Benjamin Netanyahu between 1996 and 1999, which is examined under the section "Municipal and National Policies" below. Finally, the activities of Ateret Cohanim became so extensive in both the Old City and in the surrounding parts of East Jerusalem—and the funds at its disposal through the benefactions of American Jewish millionaires such as Irving Moscowitz became so huge—that it could not help but attract attention to its work.

Torat Cohanim. Different sources give different dates as to the founding of the Torat Cohanim, which was either in 1979 or 1982. It appears that it, too, evolved from the seminars organized by Mattiyahu Ha-Cohen. Its beliefs closely resemble those of Ateret Cohanim and it has the same twin aims of studying the temple lore as laid down by Hafetz Chaim and settling in the Muslim quarters. It, too, is a Gush Emunim yeshiva but tends to attract *hesder* students, that is, Orthodox Israelis who are not ultra-Orthodox and, therefore, are not automatically exempt from military service. But instead of joining the army, they enter a yeshiva as an alternative. In 1983 it was estimated that Torat Cohanim had approximately fifteen students, though in all probability its numbers have doubled or tripled since. It is led by Rabbi Petrover and received the formal endorsement of Rabbi Avigdor Nebenzal, the former rabbi of the Old City of Jerusalem.

Torat Cohanim was also involved in establishing Atara L'yoshna and is based in Bet Ma'aravim, along the Aqabat Khalidi, which is also the office of Atara L'yoshna. Its members occupy at least three residential units there. Personal observations during the mid-1980s suggested that Torat Cohanim also occupied four apartments in the courtyard of the Diskin Orphanage, a number of apartments in the Yeshiva Hayyai Olam, and two or three apartments in Kolel Galicia. However, during the 1990s it was eclipsed by the burgeoning activities of Ateret Cohanim and maintains a lower profile and is thought to be concentrating less on property acquisition than on preparation of temple rituals.

Young Israel Movement. This settler group was formed by Rabbi Nachman Kahane, reportedly the brother of the late Meir Kahane and former leader of the ultranationalist and racist Kach Party. In the mid-1980s, he and his wife took up residence in the Kolel Georgia on Tariq al-Wad. The Kolel has a synagogue, a library, and a number of small rooms leading off from a courtyard. Rabbi Kahane taught a mixture of Greater Israel theology and temple lore, and by the late 1980s approximately twelve students attended. Rabbi Kahane was also a founding member of Atara L'yoshna, from whom the movement rents its premises.

The Young Israel Movement also ran a small information center in the post office in the Jewish Quarter. From there they organized tours of the Temple Mount, the Jewish Quarter, and sites of Jewish interest in the Muslim quarters, for which they collected donations. The tour, led by Kahane's wife, consisted largely of bringing tour members to all the sites where Jews can get close to the Western Wall of the Haram ash-Sharif. At times this is done in an extremely provocative manner. The narrative is one of extreme chauvinism and presents strongly anti–Palestinian-Arab views. After the tour, postcards of the Haram area with a superimposed picture of the proposed temple are sold at the information center.

The politics and theology of this, the most extreme of the settler groups, have been very disruptive to life in the Muslim and Christian quarters of the Old City. In April 1983, a procession organized by Rabbi Nachman Kahane for the installation of a Torah in the Kolel Georgia synagogue provoked a violent confrontation with its Palestinian neighbors. It is, in addition, interesting to note that during the same week, Rabbi Kahane's son was charged with firing a gun at a crowd of Palestinians in the Old City. As with Torat Cohanim, during the 1990s, the Young Israel Movement was overshadowed by the higher profile of the Ateret Cohanim, whose views, though only slightly less extreme, received greater official support.

Yeshiva Birkat Avraham (also known as Shuvu Banim). This group comprises Hassidic followers of Rabbi Nachman of Bratslav (no connection with Rabbi Nachman Kahane). Their extreme and violent behavior has given them a bad reputation among mainstream Bratslav Hassidim who view them as aberrants. Members of the Yeshiva Birkat Avraham believe in attaining a communion with God by wandering in open spaces shouting their thoughts and emotions, but they also pray loudly with musical instruments and drums when in their yeshiva premises. Many of the members were reformed criminals who are newly converted to Orthodox Judaism. In 1983, they numbered approximately sixty-five students, all of whom were unmarried and some of whom were not resident in the Muslim quarters. Their current number is not known.

They have no living leader or rabbi, though in the mid-1980s the group admitted to being counseled by a Rabbi Leizer Berland. The financial patron of the group was an American Jew from New York, Abraham Dwek. The group differs from the other groups described above in that they do not have a clear political strategy to complement their religious beliefs. It is unclear whether their beliefs are messianic, yet in the absence of a Jewish temple in the Haram area, they promoted the belief that a synagogue should be constructed on stilts so that it would be the highest building in the surrounding area.

It is not clear what their relations with the other settler groups have been, but one indication of what relations may be is that they do not belong to Atara L'yoshna. Another indication is that during the mid-1980s, members of the Birkat Avraham squatted in the former Yeshiva Hayyai Olam courtyard and attacked the remaining Palestinian tenants there. They also began to construct a new floor to their apartment. The Israeli Jerusalem Municipality opposed both the construction and their presence and tried to force an eviction. During a highly complicated court case, Dwek was remanded in custody for four days. The new floor was eventually demolished, but the municipality was unable to remove the actual yeshiva. They found that could only be done if the lessor, Atara L'yoshna, would refuse to renew the yeshiva's lease, which it did not do. Since this incident, very little has been heard of the Birkat Avraham, which suggests that Atara L'yoshna and the other settler groups have put pressure on it to tone down their violent behavior.[17]

The Settler Front Organizations

There are a number of settler front organizations that, once a property has been identified for takeover, take responsibility for the financing of the acquisition and its restoration. The most well known and longest established is Atara L'yoshna, but in the late 1990s two others were also established, Even Rush and Mordot Moriah.[18] Much less is known about these latter two, and further research is required as to the exact nature of their operations and executions of the settler group objectives. For the purposes of this study, the operations of Atara L'yoshna are taken as indicative of the activities of these front organizations in general.

The Atara L'yoshna organization, the "Society for the Renewal of Jewish Settlement Throughout the Old City of Jerusalem," was founded in 1979. According to its own literature, it seeks to "redeem, rebuild and restore Jewish settlement in those areas which are no less 'Jewish' than the 'Jewish' Quarter itself."[19] Among the founders of the society were the Sephardi chief rabbi, Rabbi Mordechai Elihayu; the rabbi of the Old City of Jerusalem, Rabbi Avigdor Nebenzal; an Israeli honey producer and current director of Atara L'yoshna, Yisrael Feuchtwanger; and a lawyer and amateur historian, Shabtai Zacharya. The first president of the society was the chief rabbi of Rechovot, Rabbi Simcha Ha-Cohen Kook.[20]

The organization is registered as a nonprofit and has served as a real estate front for the settler groups operating in the Muslim and Christian quarters. Atara L'yoshna is closely associated with Ateret Cohanim, Yeshiva Torat Cohanim, and the Young Israel Movement. Yet the exact structural relationship between these groups and the society is unclear. The early days of the society were characterized by rivalries between settler groups that led to disputes as to their respective rights and entitlement to properties.[21] By the late 1980s it was clear that Ateret Cohanim had become the dominant group within Atara L'yoshna. Irrespective of these different relations, it is clear, however, that Atara L'yoshna plays a leading role in the Israeli settlement activities in the Muslim quarters.

The settlement program of Atara L'yoshna is well developed and consists of five stages:

1. Locating former Jewish properties in the Muslim quarters
2. Purchasing or leasing of the properties
3. Removing protected and unprotected Palestinian tenants
4. Renovating and reconstructing the properties
5. Settling selected families in the renovated residential units

In terms of locating property, Atara L'yoshna is assisted by the fact that most of the former Jewish properties they have targeted are under the trusteeship of the Custodian of Absentee Property or the Israel-Lands Administration. Atara L'yoshna has had good relations with individual officials in both these departments and who have been instrumental in informing Atara L'yoshna of the existence of several properties.

The cooperation between Atara L'yoshna and the two government departments developed considerably, to the extent that the Israel-Lands Administration has given Atara L'yoshna formal recognition for its work. The director of the Israel-Lands Administration Jerusalem District, Yehuda Zeev, signed an official letter authorizing Atara L'yoshna to conduct negotiations both with Palestinian tenants living in the former Jewish properties and with the Awqaf Administration in the name of the State of Israel. Furthermore, it was authorized to take over the management of property already managed by the Israel-Lands Administration. In this way, Atara L'yoshna has been able to act as an unofficial arm of the Israel-Lands Administration, a state institution, without the political repercussions direct government intervention would excite.[22]

The process of evicting Palestinian tenants from the buildings that Atara L'yoshna has bought or leased has been expensive and slow. The Palestinian tenants have been, in the main, legitimate tenants. However, a pattern of behavior can be discerned: For Atara L'yoshna, those tenants without any proof of tenancy have been simply evicted, while those with proof have been offered, according to its own documents, ample compensation. There is evidence to suggest that the sums have been indeed high and that many tenants have accepted the offer. In the mid-1980s, offers to tenants living in small one- or two-bedroom apartments with very few modern facilities frequently reached up to U.S.$50,000, a considerable sum for an unskilled laborer.[23]

In cases where compensation has not been accepted, tenants have been forced to leave by a number of means. In many cases the apartments are not properly maintained, leading to the development of even more unhygienic conditions. What is more, settlers are known to harass and intimidate tenants. As many of the properties in question consist of courtyards, once a number of settlers have moved in, iron doors are often placed at their entrances, and Palestinian tenants have found themselves locked in. Examples of these and other measures used to enforce evictions are described below under "Validity of Settler Claims to Property in the Muslim Quarters." Over a number of years, these measures have been sufficient to lead to the eviction of many protected tenants.

Atara L'yoshna adopted an ambitious renovation program. All buildings under their management were renovated using well-established and professional architects. Some of the renovations were quite extensive; for example, the Kolel Galicia was completely refurbished to create eleven family units, shops, synagogues, and a reading room. In the mid-1980s, to facilitate their renovation program, Atara L'yoshna established the Binyan Yerushalaim, a subsidiary construction and management group that oversaw their day-to-day renovation work. In doing so, Atara L'yoshna claimed to cut its costs by 30 percent by dispensing with the use of contractors. Given the political sensitivity of the organization's work, it also gave Atara L'yoshna a greater control over the choice of building companies, contractors, engineers, and workers. Significantly, ideological considerations were also applied. Binyan Yerushalaim documents state that only Jewish workers would be used "unless there is no alternative."[24]

The last stage of the settlement program of Atara L'yoshna is the process of selecting and placing suitable people in their properties. From among those who apply, priority has been given to the selection of families. A letter from one of the applying families and taken from Atara L'yoshna's publicity material is illustrative:

> First of all we would like to bless you for your important enterprise and your part in the redemption of Jerusalem in the present and in the future. We are a young couple living in Kibbutz Shalvim and we are planning to move to Jerusalem in the near future. We would like to be included in the settling project in the "muslim" quarter and thus participate in this important mitzva [good deed, religiously speaking]. We are aware that the possibilities of housing in the quarter are limited today but we look forward to the salvation.[25]

The letter itself may not be authentic, but it does indicate the ideological perspectives of those who Atara L'yoshna are hoping to attract. Despite this emphasis on families, personal observations of some of the properties owned or leased by Atara L'yoshna suggest that for security reasons young male yeshiva students are placed in locations that are some distance from other properties occupied by settlers.

An interesting example of the independence Atara L'yoshna exhibits is the way that, despite its close links with government departments, it has insisted on being solely responsible for its selection procedures. Yehuda Zeev, the director of the Israel-Lands Administration Jerusalem District proposed that representatives from the Israel-Lands Administration should sit on the selection panel of Atara L'yoshna. This proposal was submitted in light of the extensive support and quasi-governmental status the Israel-Lands Administration has given Atara L'yoshna. Atara L'yoshna rejected Zeev's proposal with no obvious damage to the spirit of cooperation that exists between them.[26]

For its renovation work on four separate projects, Atara L'yoshna drew up a budget of U.S.$1.7 million. (U.S.$165,000 of this was allocated for compensation payments to tenants.) An application for U.S.$1.8 million was submitted to different governmental departments.[27] Previous projects also included Bet Ma'aravim and Kolel Reissin. Personal observation carried out in February and March 1999 suggests that all these projects have been completed. To raise additional funds for its renovation program and perhaps to keep a measure of independence from the government, Atara L'yoshna embarked upon a fund-raising campaign. Israel Feuchtwanger, then director, visited the United States in 1987 where he launched a "Bricks for Jerusalem" scheme. A glossy pamphlet was also produced outlining the historical background of the Jewish presence in the Muslim quarters from the organization's perspective and explaining its plans to "redeem" the Old City. Contributions to Atara L'yoshna were tax-deductible if sent through P.E.F. Israel Endowments Funds, Inc., with a recommendation that they be used for Atara L'yoshna.

Atara L'yoshna amended its charter in 1983 to include properties that were not formerly Jewish owned. This decision may be, in part, a recognition that in the Old City clear demarcations of ownership within buildings are not feasible and properties are usually partially or jointly owned by different parties. In addition, it may also mark a strengthening of the Gush Emunim ideology in the activities of Atara L'yoshna and adds to the evidence suggesting that the settler groups—and through them the Israeli government—are aiming at the eventual removal of the Palestinian population from the Old City. Non-Jewish properties that may be bought are likely to be those that allow Atara L'yoshna to link up property it already holds. For example, non-Jewish property between Bet Ma'aravim, the Diskin Orphanage courtyard, and the Jerusalem and Temple College building could be bought, if possible, to create a Jewish block in the heart of the

Muslim quarters. In the same way properties around the Hayyai Olam courtyard may be bought up to create a direct link to the Jewish Quarter.

The official recognition and cooperation given to Atara L'yoshna by state institutions such as the Israel-Lands Administration and the Custodian's Office is matched by a formal endorsement of its work from the chief rabbinate of Israel. The endorsement came in the form of a letter that is reproduced in Atara L'yoshna's publicity material claiming that what it is doing is an "important mitzvah" and that anyone helping them "will merit great reward from the Almighty."[28] The letter was signed by the former chief Sephardi rabbi, Mordechai Eliyahu, and the chief Ashkenazi rabbi, Avraham Shapira.

The Temple Mount Groups

There are a number of Israeli Jewish groups currently active in Jerusalem dedicated to the destruction of the Dome of the Rock and the al-Aqsa Mosque in order to replace them with a Jewish temple. The reason they are included in this study is that not only do they share the same ideology as the settler groups, but in some instances they act as conduits for funds to the settler groups. This may have a bearing on settlement activities in the Muslim quarters.

As an interim step to the building of a temple, the groups have a number of demands: They demand Jewish sovereignty over the Haram area, the establishment of a "Temple Mount Authority," and, finally, the right of Jews to pray in the Haram area. To this end, the groups periodically attempt to enter the Haram area carrying prayer books and Israeli flags, particularly on Jewish feast days. They have close links with and are made up of members of right-wing groups and political parties such as Gush Emunim, Kach, and Tehiya and include a number of Likud Party members of the Knesset as their supporters.

Rabbi Shlomo Goren acts as a mentor for the groups, and his teachings on the permissibility for Jews to pray in the Haram area—in defiance of the chief rabbinate of Israel—give them a religious legitimacy. He has been the most vociferous rabbinical authority contesting the ban on Jews worshipping in the Haram area. The ban was imposed in 1967 to prevent Jews from inadvertently desecrating the holy of holies, the ancient location of the Ark of the Covenant, by walking over it. The ban was welcomed by the secular authorities as a means of preserving the existing arrangement over the holy places in Jerusalem. In 1986, however, Rabbi Goren and some colleagues called a press conference in which they declared that they had finally calculated the approximate location of the holy of holies. It would be possible, therefore, to construct a synagogue and worship in the Haram area without desecrating the Jewish holy site.[29] It is reported that he said, "We must establish a place, a permanent place of prayer on the Mount. It is a desecration of God to enter the Mount under the authority of an Arab guard—to enter without saying any holy words because Jews are afraid."[30] At the same press conference, more than a dozen rabbis pronounced themselves as constituting the "Supreme Rabbinical Council of the Temple Mount," challenging the authority of the chief rabbinate of Israel. This is another example of Zionist militants attempting to force the hand of the Israeli political and religious establishment. The main groups associated with these activities are discussed below.

Faithful of the Temple Mount.   Established in 1967, this is the oldest of the Temple Mount groups. A frequent spokesperson for the group is Gershon Solomon, who has publicly supported the settler activities in the Muslim quarters. The Faithful are frequently arrested trying to pray and smuggle flags into the Haram area on Jewish feast days. In 1983 they won an Israeli High Court case permitting them to pray at the Bab al-Maghribiyya, above the Western Wall plaza. They also advocate the establishment of a Temple Mount authority and Israeli sovereignty over the area. Members of the Faithful are drawn primarily from the Kach Party and Gush Emunim and tend to be less religiously orthodox than the other groups. A prominent member of the group is Stanley Goldfoot, formerly of the Stern Gang, who is also international secretary of the Temple Mount Foundation, a wealthy Christian fundamentalist organization in the United States that supports the building of a Jewish temple in the Haram area. Goldfoot is said to channel funds from the Foundation to the Faithful and settler groups in the Muslim quarters (see below). In 1993, the group sought to prevent the Awqaf Administration from carrying out restoration work in the Haram compound and took a number of Israeli bodies to court for permitting such work to carry on. Although the judgment ultimately went against the Temple Mount Faithful on the grounds of high politics and security reasons, it also established a platform from which further legal and political arguments could be made.[31]

The Temple Mount Society (El Har Adonai).   Founded in 1971, this group is regarded as more religious than the Faithful of the Temple Mount. As well as wishing to establish Jewish sovereignty over the Haram area, the Society campaigns for the building of a synagogue next to the site of the Jewish holy of holies. The group claims that the Dome of the Rock or the al-Aqsa Mosque do not have to be destroyed, as the synagogue can be built alongside the Dome of the Rock. Alternatively the Society argues that a synagogue should be built outside the Haram area but in some way that it overlooks the Dome and is the highest building in the area, presumably on stilts.

The membership of the Society is drawn from members of Ateret Cohanim and the B'nai Akiva *hesder yeshiva* (religious students exempt from army services) affiliated with the National Religious Party. It seems probable that some of the Society also live in the Muslim quarters and study at the yeshivot of Ateret Cohanim or Torat Cohanim. The Society was supported by the late and well-known rabbi Tzvi Yehuda Kook of the Marcaz Ha Rav yeshiva. No information was available as to the group's financial resources or the level of Christian fundamentalist support.

Visitors of Zion. This group was founded in response to the passing of the Jerusalem Basic Law, which declared Jerusalem as the eternal capital of Israel. Not much else is known about the group except that it has similar ideology and motivation as the Temple Mount Society and conducts on-site tours and explanations of the proposed Jewish temple in the Haram area. It is thought that this group is not as religious as the Temple Mount Society and has some non-Jewish members and supporters.

The Temple Mount Foundation. This is the main Christian Zionist group active in the plans to build a Jewish temple in the Haram area. Chaired by an American fundamentalist from Texas, Terry Reisenhoover, its international secretary is Stanley Goldfoot from the Faithful of the Temple Mount group. The Temple Mount Foundation, sometimes known as the Jerusalem Temple Foundation, was originally established to provide funds for the legal fees of the Jewish terrorists who were charged with conspiring to blow up the two Muslim sites in the Haram area and the attempted murder of three West Bank mayors.

The main beliefs of the Foundation stem from a development in Christian fundamentalist thought known as "dispensationalism." Dispensationalism places present-day Israel in the center of world events by asserting that the ingathering of the Jews is a prelude to the last days and the Second Coming of the Messiah. Rebuilding Solomon's Temple in the Haram area will hasten the arrival of the Messiah. Dispensationalists fully welcome the conflict that the destruction of the Muslim holy places would generate, seeing this as the prophetic Armageddon, which will herald the new age.

The Foundation received support from a wide range of Christian fundamentalist organizations such as Jerry Falwell's Moral Majority as well as High Adventures, Inc., and other televangelists such as Jimmy Swaggart. It also received funds from the Recanati brothers, co-owners of the Israeli Discount Bank, and support from Professor Moshe Sharon of Tel Aviv University. The Foundation sought to raise U.S.$100 million annually for its activities in Jerusalem. Since the trial of the Jewish terrorists, the

Foundation has directed its work toward assisting groups seeking to eliminate Muslim control over the Haram area. Money has been sent to the Faithful, reputedly U.S.$50,000, and plans have been drawn up to purchase the Dome of the Rock and the al-Aqsa Mosque and transfer it stone by stone to Saudi Arabia. Reportedly the Foundation has also contributed to the preparation work of Ateret Cohanim by buying cedar wood from Lebanon, which is to be used for the construction of the temple, and by direct financial contributions.[32]

There is then a clear and admitted linkage between the Foundation, the Faithful of the Temple Mount, and Ateret Cohanim. What is not clear is whether funds from the Foundation to Ateret Cohanim are used for settlement purposes. In this context it is interesting to note a *Jerusalem Post* report that in the mid-1980s Ateret Cohanim had considerable debts.[33] This suggests that Foundation contributions are either small amounts or specifically earmarked for temple research and preparation only.

The International Christian Embassy in Jerusalem (ICEJ). The ICEJ is involved with the proposed temple plans to a lesser extent than the Foundation. Established in 1980 after the refusal of most Western Christian countries to move their embassies to Jerusalem, the ICEJ seeks to mobilize Christian support for Israel. The current director is Jan Willem van der Hoeven. The group's theology and supporters are fundamentalist, equating present-day Israel with biblical Israel. The Embassy had strong South African connections.

Its main activities to date have been to attract Christian fundamentalists to the annual Jewish Feast of the Tabernacles. The program includes tours of Israel and the occupied territories, and their final ceremonies in Jerusalem are addressed by the president and the prime minister of Israel. In 1985 the ICEJ held the First Christian Zionist Conference in Basle, emulating the first Zionist congress held there in the nineteenth century. Although the ICEJ denies giving money to any of the Temple Mount groups or settler groups, it does inform people of their activities, and those wishing to donate funds are directed to Stanley Goldfoot of the Faithful. The ICEJ also sells milleniarist literature and a cassette narrated by the current director describing the proposed temple. There is no evidence, however, that the ICEJ has been directly involved in settlement activities.

While the evidence available on the organizational links between the Temple Mount groups and the settlers in the Muslim quarters is sparse, overlapping membership and common ideological purposes ensure a reasonably close coordination in activities. One can speculate that the differences that do arise are more of a question of emphasis and method rather than ultimate purpose. One can draw attention here to the position of Ateret

Cohanim, which, while being prepared to conduct services in the proposed temple, denies that it is actively seeking to remove the al-Aqsa Mosque and the Dome of the Rock. Other groups have been less circumspect.

Validity of Settler Claims to Property in the Muslim Quarters

Because any negotiated settlement on the Old City will require a clarification of the role of Israeli settler groups in the Muslim quarters and their entitlement to the property they have required, let us examine briefly the basis upon which these clams are made. It is important to recognize that the settlers operate in a framework of political protection and also of certain legal advantages that flow from that protection. By examining the legal status of their acquisitions, one can discover more the extent to which the state supplies support for their activities. This section will look only at the validity of Israeli settler claims to property in the Muslim quarters. Although in some cases the legality of such claims is itself in doubt, and the means by which occupations are affected are controversial, it is the political and partisan nature of the application of Israeli law that is the underlying and most important issue.

As we have already seen, prior to 1948 there were many Jewish institutions and families living in properties in the Muslim quarters. To understand the issue more clearly, the claims to these properties can be placed upon an imaginary scale. On one end of the scale would be the properties over which there is little dispute. These would include properties that were abandoned or leased to Palestinians by the mid-1930s and whose title deeds have been retained by the original owners. Thus, properties such as the Yeshiva Hayyai Olam courtyard and the Bet Ma'aravim, which were Jewish endowments, would fall in this category.

The settlers, however, make claims to properties whose ownership is less clear and should be placed somewhere in the middle of our scale. The Yeshiva Torat Hayyim could also be placed in this category. The building was jointly owned in the pre-1948 period by the yeshiva and a Palestinian Arab. In the late 1970s, Ateret Cohanim bought or leased the Jewish part from the Jewish owners and is now attempting to take over the remainder of the building. It has occupied areas of the building that were left empty as previously agreed with the Palestinian Arab joint-owner and has attempted to change the ownership agreement from joint-ownership to a parceling agreement.

Further along our scale there are claims to property that become more tenuous. These can be illustrated by the Ezrat Nashim Mental Hospital, which was a collection of rooms rented by a wealthy Jewish benefactress and which moved several times in the Old City before finally moving out of the walls in 1896. The fact that this claim is more historical than legal does not appear to deter the settlers. It is still said to be Jewish. At the furthest end of the scale there are properties whose Jewish connections are extremely tenuous and almost incidental. Here one can cite the examples of the public baths, the Hamam al-Ain and the Hamam al-Shifa off the Suq al-Qattanin. The claims to these properties appear to be based simply on the presence, in part, by the baths of Judaic ritual cleansing areas, or *mikvaot*. It is clear, though, that rather than forming the basis of ownership, commercial considerations, due to the proximity of the baths to the Jewish Quarter and Western Wall, led to the construction of *mikvaot* in their interiors. However, the ingenuity of the settlers' lawyers in pressing these claims should not be underestimated.

To fully understand the legal position of these properties, we must return to the situation immediately after the 1948 war, when the Jordanian Guardian of Enemy Property took over the care and management of these buildings. The huge influx of refugees as a result of the war meant that many refugees squatted in the deserted premises. In cases where the emigrating Jewish owner had leased the properties to Palestinian tenants, the tenants were obliged to continue paying rent to the Guardian. In many cases the position of the refugee-squatters was regularized by giving them formal tenancies. Whether the Guardian maintained these former Jewish properties in good condition is uncertain. It is likely that the Jordanian government policy of building up Amman at the expense of Jerusalem during this period resulted in the minimum amount of funds being made available to the Guardian for the maintenance of "enemy property," and a minimum of repairs were carried out.

Following the Israeli occupation of the Old City in 1967, the Israeli government passed the Legal and Administrative Matter (Regulation) Law (Consolidated Version) in 1970. Article 5 of this law caused property that was managed by the Jordanian Guardian to be handed over to the Israeli Custodian for Absentee Property. The Custodian was charged with turning over the former Jewish-owned properties to their original owners, if they could be found. Some of the properties were put in the hands of the Israel-Lands Administration, which has the right to sell or lease properties to Israeli Jews only.

There are three reasons why occupation of these properties did not take place immediately by Israeli settlers. First, as we have seen, Israeli attention and energies were directed mainly at the reconstruction of the enlarged Jewish Quarter and settlement in the West Bank and Gaza Strip. With so many opportunities elsewhere, settlement in the heart of the Muslim quarters was not an attractive prospect. Second, as will be discussed in the next section, the former mayor of Jerusalem, Teddy Kollek, wielded great authority over the development of the Old City and his "mosaic" principle was opposed to ethnically or communally integrated residential quarters. Third, the Custodian is obliged by Israeli law to recognize the existing tenants of a property as protected tenants. In cases of properties that had been owned by Jews, if the tenants had been recognized by the Jordanian Guardian as protected tenants, these same protected rights were carried over and recognized by the Custodian. Thus, former Jewish owners were not free to simply move into their former premises.

Within these constraints and before the handing over of property to the settler groups began, there is some evidence to suggest that the Custodian and the Israel-Lands Administration were preparing the ground for the eviction of the Palestinian tenants. In many cases properties were poorly maintained, adding to the neglect already experienced under the Jordanian Guardian, and tenants were even taken to court for attempting to improve the safety and sanitation of their apartments. Such a policy encouraged those tenants with possibilities of alternative accommodation to move out. Furthermore the Custodian and the Israel-Lands Administration applied the tenancy regulations with extreme rigor. Children of protected tenants, for example, were denied the right to live with their parents once they were married. Moreover, parents were not permitted to transfer their tenancies to their children as is usually the case in the Old City. These policies meant that by the late 1970s many of the properties were tenanted by the elderly, or those with poor family connections or who were less well-off. These tenants were easily subjected to pressure and harassment. Few of them could afford court cases.

As was described, compensation has been offered to the Palestinian tenants by the settler groups if they agree to leave. If they refuse, there have been a number of incidents that lead one to conclude that the tenants are subject to a wide range of abuses and physical harassment. Below are three examples of physical intimidation. Two of them are well known, and the details have been checked with the lawyers that covered their cases; the third example is extracted from a personal interview.

1. In April 1983, a sixty-year-old tenant of Atara L'yoshna in the courtyard of Yeshiva Hayyai Olam, Fatmeh Abu Mayyali was stabbed and beaten unconscious by students of the Yeshiva Birkat Avraham. The students claimed that the woman's husband from whom she was separated had sold the apartment to the yeshiva. Fatmeh was contesting the legality of the sale when she was attacked, as it was agreed without her consent. She later died from her injuries.

2. Two months later in the same courtyard, Mahmoud Abu Sneineh was attacked by students from the same yeshiva because he refused to accept compensation and leave his apartment. The students also ransacked

his rooms. Two students were charged and sentenced, and the deputy attorney general of Israel ordered that police protection should be provided for several days for Abu Sneineh, and, thereafter, regular patrols should call at his apartment. But the district police commander claimed that he did not have the resources to enforce such a ruling, with the result that even after eighteen years Abu Sneineh is too frightened to return to his apartment. His lawyer fears that Abu Sneineh may still be prosecuted for abandoning his tenancy.

3. Raqifa Radwan Salaymeh lived with her daughter in a room off the Diskin Orphanage courtyard. She claimed her room was ransacked by Israeli settlers who had moved into the courtyard after evicting other Palestinian families from the courtyard. Her belongings were thrown out of the rooms and she was prevented from reentering. After some weeks of living on the streets, she cleared a derelict room in the courtyard and moved in there. She claimed she was constantly abused and frequently attacked. She stopped paying rent, as the previous "owner" (it is likely she meant the first tenant, as she turned out to be the subtenant), a member of the Nabulsi family, refused to accept it, and she did not know to whom it should be paid. It may be that the Nabulsi concerned was, in fact, a tenant of the Custodian and accepted compensation from Atara L'yoshna without any consideration of subtenants of his, such as Salaymeh.[34]

As important as the personal suffering caused, the following two points should be noted. First, the application of Israeli law to repossess Jewish property in the Muslim quarters is highly partisan. As the former mayor Kollek has frequently pointed out, there is no reciprocity allowed in these claims. Indeed, a law was passed to expressly deny the inhabitants of the annexed East Jerusalem the opportunity of regaining the properties they had lost in West Jerusalem.[35] Second, the mosaic policy, which was used to exclude Palestinians from living in the enlarged Jewish Quarter, is being openly flouted to the detriment of Palestinians in the Muslim quarters. What was given the force of law in the Jewish Quarter is now being side-stepped in the Muslim quarters.

Municipal and National Policies

In light of these activities, it is also important to establish the degree of Israeli government involvement. To what extent were the settler groups proxies of the state in a covert policy to acquire property and extend Israeli influence in the Old City? Or, were they acting independently but attempting to shift political and public perceptions against the constraints of

Israelis adopting a higher profile there? A number of phases can be identified beginning with minimal state involvement but ending in the past few years with active support and collusion. The implications for this on a negotiated settlement are quite profound. It is clear from the discussion earlier that the settler groups are aware of the danger of too warm a government embrace. They have sought to broaden their financial and political constituency to include support from the Diaspora and thus from groups beyond Israeli state control. Ironically, active state involvement may make a reversal of the settler gains more achievable.

It is clear that at their inception the settler groups lacked material support from the Israeli state. This was partly due to the political and ideological domination of Jerusalem by the former mayor, Teddy Kollek. He held the view that coexistence between Palestinian Arabs and Israeli Jews could be best served by a mosaic principle that recognized different styles of living and, more important, a certain territorial homogeneity. The optimum conditions for such social harmony could be fashioned through careful planning along these lines. The mosaic principle provided the rationale for the eviction and subsequent exclusion of Palestinians from the Jewish Quarter, indeed, and is entirely consistent with a pragmatic Zionist occupation policy. Yet the surfacing of the settler groups marked the end of Kollek's ideological hegemony and the decline in his political authority. It also marked a shift in the internal debate between the establishment Zionist position, as represented by Kollek, and the militant Zionist position, represented by the settler groups, in the latter's favor.

In spite of the fact that during the late 1970s and early 1980s the Likud government was positively encouraging settlement in general, Kollek's position on Jewish settlement in the Muslim quarters was crystal clear. He insisted that a quotation from him should be included in the manifesto of his "One Jerusalem" electoral list. It read (unofficial translation):

> I don't believe in the infiltration of [Jewish] individuals into the Muslim Quarter, and I strongly oppose this. Each *yeshiva* there requires more policemen than students. . . . Do you know how much property is registered in the names of Arabs in the western part of the City? What will happen if they come one day and demand to restore them?[36]

This unequivocal public position has been backed up by the application of municipal planning regulations where necessary. A measure of Kollek's success in this internal Israeli debate was the opprobrium heaped upon him by the militant settler groups.[37]

Kollek's influence, however, had two weak points. First, it meant that the government was saved the embarrassment of taking a clear stand on the issue, which resulted in it having no policy for it at all. This is a crucial factor when government intervention is necessary. In addition, it is thought that in the long term the municipality would like to clear much of the Muslim quarters of its so-called slum conditions, leaving the market areas and the Via Dolorosa for touristic purposes. The areas thus vacated by Palestinians would be reconstructed and settled by Israeli Jews. In this context, then, the Israeli settler groups are merely speeding up the process of Palestinian resettlement and forcing the municipality and the government to follow in their wake. Second, the settlers were able to exploit the fact that acting as a private and nonprofit organization they were frequently not accountable to the Israeli Municipality and could both pursue their settlement aims and obtain grants from government ministries. Thus, as Kollek's power over them was circumvented and the government was not acting to prevent them, the settlers were given a free hand to expand their activities in the Muslim quarters. In an editorial, the *Jerusalem Post* had this to say:

> In the past two years, this mosaic pattern has been disturbed at its most sensitive point—the Moslem Quarter of the Old City. Some 200 Jews, most of them yeshiva students, have settled in formerly Jewish-owned buildings in the quarter. The motive of some of them may be confined to repossessing the buildings, but others would like to turn the Moslem Quarter into a thoroughly mixed neighbourhood, and ultimately perhaps to make it as Jewish as the Jewish Quarter itself.
>
> In any case, their presence in the Moslem Quarter constitutes a grave danger to the peace of Jerusalem—they are, as a senior government official has put it recently, "the fuse in the powder-keg. . . ."
>
> This still relatively limited presence could spread uncontrolled without a clear official stand. With all the difficulties now facing the country, from the economy to Lebanon, it should be spared trouble in Jerusalem too. The situation calls for urgent preventative action by the government.[38]

Another factor leading to an increase in attention toward settler group activities was the appointment of settler supporters to the key state ministries and agencies under the Likud Party in 1977. This increase in the profile of these groups necessitated a coordination strategy between government ministries, the police, and the municipality.[39]

The settler groups also agreed to sit on an interministerial committee set up to discuss the subject of their activities in the Muslim quarters. Members of the committee included representatives from the Housing, Justice, and Interior Ministries; representatives from the municipality, the army, and the police; the district archaeologist; and representatives from the different settler groups. The meetings were chaired by the coordinator of Activities for Jerusalem Affairs in the Ministry of the Interior, Ephraim Shilo. One can speculate that this committee was set up at the instigation of the municipality to assert some control over the settlers' activities. If this was the case, it failed to do so.

Four secret meetings were held and the minutes were classified as highly confidential, but some details were leaked to the Israeli press.[40] The following decisions concerning Jewish settlement in the Muslim quarters were agreed upon with the representative of the municipality dissenting:

1. Buildings classified under municipal regulations as dangerous would be demolished and not renovated.
2. The settlement of Jewish families would be given priority over the establishment of institutions.
3. No settlement or renovation would take place near the Haram ash-Sharif.
4. No settlement would take place in property sealed off by the army.
5. For security reasons, only properties close to the Jewish Quarter would be occupied and renovated.
6. No government support would be given to properties not close to the Jewish Quarter.
7. A follow-up committee would be set up and coordinated by Ephraim Shilo of the Ministry of the Interior.

These decisions raise a number of interesting points. First, the agreement to demolish rather than renovate "dangerous" buildings adds to the impression received by many residents of the Old City that plans for the depopulation of the Muslim quarters do exist. Second, the committee marked the beginning of a covert government policy to develop the area contiguous with the Jewish Quarter, the Hebron Market Area of settler parlance, and to eventually absorb it into the Jewish Quarter. One can observe that linking up areas of settlement has long been a Zionist strategy for expansion and occupation, and as a senior official in the Awqaf Administration has observed, this is already taking place in the area around the Bet Ma'aravim. The third point listed above is of particular interest and was probably included on the insistence of the army and by members of the committee with more establishment Zionist views. However sympathetic they might have been to the Greater Israel views of the settlers, they would certainly draw the line at their messianic plans to build a Jewish temple on the Haram. Settlement in areas close to the Haram would be bound to increase the agitation for Jewish sovereignty over the Haram area. The settlers' concession on this point seems to confirm the view that the government, on its part, has agreed to support the gradual absorption of the area just north of the Jewish Quarter into the Jewish Quarter itself.

The extent to which these decisions were adhered to is difficult to judge. The facts on the ground suggest that some have been ignored, not least that there has been no follow-up committee set up as agreed. Furthermore, some settlement has taken place close to the Haram, notably in a courtyard known as Tzadik's Damen and in Beit Rand, beside the Suq al-Qattanin.[41] One can imagine that the settler groups were unhappy to be constrained by the committee's decisions. Given the uncertain political conditions prevailing in 1985–1986 with no clear government policy on settlements, even in the occupied territories, the settlers may have hoped to return to the former unrestrained and low-profile settlement that suited their goals better. If, as seems to have been the case, they could continue to circumvent Kollek's authority over the matter and still obtain the cooperation of sympathetic officials in government departments, they would, in fact, be in a stronger position than in the previous state of affairs.

In retrospect, one can see how the issue of the Yeshiva Birkat Avraham had the ingredients of a test of strength between the settlers and their opponents. That the result was not conclusive—their illegally constructed floor was demolished but they remained in the Muslim quarters—indicated that the settlers had obtained a partial reprieve that they could convert into a secure foothold in the Muslim quarters. A strongly worded editorial in the *Jerusalem Post* declared:

> The public has lately become aware of the problem from reports about the crude harassment by "penitent" students of the Birkat Avraham Yeshiva of their neighbours in the Moslem Quarter. But these pious, if still violent yeshiva students appear to have no particular nationalist ambitions. The notoriety they have acquired in fact spoils it for the young Gush Emunim zealots who are quietly hoping to set up yeshivot tinged with nationalist activism amid the Moslems of the Old City. . . .
>
> The Jerusalem Municipality hoped that the inter-ministerial committee would act as a brake on extremist elements seeking to set up house within the Moslem Quarter. This hope has been dashed. The way now seems open to the settling of the other former Jewish buildings. And this, municipal officials realise, could well be not the end but only the beginning of a major move of expansion near the Mount by Gush Emunim.
>
> Jerusalem's Mayor Teddy Kollek is disturbed. Action by a tiny minority trained in the art of imposing their will on the majority of the nation threatens to produce friction and tension and upset the delicate inter-communal balance on which the peace of Jerusalem largely depends.[42]

From the mid-1980s onward, there is evidence for strong but covert government support for the settlers. Such support has circumvented the authority of the municipality and taken the form of grants for housing, educational courses, and religious subsidies. The settler groups have the support of many individuals in different government departments who have been able to provide financial pledges through administrative rather than legislative means. For example, the U.S.$40,000 grant to Ateret Cohanim from the Ministry of Housing for the purchase of apartments in the Muslim quarters, as mentioned previously, was a unilateral decision by a committee and not authorized by the state budget.

The close relationship between the settler groups and Israeli state institutions continued to flourish until 1992, when the Likud government under Prime Minister Yitzhak Shamir was replaced by Yitzhak Rabin and a Labour coalition government. Although the government held a hawkish position on Jerusalem, it initially sought to put a brake on settler activity in the Old City and other parts of East Jerusalem. In addition, at the urging of Kollek, in 1993, it set up a Commission of Enquiry into state support for the settlers, headed by a respected official, Haim Klugman. The report of the Klugman Commission more than confirmed the level of state support received by settlers that had been suspected in the 1980s. It also revealed the extent to which it had been both thoroughly institutionalized and in many areas quite illegal.[43] The two main findings were (1) that the Ministry of Housing under Ariel Sharon channeled in excess of $22 million to various settler groups for acquisition and renovations in the Old City and East Jerusalem, and (2) that the Office of the Custodian of Absentee Property sold or rented property to the settler groups in breach of normal government guidelines.

The report admitted difficulties in tracing all the financial transfers due to the complexity of the accounting procedures. But it did discover a number of transgressions: Accounts were specifically allocated for settler groups; funds were transferred from funds earmarked for new immigrants and hardship families; and some funds were also directed to settlers through the state-owned Company for the Redevelopment of the Jewish Quarter. In addition, to this hard cash, the settler groups saved additional significant funds through the sale and rent of property for nominal sums. Finally, the Klugman Report also confirmed the existence of logistical, legal, and administrative support for settler activities through the workings of a special committee set up in July 1991 to oversee the acquisition and transfer of Palestinian property to settler groups.

Despite the hard-hitting nature of the findings and the attempts by Kollek and pressure groups opposed to the settlers in forcing the government to take action, there was no decision to reverse the gains made by the settlers.[44] For example, the Hospice of St. John, belonging to the Greek Orthodox Patriarchate and occupied by settlers in April 1990 by means of a Panamanian shell company, still remained in settler hands despite many legal petitions (see also Chapter 5).[45] While during the period 1992–1996 some of the settlers' development plans were stymied and the overt financial support from the government dried up, they were now in a much stronger position and could point to solid achievements on the ground in their fund-raising campaigns. This track record led to the mobilization of external support from wealthy individuals such as the Florida-based Jewish billionaire Irving Moskowitz.

The late 1990s also saw the conjunction of a Likud-led national government, under Prime Minister Netanyahu, and a Likud mayor of Jerusalem, Ehud Olmert. While much of the activities of the settler groups under their joint tenure were directed outside the city walls, the process of identifying properties to be acquired and renovating those already acquired continued. The consolidation of the settler position in the Old City went unabated. The strength of their position can be seen in the way that even during the aftermath of the riots following the opening of a tunnel along the whole stretch of the Haram's Western Wall, they were able to act decisively to prevent a Palestinian welfare center being constructed in an area of the Muslim quarters (Burg al-Laqlaq) and quickly throw up a building in its place.[46] What this incident demonstrated was that the settler groups had both become part of the political mainstream and that neither Netanyahu nor Olmert could afford to be seen to be outflanked by them in their support for a "Jewish" Old City.

Implications

Irrespective of their militant religious and chauvinistic ideology that mitigates against harmonious coexistence with the Palestinian community, the presence of the settler groups adds to the pressures on the Palestinians that already exist in the Muslim quarters. Furthermore, the vulnerability of their residence in an unsympathetic environment will inevitably lead to demands for further protection and government intervention. In the short term, their presence may lead to the establishment of more army checkpoints and settler patrols. In the long term, Palestinian residents fear that continued Israeli settlement in the Muslim quarters will trigger municipality development projects in the area, which will diminish the Palestinian presence in the area and alter the Arab and Islamic character. Manifestations of the Arab and Islamic character will remain only for touristic purposes. In addition, the agreement between the settler groups and the government not to settle close to the Haram ash-Sharif is likely to be a tactical concession that the settlers will ignore once they have consolidated their finances and their hold on current properties.

The chief area of future settler activity will be in the Aqabat Khalidi–Aqabat Saraya rectangle. This area was the most populated by Jews in the late nineteenth century and lies contiguous to the Jewish Quarter. It contains the most Jewish properties and, as previously mentioned, in settler circles it is often referred to as the Northern Jewish Quarter. Settler groups have already taken over the Diskin Orphanage courtyard, the Yeshiva Hayyai Olam courtyard, Bet Ma'aravim, and Kolel Galicia.

Other former Jewish-owned or -leased properties are in close proximity to these properties as well. They are, therefore, prime candidates for future resettlement. They include the Aguna Synagogue, the Vishnitz Synagogue, the Ezrat Nashim Mental Hospital, and Rabbi Rechtman's courtyard. If their status is as the settler historians and lawyers claim, then these properties have been managed by the Custodian or the Israel-Lands Administration and are most probably already in the process of being handed over to one of the settler groups. Given the close relationship between Atara L'yoshna and government bodies such as the Israel-Lands Administration, the most likely means by which this handover will be effected is that the Atara L'yoshna will be made chief tenant and it will go on to lease the properties to the other settler groups.

Once these latest properties are fully occupied and settled, the settlers will attempt to consolidate their hold over them and the Aqabat Khalidi–Aqabat Saraya area by linking each of them up. In some cases the linking-up process will not involve the purchase of new properties. For example, the Diskin Orphanage courtyard has already been linked up with Bet Ma'aravim by means of a short underground passage. Linking up other former Jewish properties will be more difficult, for it will involve the purchase and occupation of a considerable number of Palestinian-owned properties. This did not deter Atara L'yoshna, which, as we have seen, changed its charter to allow it to purchase property that had no historic or legal connections to Jews. With this obstacle already cleared, the settlers will attempt to buy or find legal means to take over property between Bet Ma'aravim and the Jerusalem and Temple College and between Bet Ma'aravim and Kolel Reissin. Already settlers have illegally occupied some apartments next to Bet Ma'aravim that belong to the Rsass *waqf*.[47] These attempts will be replicated in many other instances resulting in that many of the Palestinian properties in this area will be partially settled or undergo court proceedings as a result of such illegal occupations.

Although not of the same priority as the former Jewish properties in the Aqabat Khalidi–Aqabat Saraya area, other areas will also be the target of settler activities. Ateret Cohanim will continue its efforts to take over the remainder of the Yeshiva Torat Hayyim building on Tariq al-Wad, which it now shares with a Palestinian owner. Similarly, it will continue to attempt to persuade the Palestinian residents living in Tzadik's Damen House to leave. Due to their Jewish association and their proximity to the Yeshiva Torat Hayyim building and the Kolel Georgia, two other former Jewish properties in that area will be targeted for occupation. These are the Frumkin Press and Synagogue courtyard and the Leider Synagogue courtyard, which will set in motion the linking-up dynamic in this area.

According to the historian Shabtai Zacharya, one family has already moved into the Leider Synagogue courtyard. Although no evidence has surfaced to corroborate the claim, the intention is clearly there.

Renovation of the Bet Warsawa courtyard in the Bab al-Huta area, begun in the mid-1980s, will also continue. During fieldwork the legal status of the adjoining properties was not discovered. But judging from maps of the area hanging in Atara L'yoshna's office, these are also being claimed as former Jewish properties. The purchase or leasing of the adjoining properties is likely to be a high priority. Settler groups will be keen to both establish their presence in the area, regarded by them as the tenth-century Jewish Quarter, and to precipitate municipality development plans and "slum clearance" projects. Provocative incidents to encourage Palestinians to leave their homes may be engineered, which may compel the army to set up an army checkpoint. This would give the settlers further security.

The above-mentioned properties and areas can be regarded as part of the first wave of settler residency. Following their renovation and settlement, the second wave took the form of occupying former Jewish properties close to the Haram ash-Sharif. These include Rabbi Lapin's courtyard, Rabbi Beer's home and synagogue, David Boimgarten's shop, and the Bet Rand courtyard. Not all parts have been acquired yet. A third wave of properties may be targeted for occupation by the settlers in the long term and has been mentioned previously as being at the far end of an imaginary scale. These include buildings such as the Hamam al-Ayn, which have had historical associations with the Jewish presence in the Muslim quarters but without being legally owned by Jews. Occupations of such buildings would not be likely without government or municipality connivance.

Purchasing or leasing non-Jewish property still remains a difficult task for the settler groups at this stage. Communal pressures mitigate against any public sales, and the PNA and Jordanian government have reinforced this stand by passing the death sentence on a number of individuals who have sold property to Israelis. The Awqaf Administration, too, plays a role in keeping this communal pressure alive. In this context one can imagine that the settler groups will be willing to purchase any property that becomes available.

Departing from existing precedents, another likely means in which the settlers will step up their presence in the Muslim quarters is by involving the East Jerusalem Development Company for the Reconstruction of the Jewish Quarter. In the past, the company has attempted to develop the roofs of the shops managed by the Awqaf Administration in order to build a rooftop promenade, linking the Kolel Galicia to the Jewish Quarter.[48] It is clear that the municipality and the East Jerusalem Development Company would like to proceed with the construction of similar open spaces in certain areas of the Muslim quarters, particularly alongside the city walls. The settlement of Jews in areas close to those designated for such development would increase the incentive and the pressure for the East Jerusalem Development Company to implement its plans.

The settlers may also use provocative incidents to precipitate a greater army presence in the Muslim quarters. A greater Jewish presence in the Muslim quarters may provoke spontaneous retaliations by Palestinian residents. Certain areas next to the Haram ash-Sharif of mutual religious and national significance are likely flash points. In this regard the Small Kotel is of particular interest. This is a place where nationalist Jews are coming to pray in increasing numbers. I accompanied a member of the Young Israel Movement settler group to the Small Kotel and was told how, on the Jewish feast of Succoth, the settler groups met for worship in the courtyard of Ribat Kurd and along the Tariq Bab al-Hadid. Numbering approximately 200 people, the festivities were accompanied by dancing, singing, and music. It is highly probable that open manifestations of the Jewish presence in the Muslim quarters such as these will eventually lead to an incident resulting in a permanent army post at the gate or in the street. As it is, the Awqaf Administration has had the key to a small room next to the Small Kotel courtyard that was confiscated by the police after a dispute with the settlers over the room's use.

The occupation of army-sealed buildings may also provide the settlers with further means of increasing their presence in the Muslim quarters. As we saw earlier, this kind of action by the settlers was ruled out by the interministerial committee. The ambiguous role of the army in settlement activities has been amply demonstrated in the occupied territories, notably in Hebron. A further flouting of the interministerial guidelines may result in the occupation of abandoned, derelict, or unsafe buildings in the Muslim quarters. The personal opposition of former mayor Teddy Kollek to the uncoordinated settlement activities of the settler groups stems partially from their possible interference with long-term municipal plans for redevelopment in the Muslim quarters. The plans often include keeping abandoned, derelict, or unsafe buildings in that condition until a project can be fully implemented. The current mayor, Ehud Olmert, with his close relations to members of the settler groups, is unlikely to be so deterred. It is quite plausible, for example, that the settlers may receive a grant from a government body or international foundation to reconstruct an area, which although conflicting with specific municipality projects could still be presented by the settlers as slum clearance and redevelopment and, therefore, not inconsistent with the long-term goals of the municipality. In this way such unilateral action in occupying abandoned buildings would receive widespread support and trigger the municipality's own plans.

It is too early to say if the situation in the twenty-first century will constitute a new phase in settler activity. Under Israeli prime minister Ehud

Barak, state support for settler activity diminished but government passivity toward their activities, already heavily institutionalized and incorporated into the political mainstream, led to greater entrenchment and consolidation of their operations. In light of this, the role of the settlers becomes crucial to the future allocation of sovereignty in the Old City. Since the failure of the Camp David summit and the election of Ariel Sharon, this role has been enhanced.

To sum up the previous discussion, one can safely assume there will be a greater push by the settler groups in two spatial directions. One, they will seek to acquire as much property as possible in the Aqabat Saraya–Aqabat Khalidi area. This area contains the highest concentration of former Jewish properties in the Old City and is also immediately adjacent to the Jewish Quarter. Already, as a result of settler acquisitions during the 1980s and 1990s, the area is approaching the mixed population balance that was recorded during the mandate period. The de facto absorption of this area into the Jewish Quarter is likely to be the top priority for the settler groups, probably with covert financial support from the government. Two, it will be considered critical to establish a territorial corridor from the Jaffa Gate to the Jewish Quarter and the Kotel. Acquiring property from the Armenian Patriarchate in order to establish territorial contiguity has had only limited success in the past and is unlikely in the current climate.[49] Thus, the acquisition of properties along David's Street is likely to be the next priority.

From this chapter, one can see how the Israeli state has successfully consolidated its hold over parts of the Old City. While it confined its presence to the area of the Jewish Quarter, despite its enlargement, there was a prospect of a modus vivendi being established between the different parties in the peace process. However, the Israeli settlers operating in other parts of the Old City have upset the delicate balance and a political settlement that recognizes their acquisitions is not achievable. Indeed, their continuing operations are likely to serve, in the medium to long term as a catalyst for the further expulsion of Palestinian residents from the Old City. Judged by their own terms, the settler groups have been a success in that not only have they acquired up to eighty properties in the Old City, but they have also obtained extensive state subsidy, administrative support, and an acceptance into the political mainstream. Yet measured in other ways, their acquisitions amount to little more than 1 percent of the total properties in the Old City, and the total Jewish population in the Old City has remained less than 10 percent of the total population. Indeed, one result of the activities of the settlers has been to galvanize and reinvigorate the Muslim and Christian Palestinian populations in the Old City following a period of disorganization and stagnation. It is to the response of these residents of the Old City that we now turn.

Notes

1. See Y. Ben Arieh, *Jerusalem in the 19th Century: The Old City* (New York: St. Martin's Press, 1984), 283–284, 360. A brief summary of the system can be found in R. Nyrop, *Israel: A Country Study* (Washington, D.C.: The American University, 1979), 66.

2. Arieh, *Jerusalem: The Old City,* 290.

3. J. Halper, "Jewish Ethnicity in Jerusalem," in *Jerusalem: City of the Ages,* ed. A. L. Eckhardt (New York: University Press of America, 1987), 186.

4. Y. Ben Arieh, *Jerusalem in the 19th Century: Emergence of the New City* (New York: St. Martin's Press, 1989), 390.

5. M. Romann, "The Economic Development of Jerusalem in Recent Times," in *Urban Geography of Jerusalem,* eds. D. Amiran, A. Shachar, and I. Kimhi (Berlin: De Gruyter, 1973), 92–96.

6. See R. Kark's monograph on this subject in *Jerusalem Neighbourhoods: Planning and By-Laws (1855–1930)* (Jerusalem: Magnes Press, 1991); see also reservations expressed in my review of her book in *Journal of Palestine Studies* 22, no. 1 (autumn 1992): 108–109.

7. M. Dumper, *Islam and Israel: Muslim Religious Endowments and the Jewish State* (Washington, D.C.: Institute for Palestine Studies, 1994), 119.

8. *Burkan v. the Minister of Finance,* Israel Supreme Court, 4 July 1978, cited in R. Lapidot and M. Hirsch, eds., *The Jerusalem Question and Its Resolution: Selected Documents* (Dordrecht, Netherlands: Kluwer Academic Publishers, 1994).

9. Dumper, *Islam and Israel,* 119.

10. *Jerusalem Post,* 2 February 1974.

11. For further details, see E. Sprinzak, *The Ascendance of Israel's Radical Right* (Oxford: Oxford University Press, 1991), 107ff.

12. Ibid., 258–259.

13. Welfare Association, *Jerusalem Old City Revitalisation Plan: Interim Summary Report,* Jerusalem, January 1999, 19. According to this survey there are about 600 Israeli Jews living in the Armenian Quarter, but because their residency followed the expansion of the Jewish Quarter in 1969, they are not regarded as settlers in the same way as is being discussed in this chapter. See Table 2.2.

14. Cited in "Israeli Settlement in the Old City of Jerusalem" (manuscript, World of Islam Festival Trust, London, 1987), 15.

15. *Jerusalem Post,* 27 March 1986.

16. Ibid., 12 December 1983.

17. "Israeli Settlement in the Old City of Jerusalem" (manuscript), 18.

18. These organizations are briefly mentioned in A. Cheshin, A. Melamed, and W. Hutman, *Separate and Unequal: The Inside Story of Israeli Rule in East Jerusalem* (Cambridge, Mass.: Harvard University Press, 1999), 217.

19. Leaflet issued by the Atara L'yoshna organization, no date.

20. Leaflet issued by the Atara L'yoshna organization in 1986.

21. Letter sent to Ehud Shilat, the registrar of nonprofit organizations, Ministry of Interior, Jerusalem (undated, but probably 1979), disputing the right of a rival group calling themselves Torat Cohanim: "Their aim is to jeopardize the existence of our association and then take hold of the properties listed above as well as the yeshiva." Copy in author's possession.

22. *Ha'aretz,* 23 April 1986.

23. Letter reproduced in a brochure issued by the Atara L'yoshna organization in 1986. Copy in author's possession.

24. Leaflet titled "Binyan Yerushalaim: Group for Building Projects Founded by Atara L'yoshna Organisation." No date, but obtained in 1986.

25. Letter reproduced in a brochure issued by the Atara L'yoshna organization in 1986. Copy in author's possession.

26. N. Shragai, "Who Will Buy: Who Will Buy Me a House?" *Ha'aretz,* 23 April 1986 (translated from the Hebrew by Professor Israel Shahak).

27. The four projects to be renovated were: 537 square meters in Bet Warsaw; four apartments in the Diskin Orphanage courtyard; several apartments in the Yeshiva Hayyai Olam courtyard, Kolel Georgia; and thirteen apartments amounting to 1,600 square meters in Kolel Galicia. Taken from Atara L'yoshna's publicity literature.

28. Letter reproduced in a brochure issued by the Atara L'yoshna organization in 1986. Copy in author's possession.

29. *New York Times,* 6 August 1986.

30. Ibid.

31. See "Temple Mount Faithful v. Attorney-General et al.," in *Catholic University Law Review* 45, no. 3 (spring 1996): 861–941.

32. "Israeli Settlement in the Old City of Jerusalem" (manuscript), 39.

33. *Jerusalem Post,* 27 March 1986.

34. I was not able to find her lawyer, an Israeli called Mr. Aron, to confirm all the details of her case.

35. Article 3a, Legal and Administrative Matters (Regulations) Law (Consolidated Version) 1970.

36. Cited in N. Shragai, "Who Will Buy: Who Will Buy Me A House?" *Ha'aretz,* 23 April 1986.

37. There is some evidence that initially Mayor Kollek was sympathetic to the aims of the settler groups in that he thought they might promote Palestinian-Israeli coexistence in the Old City, but he changed his mind when confronted with their aggressive behavior. See *Ha'aretz,* 29 May 1998, cited in H. Abu Shamseyeh, "Settling the Old City: The Policies of Labor and Likud," *Jerusalem Quarterly File,* no. 6 (autumn 1999): 41.

38. *Jerusalem Post,* 27 January 1984.

39. See M. Dumper, "Israeli Settlement in the Old City of Jerusalem," *Journal of Palestine Studies* 21, no. 4 (summer 1992): 43, for further details of disputes between the municipality and the settlers, particularly the Shuvu Banim yeshiva.

40. See, for example, N. Shragai, "One House After the Other," *Ha'aretz,* 25 April 1986.

41. It may also be significant that Ephraim Shilo resigned from his post soon after the follow-up committee failed to meet, though there is no evidence of a direct correspondence between the two events, as he was known to have been largely sympathetic to the settlers.

42. *Jerusalem Post,* 13 December 1983.

43. "Report on Settlement in East Jerusalem," October 1993, known as the Klugman Report. Attached to the report were copies of key memoranda recording meetings of special committees overseeing the acquisition of Palestinian properties and of details of financial transfers from the Ministry of Housing to settler groups.

44. See A. Cheshin et al., *Separate and Unequal: The Inside Story of Israeli Rule in East Jerusalem* (Cambridge, Mass.: Harvard University Press, 1999), 221–224, on Kollek's attempts to restore property to Palestinian owners and tenants. Lawyer Daniel Seideman and the Ir Shalem group appealed to the Israeli High Court to force the government to take action on the findings of the Klugman Report.

45. M. Dumper, *The Politics of Jerusalem Since 1967* (New York: Columbia University Press, 1997), 194–195.

46. See the article by G. Usher, "Israel's Jerusalem Pyromania," *Middle East International*, 5 June 1998, 3–5.

47. For further details, see Dumper, "Israeli Settlement in the Old City of Jerusalem," 49–50.

48. For further details, see Chapter 4 herein.

49. A possible additional linkage from Jaffa Gate directly to the Jewish Quarter is through the property belonging to the Anglican church, Christ Church Cathedral, near Jaffa Gate. This cathedral has been taken over by Hebrew-rite Christians who are, in the main, Israeli citizens. There is only a small car park, owned by the Armenian Patriarchate, separating the cathedral from outlying parts of the Jewish Quarter.

4

The Muslim Community: Religious Endowments and the Awqaf Administration

In viewing the position of the Muslim community in the Old City since 1967, the picture is very mixed. On the one hand, the community has clearly lost its preeminent political role and significant amounts of actual geographical territory. The loss of the Jewish Quarter, the destruction of the Magharib quarter, the attacks on the Haram enclosure itself, Israeli excavations around the walls, the dramatic encroachments of the Israeli settlers examined in the previous chapter, and the opening of the Hasmonean Tunnel along the Western Wall of the Haram enclosure have all been manifestations of its gradual social and political decline in the Old City. On the other hand, there are areas of consolidation and expansion that are quite remarkable given the forces ranged against it. There is evidence of a revived Islamic cultural life and extensive renovations to the historical monuments and residential areas. The main agent in these areas is the Awqaf Administration, the administrative structure in charge of the religious endowments and the single largest property owner in the Old City. Furthermore, the social and political decline has not been matched by a demographic decline of the Muslim community. Indeed, more recent statistics indicate that the opposite is occurring at the expense of the quality of life in the Old City. This mixed picture is further obscured by a transition in the political allegiances of the religious hierarchy in the post-Oslo era. The gradual establishment of a Palestinian state apparatus on the borders of Jerusalem is precipitating a slow transfer of loyalties from the Hashemite Kingdom of Jordan to the PNA.

This chapter consists of two main parts and a shorter concluding part. The first part examines the decline in the role of the Muslim community in the Old City. It delineates the historical and wider contemporary political context by looking at trends from the British Mandate period and the events that took place immediately after the occupation in 1967. It also refers to a number of points of contention with the Israeli government, such as the development of open space in the Old City, the Haram massacre, and the opening of the Hasmonean Tunnel. The second part examines the areas of consolidation and expansion in the Muslim community. It consists mainly of an in-depth study of the Awqaf Administration with a particular focus on the work of the Department of Islamic Archaeology (DIA) set up in the mid-1980s. In addition, there is an examination of the attempts by the Awqaf Administration to adapt to new commercial and organizational realities and the lack of funding by ushering in gradual reforms to the extensive endowment, or *waqf,* system. The third and final part examines the impact of the post-Oslo situation and some of its responses to the new political configurations. In addition, reasons are posited for the failure of the administration to realize its full potential, both as an agent of social and political change but also as a base for the consolidation and expansion of a Palestinian national presence in the Old City.

Challenges Facing the Muslim Community

The decline of the Muslim community in the Old City has its antecedents in the British Mandate period. The decline accelerated in 1967 with the expropriation of the Jewish Quarter and the destruction of the Magharib quarter. Although these are the most dramatic instances, there are many examples of how the community is unable to protect its assets and its integrity. In Chapter 3, we saw how the covert operations of the settler groups began to make serious inroads into the life of the largely Palestinian Muslims living in the Muslim quarters. In addition, there have been a number of other attempts to infringe on the community's space through the activities of the Israeli Municipality and more dramatic events such as the massacre in the Haram ash-Sharif in 1990 and the opening of the Hasmonean Tunnel in 1996. Let us now examine these events as illustrations of this decline.

The Decline of the Muslim Community

It is to be expected that shared sites should create the most difficult challenges in maintaining mutual respect between religious communities, and the conflict over the Western Wall of the Haram ash-Sharif has been a source of conflict from at least the early days of the mandate. In view of the drama that continues to surround this area, a brief look into some past events is required.

There are three main issues in the Western Wall incident of 1929 that are relevant to the contemporary situation:

1. The site is shared between Muslims and Jews, and competing reli-

gious claims have provided a vehicle for more secular nationalist claims.

2. The increased use of the site as a result of demographic growth has led to demands for greater access; this, in turn, has led to confrontation and changes in jurisdiction and control.

3. The preservation of the religious status quo was dependent upon the willingness of the dominant state authority to enforce it.

Muslims call the Western Wall al-Buraq, after the horse of the Prophet Muhammad. Tradition has it that the horse was tethered to the wall during the prophet's ascent to heaven and, thus, has become a Muslim holy site. In, addition the pavement adjacent to the wall is part of the Abu Madyan Sufi *waqf*, which made up the whole area west of the wall. The pavement in front of the wall was used as a means of access to dwellings along and attached to the wall.

At the same time, the wall is sacred to the Jews because sections are believed to be formerly part of the Temple of Solomon. During the Ottoman period, Jews were traditionally permitted to use this area for the saying of prayers, provided that no fixed religious equipment was used that would block the pavement. In general, both religious Jews and Muslim residents of the area displayed mutual respect. But the circumstances ushered in by the British Mandate period disturbed this equilibrium and the area, sacred to both religious groups, and became the focus of national and religious tensions.

As we have seen in Chapter 2, the British Mandate authorities were formally obliged to preserve the religious arrangements surrounding this site, which had existed during the Ottoman period, but the events of 1929 placed this commitment under great strain. As the mandate period progressed and more Jews arrived in Jerusalem, it was possible to see how Zionist Jews, with their increasing numbers and their self-conscious religious nationalism, began to assert themselves more forcefully along the wall. Although previously there had only been small groups of Jews and then only intermittently, there was now a constant presence throughout the night and day with large crowds during Sabbath and feast days. This growing presence began to cause offense to both the Muslim residents and the Muslim authorities responsible for the site and the *waqf*—at that time known as the Supreme Muslim Council. Discussion among Zionist circles as to the possibility of buying the Western Wall and pavement transformed this sense of offense to alarm.[1]

The catalyst for Palestinian Muslim opposition was the erection of a screen on the pavement that would separate Jewish male and female worshippers. This was an infringement of the existing religious arrangements that, as in all cases like this, needed to be halted, if it was not to become a new status quo. The Muslim response was to reassert their presence by practicing Sufi prayer rituals, which included the banging of cymbals and drums. This, in turn, provoked a large Jewish demonstration to protest against British inaction.

In essence, the incident became a test of which religious community was dominant in Jerusalem. The Supreme Muslim Council organized a nationwide campaign and set up a committee specifically to rally support from the international Muslim community. Thus, added to the Palestinian dimension, which reflected the Muslim fear of Zionist Jewish immigration and encroachment, was a general Islamic dimension, purporting to prevent the desecration of Islamic sites by Jews. In August 1929, riots broke out and nearly 100 Jews were killed and Jewish settlements were attacked. The British acted quickly to put down the violence and commissioned an inquiry to discover the causes of the incident and make recommendations.[2] The status quo ante was restored and Jewish access to the area monitored carefully.

What had been at stake in the Western (Wailing) Wall incident was clearly more than the question of access to a holy site, though this was very important. Much more profoundly, the incident reflected the tensions brought about by the changes wrought by the Jewish National Home policy of the British on Jerusalem and in Palestine. It brought into sharp relief the underlying structural alterations taking place in the relationship between the Muslim and Jewish communities, where the total and unquestioned dominance of the former was now being challenged by the latter. The British Mandate authorities may have held the line during their period of jurisdiction and over this particular site, but the pressures continued to build up all around. While the status quo ante was restored for the Muslim community, it was clear that the pressure from the Jewish community for greater access would continue to build. The outbreak of fighting between the Zionist settlers and Palestinians in 1948 was simply this early confrontation writ large. While between 1948 and 1967 the question of increased access was postponed due to the division of the city, it returned with a vengeance in 1967. From the point of view of the Muslim quarters, the events of 1929 constitute a precursor of the destruction of the Magharib quarter in 1967 and the later attempts to infiltrate the Muslim quarters in order to surround and take over the Haram compound.

The Magharib Quarter

A further example of the gradual decline of the Muslim community in the Old City is illustrated by the destruction of the Magharib quarter. The Magharib, or Moroccan, quarter was one of the oldest quarters in the Old City and lay immediately in front of al-Buraq, or the Western Wall. It was inhabited primarily by people who could trace their lineage to families of North African descent. During the Ayubid period, the quarter, an area of approximately 10,000 square meters, was endowed for the benefit of the community and Moroccan pilgrims. It was completely demolished by the Israeli government within days of the start of the 1967 war, and it was an indication of the ruthlessness and efficiency in which the Israeli government was prepared to act to extend its control over the Old City when political factors were propitious.

On 11 June 1967, even before the hostilities were over, the Palestinian inhabitants of the quarter were ordered to evacuate their houses. Israeli army sappers laid and detonated explosives in the houses and courtyards, and bulldozers appeared at the Dung Gate and proceeded to clear away the rubble. When the dust had settled, a large plaza leading up to the great Herodian blocks of the Western Wall was revealed, the only remnant of the former quarter being a Sufi *zawiya* (prayer room) perched above ground level and clinging to the entrance to the Haram ash-Sharif.[3]

To Jews and Israelis, the creation of the plaza in front of the wall was a form of redemption. Cut off from their holiest site for years, they could not only return but also congregate unimpeded and in large numbers. The Western Wall plaza, as R. Freidland and R. Hecht write,

> penetrated to the very core of the state's civil religion. Israel's elite military units are initiated in complex ritual ceremonies in the plaza in front of the wall and the state's new memorial festivals—Holocaust Memorial Day, the Memorial Day for Israel's soldiers who have fallen in war, Independence Day, and Jerusalem Day—all have important ritual ceremonies at the Western Wall.[4]

To Muslims and Palestinians it was a portent of the nature of Israeli rule: 135 homes were destroyed, the ancient Buraq and Afdali mosques were demolished, and approximately 650 people were evicted without warning.[5] Israeli responses to this act are interesting. Meron Benvenisti, the former deputy mayor of Jerusalem, for example, justified it in the following terms:

> The move was the settling of an historic account with those who had harassed the Jewish people over the centuries, restricting it and humiliating it at its holiest place, as well as with those who had prevented access to the wall for nineteen years. The displaced inhabitants of the Mugrabi Quarter were not personally to blame, but it was their fate to be additional victims of the Arab-Israeli conflict.[6]

Yosef Schweid, the senior municipal architect and town planner, expressed similar sentiments:

It was not just the practical aspect—the need to absorb large numbers of people [in front of the wall], which was the deciding factor here; even more important was the sense of the historic necessity of the act, a sense of expiation and restitution, and that was what motivated the decision.[7]

Teddy Kollek, the Israeli mayor of Jerusalem at that time, has admitted that he ordered the demolition of the Magharib quarter to be carried out quickly before international bodies like the UN Educational, Scientific, and Cultural Organization or the UN itself could intervene.[8]

The destruction of the Magharib quarter highlights a number of issues relevant to the discussion over the erosion of the Muslim presence in the Old City. First, it is clear that the religious sanctity of a site is of no guarantee of its survival; second, given opportune political circumstances, the Israeli state did not hesitate to assert its control in favor of the Jewish community; and, finally, to establish physical control and demographic dominance over the city, it was willing to risk international opprobrium and condemnation.

Expansion of the Jewish Quarter

Another measure of the decline of the Muslim community in the Old City was through the acquisition of *waqf* property and specifically the enlargement of the Jewish Quarter. When one visits the expanded quarter today, with its swish shops and luxury apartments, it is hard to believe that it was once also part of a busy Arab area, albeit poor and dilapidated in parts, or that it was also the ancient home of many well-known Jerusalem families, such as the Abu Su'ud, Hariri, Ja'ouni, Nummari, and Dajani. It is difficult to be precise about the exact location of the traditional Jewish Quarter because, as already has been noted, the borders between all the quarters of the Old City fluctuated according to immigration and political circumstances of a given period, but there is no doubt that it was smaller than its modern Israeli counterpart.[9]

As was described in Chapter 3, during the latter part of the nineteenth century and the beginning of the twentieth, Jews started to settle well outside the traditional quarter, in areas to the north near the soup kitchen of Khaski Sultan and along the Tariq al-Wad. Indeed, in the middle of the nineteenth century, the smallness of the Jewish Quarter was much commented on by Western travelers.[10] During most of the nineteenth and twentieth centuries up to 1948, it was surrounded in the west by the Armenian St. James Cathedral and the adjacent residences of Armenians, as well as the Syrian and Maronite convents around which also lived their communities and four small quarters named after the Muslim families living there; in the north it was bordered by the Tariq Bab al-Silsilah and the central market area; in the east by the Harat al-Sharaf along the slopes overlooking the Magharib quarter; and in the south by the city walls and another small *hara* called Abu Maidun.[11] As well as being small and centered largely in one area, the Jewish Quarter was made up mostly of property rented from Palestinian Arab landlords and from public and family *waqf*s.[12]

Following the 1948 war and the evacuation of the Jewish Quarter by the Jewish inhabitants, many Palestinian Arab refugees from residential quarters in West Jerusalem took up residence in empty Jewish properties in the quarter. Initially, their residence was administered by the International Red Cross, but later and until their eviction in the 1960s and 1970s it was placed under the jurisdiction of the United Nations Relief and Works Agency (UNRWA).[13] Property that had been owned by the former Jewish inhabitants was put into the care of the control of the Jordanian Guardian of Enemy Property. In many cases, the Guardian rented it out to both individuals and to UNRWA.

On 18 April 1968, the Israeli minister of finance, Pinchas Sapir, issued an order expropriating twenty-nine acres (or 116 *dunum*s) of the southern part of the Old City for "public purposes." The declared reason was to develop this area to house Israeli Jewish families and to reestablish a Jewish presence in the Old City. The boundaries of the expropriation zone stretched from the Western Wall in the east to the edges of the Armenian monastery in the west, and from the Tariq Bab al-Silsilah in the north to the walls of the city in the south. The expropriation included 700 stone buildings, only 105 of which were owned by Jews before 1948. Of the Palestinian Arab properties expropriated, there were 1,048 flats or apartments housing 6,000 Palestinians, and 437 workshops or commercial stores providing employment to approximately 700 workers.[14]

The former mayor of Jordanian East Jerusalem, Ruhi al-Khatib, protested in the following way:

> By these new expropriations Arabs in the City will lose properties which have belonged to them for hundreds of years, and more than 6,000 Arabs will be evacuated from the City and dispersed . . . while more than 700 employers and workers will be deprived of their means of livelihood, and forced to swell the ranks of the homeless . . . while the landlords and beneficiaries of Waqfs, who used to enjoy and live on the rent of their properties and Waqfs, will be deprived of their sources of livelihood and forced to join the ranks of the needy, if not of the refugees.[15]

The eviction of the Palestinians inhabitants and *waqf* tenants was not carried out in one day, as in the Magharib quarter, but was spread out over a decade as houses became earmarked for renovation and reconstruction.[16] Taken together with the loss of the Magharib quarter, this loss of assets for the Muslim community was a severe blow.

Encroachments on Waqf *Property*

As already noted, following the Israeli occupation of the city in June 1967 and its reunification policies, the new extended Israeli Municipality attempted to incorporate the functions of the Awqaf Administration into its jurisdiction.[17] The chief *qadi*, the director-general of the Awqaf Administration, and the mufti of Jerusalem took a firm line and insisted that Awqaf property and the ordering of the Muslim community was beyond the jurisdiction of the Israeli Municipality and the Israeli government. Instead, they called a meeting of the heads of the Muslim community in Jerusalem and the West Bank to establish a governing Muslim body to guide the interests of the Muslim community under occupation. This action was in accordance with a *fatwa* enunciated by the chief *qadi* in which he declared that under non-Muslim occupation, the Muslim community must elect a leading body to look after its interests. The body became known as the Higher Islamic Board ('al-Ha'i al-Islamiyya al-'Ula) (HIB) and was composed of twenty-five people drawn from leading families, notables, and Jordanian members of parliament.[18] The HIB received telegrams and letters of support from trade unions, cultural clubs, and cooperatives legitimizing its representativeness.[19] After declaring its opposition to the Israeli occupation and the formal annexation on 28 June 1967 of Jerusalem by the Israeli government, the HIB's main task was to reactivate the Shari'a courts and to establish an executive council that became known as the Awqaf Council.[20] The purpose of the Awqaf Council was to oversee the administration of *waqf* property on the West Bank through the Awqaf Administration, and of the *waqf* schools and the al-Aqsa restoration project.

Relations among the Israeli government, the Israeli Jerusalem Municipality, and the Awqaf Administration are of a unique nature and, in Israeli law, anomalous. If East Jerusalem had been properly annexed, the Awqaf Administration would have been absorbed by the Israeli Ministry of Religious Affairs. The legal anomaly that constitutes this relation can be expressed briefly by saying that neither body recognizes the other as having any authority in the Old City and East Jerusalem.[21] Thus, while the Ministries of Religious Affairs and of the Interior claim jurisdiction over the upkeep and administration of the Islamic monuments and archaeological remains, many of which are *waqf*, the Awqaf Administration continues to administer them regardless of any counterclaims.[22] The Awqaf Administration is often in conflict with the municipality and other Israeli government bodies. The confiscation of its *waqf* property is an obvious cause of friction. For security reasons, property such as the *madrasa* (religious school) Tankiziyya, beside the Bab al-Silsilah, has been expropriated, and part of the Islamic museum in the Haram ash-Sharif cannot be used, as it overlooks the Western Wall. The enforcement of public safety measures also results in confiscation of dilapidated Awqaf Administration properties. Finally, the expropriation carried out in the Magharib quarter and the Jewish Quarter and the loss of communal assets there, from mosques, mausoleums, and residences, made cooperative relations very difficult.

However, many informal contacts do exist and much courtesy has been shown, at least in the higher echelons, by the Israelis for the Awqaf Administration. A former mayor of Jerusalem, Teddy Kollek, frequently visited the mufti during times of political crisis, and the Awqaf Administration's Department of Islamic Archaeology still has informal contacts with Israeli academics who subject their work to professional criticism.[23] The result is that not all the encroachments upon the Muslim community in the Old City have been as dramatic as the preceding examples. Much give-and-take takes place. An example of the subtle and constant erosion of the position of the Muslim community can be seen in the dispute over the Roof Top Promenade in the Old City. This was a proposal to develop the area above three parallel *suqs* (markets) in the heart of the Old City, al-'Attarin, Suq al-Lahamin, and Suq al-Khawajat. Municipality architects and planners argue that this is a neglected space that could be used as a park and garden area to ease congestion in the Old City, particularly in the expanded Jewish Quarter. They proposed that it should be paved and that flowerbeds and shrubs be introduced between seating areas to create a promenade.

As manager of the *waqf* shops beneath the area, the Awqaf Administration objected to the proposals on a number of grounds. First, the Western-style design of the promenade was out of keeping with the surrounding styles and would undermine the Islamic and Arab character of the Old City. It is interesting to note that the designs harmonized much more with the refurbished and expanded Jewish Quarter, which is adjacent to the area. The project could be seen, therefore, as a form of architectural "Israelization" of the remaining parts of the Old City. Second, the Awqaf Administration did not wish to cooperate in relieving the congestion in the expanded Jewish Quarter while the Israeli state still retained properties expropriated from the Awqaf Administration. More important, the Awqaf Administration was not prepared to relinquish responsibility for the maintenance of the roofs of the *suqs*, anticipating that it might lead to further encroachments by the Israeli government. This was particularly the case in view of the establishment of an Israeli settlement in the former Kolel Galicia beside the market area, whose members used the rooftop as their main access to the Jewish Quarter. In view of these objections, in 1986, the Awqaf Administration's DIA began to carry out a simple retiling of the rooftop area without the walkways and planted beds as a preemptive measure and as a means of asserting its jurisdiction and control over the area.

For most of the period under review, the Awqaf Administration regarded itself as part of the Jordanian Ministry of Awqaf in Amman and continues not to recognize Israeli occupation over Jerusalem and is reluctant to go to an Israeli court to defend its own jurisdiction. Thus, in a situation of conflict with, for example, the municipality, the Awqaf Administration cannot take it to court and has to accept many unpalatable measures such as expropriation or demolition by administrative diktat. However, in 1987 it broke with precedent and defended itself in an Israeli court.[24] In addition to these encroachments, there were two more direct incidents that took place in the 1990s that have seriously threatened the role of the Awqaf Administration. The first is the Haram ash-Sharif massacre and the second is the opening of the Hasmonean Tunnel, which runs along the Western Wall of the Haram.

Direct Confrontation with the Israeli State

On 8 October 1990, seventeen Palestinians were killed and more than 150 were injured as a result of Israeli border police gunfire at the Dome of the Rock compound in Jerusalem.[25] The violence erupted when a large crowd of Palestinians (between 2,000 and 5,000) had gathered in the Haram compound to prevent the entry of the Temple Mount Faithful, discussed in Chapter 3.[26] Public calls from mosques and schools were issued in order to gather Muslims to defend the Haram in what was perceived as an attempted takeover, as the Temple Mount Faithful group has threatened to do on several previous occasions. During the course of the demonstration, stones were thrown at Jewish worshippers at the Western Wall. As the demonstrations spread through the West Bank and Gaza Strip, two more Palestinians were shot dead by Israeli Army soldiers in Gaza, and more than forty leading Palestinians were arrested, including Faisal Husseini, the leading Palestinian politician in Jerusalem, and the deputy mufti of Jerusalem. In addition, the most densely populated areas of the West Bank and Gaza were placed under curfew.[27]

Israelis and Palestinians disagree on how violence erupted and about the necessity of the force used by the Israeli paramilitary police. The Israeli government blamed the PLO for what they said was a deliberate attack on innocent Jewish worshippers. Prime Minister Yitzhak Shamir appointed the official Israeli Commission of Investigation on 10 October, which was headed by Zvi Zamir. The results of this investigation differed from the reports of the Palestinian al-Haq and the Israeli B'Tselem, both human rights organizations, in almost all aspects. Most important, the *Zamir Report* states that "the incident itself began when, suddenly, violent and threatening calls were sounded on the speakers ('Allahu Akbar,' 'Jihad,' 'Itbakh al-Yahud' [Slaughter the Jews]). . . . The actions of the rioters, and certainly the inciters, constituted a threat to the lives of the police, the thousands of worshippers at the Western Wall and to themselves."[28] It prevailed a few days later after other investigations that the attack, in fact, had been spontaneous and unplanned. Indeed, when the paramilitary police opened fire on the Palestinians inside the Haram, the Jewish worshippers at the Western Wall, who the paramilitary were ostensibly protecting, were no longer in danger, as they had been evacuated earlier on. Nor was the paramilitary police force in danger at this time.[29] Similarly, it was discovered that the Palestinian crowd had not been incited to "slaughter Jews" by the loudspeakers.[30] However, the Israeli government rejected accusations of blame or responsibility for the massacre and reacted angrily to a UN Security Council Resolution condemning Israel for the Haram al-Sharif killings. It refused to cooperate with the UN team that was supposed to launch an investigation into the incident.[31]

The second incident that also directly undermined the role of the Awaqf Administration and the development of the Muslim community in the Old City was the opening of the Hasmonean Tunnel and the subsequent riots on 24 September 1996. The twelve-year-old excavation project of a tunnel running along the Western Wall of the Haram compound was completed on the personal orders of Prime Minister Benjamin Netanyahu. Palestinians perceived this act as a message to them that Israel was to be the sole sovereign in Jerusalem.[32] The PNA denounced the opening of the tunnel and called for a general strike in protest, during which Palestinians clashed with the police and the Israeli Army in Jerusalem. The worst fighting since the peace process began ensued throughout the occupied territories.[33] As a result, Ramallah was declared a closed military zone, and the West Bank and Gaza were sealed as a security measure. Heavy fighting also took place in Nablus where six Israeli Defense Force soldiers were killed. The confrontations continued throughout the West Bank and Gaza Strip in sporadic outbursts, resulting in the death of eighty-six Palestinians and fifteen Israelis, as well as thousands of wounded in the first week after the opening of the tunnel.[34] Nevertheless, Israel accused the PNA of instigating the violence and Foreign Minister David Levy stated that the tunnel would stay open.[35]

For Palestinians, these confrontations with Israel were simply the latest manifestations of the struggle with Jews and the Israeli state over the control over the Haram compound and the Old City. Following the precedent set by the Western Wall incident in 1929, the demolition of the Magharib quarter, the expansion of the Jewish Quarter, the penetration of settlers into the Muslim and Christian quarters of the Old City, the activities of the Temple Mount Faithful groups, and the Jewish underground to take over the Haram all were part of a broad strategy for their ultimate dispossession in the heart of Jerusalem.

**Consolidation: Developing the
Assets of the Awqaf Administration**

Despite the gradual usurpation of the Awqaf's role, the undermining of its
ability to preserve the existing religious arrangements for its worshippers,
and the creeping penetration of Israeli state-supported projects in the Old
City, the Awqaf Administration has had some success in other areas. This
section will start with a brief overview of its role as landlord and provider
of religious, educational, and welfare services. It will then focus on the
restoration program of the Awqaf Administration's DIA to draw out the
range of responsibilities and physical impact that the Awqaf
Administration's activities have on the Old City. Finally, it will look more
generally at some of the jurisprudential changes that have taken place that
allow the *waqf* institution to respond more creatively than is often imagined
to changes to political, legal, and commercial practice.

Structure and Programs

The basic administrative structure of the Awqaf Administration was introduced in 1966, and although several reforms were enacted, the structure
remained the same until the Oslo Accords. A director-general in Jerusalem
oversees the work of each department, and he is responsible directly to the
Ministry of Waqfs in Amman. Jerusalem departments include Pilgrimage
Affairs, the al-Aqsa Restoration Project, the Department of Islamic
Archaeology, the Department of Engineering and Maintenance, as well as
separate departments for finance, education, public relations, and research
into Islamic sciences. Including guards for the Haram area but discounting
contract labor, in the mid-1980s the Awqaf Administration employed
approximately 200 people in Jerusalem. Since then, this has decreased due
to budgetary cuts imposed by Amman. Since the Oslo Accords, there has
been no formal change in this structure, though informally there is much
consultation. The late Shaykh Hassan Tahbub, who was appointed the minister of religious affairs by the PNA, was formerly the director-general of
the Awqaf Administration and worked closely with the current director-general.[36]
     For the post-1967 period, some estimates for the extent of *waqf* proper-
ties in the Old City were obtained from former officials in the Jordanian
government and the Awqaf Administration. Including properties now confiscated by the Israeli government in the area developed as the Jewish
Quarter, but excluding the Haram ash-Sharif, the late Anwar Khatib, the
former governor of Jerusalem, estimated *khayri waqf*, that is, a public *waqf*,
at 30 percent, and *dhurri*, that is, a private or family *waqf*, at 40 percent of

the Old City. Tahbub estimated *khayri* at 30 percent but *dhurri* at no more than 15 percent.[37]

From interviews I conducted during 1986 with six *mutawalli*s, or administrators, of major *dhurri waqf*s in the Old City, Khatib's figure for *dhurri* would appear to be too high. A figure between 15 and 20 percent would be much more accurate. Taking these figures together, the total of *waqf* property in the Old City excluding the Haram area can be estimated to be approximately between 45 and 50 percent. Including the Haram area, which amounts to 17 percent of the Old City, the grand total of *waqf* property in the Old City comes to approximately 67 percent, or more than two-thirds.[38] A more recent figure has been offered by veteran Israeli journalist of the Old City Nagav Shragai. He gives the figure of 210 *dunum*s of the Old City (52.5 acres) as belonging to the *waqf*, presumably the Awqaf Adminstration.[39] Whatever the percentages, the Israeli scholar Yitzhak Reiter, who studied the archives of the Awqaf Administration in the Department of Islamic Heritage, was able to show that from the mid-1980s, the Awqaf Administration was responsible for the following properties in Jerusalem:

- 376 shops in the Old City, including 129 in Bab al-Zahra business district
- 66 residences, of which 350 were in the Old City (48 as Awqaf Administration offices, 76 rented to the Israeli Jerusalem Municipality)
- 116 units serving as offices in the Bab al-Zahra area
- 4 large houses rented to banks
- A number of hotels
- The Shari'a court building on Salah ed-Din Street
- Several school buildings
- 1 car park
- The central bus station and surrounding shops

In addition, the following are administered by the Awqaf Administration but only produce nominal rents as a result of long-term leases (*hikr*): 625 shops, 171 homes, 19 workshops, 22 businesses, and 30 miscellaneous buildings. Property not generating incomes includes the Haram ash-Sharif compound, 65 mosques, 3 cemeteries, 27 fountains, 34 wells, 9 educational institutions, and an unspecified number of *zawiya*s and saints' tombs.[40]

The Awqaf Administration was concerned with the provision of facilities for prayer and worship. Accurate and up-to-date data on all the construction and maintenance projects carried out by the Awqaf Administration in Jerusalem are unavailable, but by turning to its official report covering the period 1977–1982, it is possible to obtain an idea on the range of work undertaken. In 1982, there were in all 103 mosques in the Jerusalem *mudiriyya* (province), and the Awqaf Administration employed some 473 people, a rise from 245 employees in 1976.

The Awqaf Administration has invested considerable effort and funds in the provision of religious instruction on the West Bank. It recognized that a vigorous religious education program would play an important role in maintaining its influence in the Palestinian Muslim community. By educating and informing a new generation of Palestinians of the importance and centrality of Jerusalem—and hence its *waqf* property—to Islam and to the Arabs, the Awqaf Administration's role would be valued and respected.[41] This emphasis on education is exemplified by the fact there are twenty-two schools under the aegis of the Awqaf Administration.[42] In addition, the Awqaf Administration runs a small but expanding school for disabled children in the Khanqah Dawadariyya and several preschools and elementary schools in the Haram compound.

The Awqaf Administration has more directly supported religious instruction in the Old City by establishing a Shari'a college and several schools of religious commentary and jurisprudence. It has also established a Department of the Revival of Tradition and the Islamic Sciences, which is collecting and publishing copies of ancient manuscripts, archival material, and commentaries. A journal on contemporary Islamic issues, *Hoda al-Islam,* is published once a month and provides a forum for discussion and debate on contemporary Islamic affairs. Although not necessarily of a standard to rival other major seats of Islamic learning in the Muslim world, the result of this emphasis on education has been to generate, at least in the Haram courtyard, a visible atmosphere of study and discussion. One very important spinoff from these activities has been the attraction of significant numbers of young men to the Old City and the Haram courtyard, whose very physical presence serves as a deterrent against attempts by militant Israeli nationalists to establish some kind of Israeli foothold in the Haram courtyard.

An ancient and important responsibility in the educational program of the Awqaf Administration is the Dar al-Aytam, or Muslim Orphanage and Vocational School.[43] Since its establishment in 1922, it has undergone considerable expansion, particularly in the past twenty years. It originally provided residential accommodation and vocational courses for orphan boys in the Dar Sitt Tunshuq in the Old City, the site of the old soup kitchen of the Khaski Sultan *waqf.* Following the Israeli occupation, it has expanded with premises in ar-Ram and al-Azariyya on the outskirts of the city.[44] The Dar al-Aytam is now undergoing extensive renovation with support form the Palestinian Welfare Association (see below for further details).

One should also note the variety of ways in which the Awqaf Administration is involved in the lives of most Palestinian residents and workers in the Old City. All *khayri waqf* properties are registered at the administration's finance office. The finance office must be notified of all changes of tenancy or of use. Changes of use must also be carried out in consultation with the Engineering and Maintenance Department. The Engineering and Maintenance Department is responsible for the repair and upkeep of outside and inside walls, roofs, floors, windows, and doors; interior and exterior decoration are the responsibility of the tenants. However, because of the low rent levels, the department is not able to fulfill its management responsibilities as it should, and intense negotiations often take place between the tenants, the Engineering and Maintenance Department, and the finance office.

Due to the overcrowding in many of the properties of the Old City, the Engineering and Maintenance Department finds itself heavily committed in resolving problems of access and partitioning over and above its regular maintenance and repair work. Finally, the Awqaf Administration has been responsible for the al-Aqsa Restoration Project, which has been an ambitious project involving the coordination of teams of international architects and engineers and the training of local craftsmen and restorers. Its work has attained international standards, but it has also required enormous funds from overseas.

Restoration and Renovation

By far and away, however, the most important project of the Awqaf Administration in its efforts to protect the Muslim community in the Old City was the restoration program it embarked upon through a specially created department, the DIA, in the early 1990s. As early as the Jordanian period of rule in Jerusalem, the Awqaf Administration was at the forefront of efforts to economically develop the central business district in East Jerusalem between Bab al-Amoud and Bab al-Zahra and along Salah ed-Din Street. During the British Mandate period, the main commercial area of Jerusalem outside the city walls had been along Jaffa Road. The loss of this area to the Israeli state following the 1948 war dealt a severe blow to the Palestinian economy of Jerusalem. However, from the early 1950s, the Awqaf Administration became active in developing the land under its control for commercial uses. In 1953 a central bus station was erected and leased to the municipality for thirty years. The large post office building was constructed and leased to the Jordanian government in 1957. Similarly, land in the Muslim cemetery running alongside Salah ed-din Street was converted to building land, and a series of shops were built with offices on top, housing the Shari'a Court of Appeal for Jerusalem and the West Bank and in an adjacent building the offices of the Committee for the Renovation of the al-Aqsa Mosque and the Dome of the Rock.

In addition to these new constructions, the Awqaf Administration embarked upon an extensive renovation program. In 1957, the Dar al-Aytam, the Awqaf Administration offices in the Madrasa al-Manjakiyya, the secondary school in the Madrasa 'Umariyya, and a number of mosques, shops, and residences were all renovated. In 1960, the offices of the Islamic congress, the boarding premises of students at the Islamic college in the Haram ash-Sharif, and other residential units were also renovated.[45] Some of this activity was assisted by the establishment of a development council by the Jordanian government, which offered guaranteed loans for development and reconstruction work at a fixed annual rate of interest.

From these examples, it is clear that there are numerous precedents for the *waqf* institution to take an active and interventionist role in the development of the city. The combination of government support through the Awqaf Administration and the Jordanian Development Council combined with private capital and the flexible utilization of fixed assets was a major factor in the regeneration of East Jerusalem in the post-1948 period. It should be borne in mind that this was taking place in the context of Jordanian policies of enhancing the role of Amman and the transfer of former mandatory government functions from Jerusalem to Amman.

Up to 1969 various ad hoc attempts had been made to restore property in the Haram area, notably the refurbishment of the Dome of the Rock by the Supreme Muslim Council during the 1930s. However, following the arson attack on the al-Aqsa Mosque in 1969, the Jordanian government and the Awqaf Administration were galvanized into taking immediate action. Attention was also drawn to the other architectural and historical treasures in the Old City by the surveys being conducted by the British School of Archaeology in Jerusalem, which began in the 1970s. Thus, the interlocking black and white stone strips, known as "quirked ogee moldings" on the facade of the Madrasa Tankiziyya were restored and its jogglings, or *muqarnas,* were touched up.

Similarly, in the mid-1970s, the Suq al-Qattanin was made the subject of an extensive study and completely refurbished. Under the directorship of Ibrahim Daqqaq, it was the Awqaf Administration's most thorough project up to that point. The restoration of the Suq al-Qattanin was judged to be a success in terms of its conception, appearance, and rehabilitative work. Yet it has failed in the sense that it is neither functioning nor commercially viable. The restored shops are shut, and the *suq* is unused as a thoroughfare, except at the time of Friday prayers. Several explanations have been proffered for this failure: First, the planners' original conception was that the Bab al-Qattanin, which lies at the end of the *suq* and opens onto the Haram ash-Sharif, would be opened for tourists. At present, the Israeli government has determined that they can only enter the Haram by the Bab al-Magharib or the Bab al-Silsilah. If tourists were given access to the Haram through the Bab-al-Qattanin, the *suq* would benefit from the passing tourist traffic. The Bab, however, remains closed. Second, the Awqaf Administration did not budget sufficiently for the lighting, cleaning, and maintenance that the restored *suq* would require, with the result that it quickly became dirty and uncared for. Third, high municipal taxes rates are incompatible with the likely income from such a site, and enterprising shopkeepers quickly move elsewhere. Finally, projects such as these require the support of a national government to publicize their use and encourage their existence.[46]

Department of Islamic Archaeology

Although unsuccessful as a commercial center, the project did have the added value of setting in motion a series of initiatives that led to the establishment of the DIA. The work of this department was given impetus after the al-Quds Committee of the Islamic Conference Organization provided sufficient funds specifically for the restoration program to the Ministry of Waqfs in Amman. The DIA, headed by Yusuf Natshe, has its office in the Madrasa Jawhariyya on the Tariq al-Hadid. During the 1980s, the work of the department was divided into several parts: (1) a historical research unit that delved into the Shari'a court records and Haram archives to discover the foundation, development, and uses of a particular building; (2) a photographic and surveying unit that drew up detailed maps of the main features and structural history of the building; and (3) a material and design unit that prepared the different stages of restoration work.

A decision whether to include a building in the restoration program was based on three criteria. The first was whether the historical and architectural value of the building was of sufficient importance. Another criterion was the seriousness of its structural decline and, finally, and as important, was the extent of the danger that it be confiscated or occupied by the Israeli Municipality, the Israeli Army, or settlers.

By the beginning of the Palestinian intifada in 1987, five restoration projects were fully completed. They were the al-Jawhariyya, al-Muzhiriyya, al-Kilaniyya, Turba Khatun Khan, and the Ribat al-Kurd. These were large monumental buildings built either as seminaries, mausoleums, or palaces. Three had undergone gradual conversion over centuries to multiple residencies with the attendant damaging partitioning and division. The program also included the complete restoration of the Khan al-Sultan, al-Ashrafiyya, Khan Tankiz, Hamam al-Ayn, and the Madrasa Sa'addiyya. However, the program was interrupted by the intifada and the following political turmoil. The DIA also completed some restoration work on the Madrasa Tashtimuriyya, al-Lu'lu'iyya, Maktab Bayram Jawish, Hamam al-Shifa', and other minor projects.

In its heyday, the DIA consisted of three archaeologists and two architects with a number of photographers and surveyors. There were also contract laborers and two or three stone masons who had been trained in Mamluk and Ottoman masonry design by the department. The restoration program was expensive. For example, the al-Muzhiriyya cost JD 17,000 (17,000 Jordanian dinar or approximately U.S.$90,000) and the al-Lilaniyya cost JD 30,000 (approximately U.S.$150,000). The legal cessation of Jordanian ties with the West Bank in 1988 (see Chapter 2) saw deep budget cuts. Although the Jordanian government continues to support the Awqaf Administration, its major projects were put on hold pending a political settlement. The Gulf War, which led to the virtual bankruptcy of Jordan, meant an almost complete cessation of funds for the DIA. Some of the architects were put on short hours, and the size of the program was scaled down drastically and the time of completion extended.

The DIA encountered a number of challenges that give a good illustration of the problems and opportunities of a renewed restoration program. Some of the problems that hampered its work are on a purely restorative level. Many of the monumental buildings such as the *madrasas*, *khans* (hostels for merchants, normally with a warehouse), and *turbas* (mausoleums) have been converted into residences with several families occupying the inner rooms. This posed a sensitive political and logistical problem for the department. In the current political situation where the municipality and the Israeli government are seen to be encouraging the removal of Palestinians from the Old City, the Awqaf Administration could not be seen to be contributing to the same effect.

Indeed, the Jordanian policy was to encourage the reverse situation, which overrode the inconvenience caused to the DIA. Thus, the department was obliged to devise plans that both restored the buildings to their original beauty and grandeur and allowed the tenants to remain in their places of residence. For example, some of the monuments have been imaginatively converted into offices and workshops. These difficulties can be aggravated by the noncooperation of the tenants and their demands for renovation work that is not in keeping with the original design of the building. For example, in the Madrasa al-Muzhiriyya, the department was prevented from restoring two rooms because the tenant, currently living in Kuwait, refused them permission for access. Similarly, the inner courtyard of the *madrasa* contains a beautiful Mamluk *mihrab*. After restoration of the *mihrab* and the courtyard, the tenant who had been using the east-facing wall insisted that the *iwan* (covered seating area on courtyard) in front of the *mihrab* be partitioned off to make another room for her family, with the result that the *mihrab* is now completely closed from public view. What is more, despite offering to rebuild a new one, the architects could not persuade the tenants in the *madrasa* to allow them to remove a dirty cement breeze-block washroom in the middle of the courtyard.

Another major difficulty for the DIA was the erratic funding of its work by the Jordanian Ministry of Waqfs. The department was set up as part of a long-term project of restoration work in the Old City. Monthly financial reports with three monthly technical reports were followed by biannual meetings with the Awqaf Administration executive officers. It was proposed that every five years an evaluation would be made to check the direction and effectiveness of their work. This indicated a long-term strategy of funding, which permitted priorities to be drawn up and some training to be initiated. However, government budgetary constraints prevented such a strategy to be put in place.

Innovations in Shari'a Law

None of the developments described in the previous sections could have occurred without a number of jurisprudential innovations being introduced to Shari'a law pertaining to *waqf* management. There was no wholesale radical reform implemented in a single measure but a series of relatively minor decisions taken in an ad hoc way. Nevertheless, their cumulative effect was quite revolutionary and allowed the *waqf* institution to flourish in an unexpected way during the difficult economic period after 1948 and during the Israeli occupation. In particular, it allowed the Awqaf Administration to respond to the gradual urbanization of the periphery of Jerusalem where changes in land zoning would have meant that *waqf* land remained unproductive rural land, compared to adjacent plots of urban real estate.

This was particularly the case during the Jordanian period. Between 1948 and 1988, the Jerusalem Shari'a court issued more than 100 permits for economic transaction involving *waqf* property and land. Ninety-one of these permits were issued between 1948 and 1967 and only nine have been issued since 1988. However, as will be examined, there were other innovations in *waqf* management in the post-1967 period that were equally radical in that they permitted the investment of external funds in economic development.

The innovations in *waqf* management include the following economic transactions, which are strictly forbidden in Shari'a law:

- Character change of *waqf* assets: Permission was given to alter the asset by adding doors or windows (nearly one-quarter of all transactions).
- Extensions to existing *waqf* properties: Permission was given to add rooms or floors.

- Limited term rentals: To attract capital, investors were permitted to lease property for a longer period than the permitted one-year lease.
- Loans: Borrowing from public bodies was permitted.
- Long leases (*hikr*): Traditionally only permitted for dilapidated property and under certain specified conditions but permitted in 1984 to allow the Awqaf Administration to renovate the Madrasa Jawhariyya.
- Change of use: Permitted to allow the development of rural land and urban cemeteries.
- Fund-raising: Permission was given to make use of donations for specific *waqfs*.
- Exchange (*istibdal*) and sale of *waqf* assets: Normally only permitted if the property to be exchanged for is of equal value. This was interpreted flexibly and allowed to cover sales of *waqf* property when the funds received were to be invested at a later date and were the principal means of development of *waqf* property.[47]

It is clear that the flexible interpretation of *istibdal*, of the loan system, and of limited term rentals were the most fruitful way of making use of *waqf* assets for economic development. However, the use of *istibdal* to generate sales and free up land and property has been treated cautiously. The extensive presence of *waqf* land and property in the Old City and East Jerusalem has provided an obstacle to Israeli acquisition of that land and provided a reserve of Palestinian land for development. The Awqaf Administration, therefore, has been very reluctant to undermine this passive but critically important role in maintaining the Muslim community.

One response to the Israeli occupation has been the flourishing of Palestinian charitable organizations or nongovernmental organizations (NGOs). These attempted to fill the educational, humanitarian, and cultural vacuum created by the absence of a Palestinian government or municipality that would have supported or provided such services. Interestingly, of the ninety new foundations created in the Israeli period, 25 percent of them were *khayri waqf*. This contrasts with 0 percent in the Jordanian period and 10 percent during the British Mandate period. From the late 1970s onward, these associations sought greater protection for their assets and to provide greater transparency in their financial affairs.[48] Therefore, a number of them applied to the Shari'a court to register their *waqfs* as assets for the benefit of their associations. This was due to several reasons. First, by the mid-1970s, it was clear that the occupation was clearly going to be prolonged. Second, as we have seen in Chapter 3, following the election of the Likud government in 1977, the Judaization policies of the Israeli government intensified and new confiscations were feared. Third, the rise in oil price provided additional pan-Arab and pan-Islamic funds for Palestinian causes, particularly in Jerusalem. Fourth, external donors sought to have greater accountability of their funds transferred to these NGOs. The supervision of *waqf* accounts by the Shari'a courts provided a minimum assurance. As a result, the following charitable organizations have registered their assets as *waqfs*: Al-Ibrahimiyya College (1978); Dar al-Tifl (1979); Gil al-Amal (1982); Arab Women's Association (1982); and East Jerusalem Chamber of Commerce (1986).[49]

In addition to this development, there was a parallel development of people endowing their property to an existing public association such as the Muqassid Hospital.[50] The result of this has been the almost imperceptible evolution of what could be termed a modernized *waqf* system by which public and charitable organizations are subject to civil law, but their assets are subject to Shari'a law. In this way the *waqf* institution is incorporating two important changes: (1) It can be an association set up according to Jordanian law and recognized as a body that can endow assets; and (2) the *mutawalli* can be chosen by the association in a way stipulated by its regulations rather than appointed by the beneficiaries and approved by the *qadi*.[51] These changes in *waqf* law and practice have provided the necessary framework for the development of Awqaf Administration and private *waqf* property in the Old City and the consolidation of the Muslim community there.

Developments Following the Oslo Accords

The post-Oslo situation in the Jerusalem region regarding the Awqaf Administration system is one of great uncertainty and replete with transitional arrangements. The Awqaf Administration continues to be financially supported by the Jordanian government, but its future as the arm of the Jordanian Ministry of Waqfs and Islamic Affairs in Amman is clearly limited. On the one hand, the peace agreement between the Israeli and Jordanian governments affirmed the role of Jordan in the holy places of Jerusalem, presumably through the agency of the Awqaf.[52] On the other hand, the establishment of the PNA has constrained its activities in the form of two concrete political developments. First, the Awqaf Administration surrendered its responsibilities outside the municipal borders of Jerusalem to the PNA. Second, the PNA has established its own Ministry of Religious Affairs with a brief (not accepted by the Israeli government) to operate in Jerusalem. A Palestinian mufti has been appointed and offices opened in the Old City.[53]

One should recall that the position of the Israeli government is still not to recognize legally the functioning of the Awqaf Administration. This fact combined with the two developments mentioned above means that the

Awqaf Administration and, hence, the *waqf* system in general is kept in a state of suspension. Any attempt by the PNA to extend its influence may provoke Israeli intervention, but the absence of any proactive policies may open up a vacuum and that, too, will give the Israeli government or the municipality an opportunity to intervene. Without political progress in the permanent status negotiations, implementing programs to safeguard and to develop the Awqaf Administration and Muslim community in the Old City is very difficult. In these circumstance the overt involvement of official or state actors such as the Awqaf Administration and the PNA's Ministry for Religious Affairs in programs in the Old City is, therefore, too sensitive. As a result, one can see a growing involvement of nonstate actors such as the private sector and Palestinian NGOs in the future development of *waqf* land and property. To give an indication of their growing and potential role, a brief examination of two examples will be made: one from the private sector and one from the voluntary sector.

The main difficulties encountered by private sector involvement in the *waqf* institution and system are similar to difficulties encountered elsewhere in the current political circumstances. These are constraints on the transfer of capital, the absence of sufficiently large-scale projects to finance, the uncertainty of legal jurisdictions and enforcement agencies, and, finally, the political constraints on recognizing an Israeli regulatory regime. In addition to these, a further constraint associated with *waqf* property and land is that the religious nature of the property places restrictions on the kinds of use of the property. However, set against these problems is the knowledge of the precedents set during the Jordanian period where the Awqaf Administration showed considerable enterprise in helping to build the new business district along Salah ed-Din Street. A brief examination of the operations of the Palestinian company, the Jerusalem Development and Investment Company (JEDICO), will illustrate these issues.

JEDICO is a private Palestinian-owned company registered in the Virgin Islands and set up in 1998. It has a capital base of U.S.$100 million, 40 percent of which is already deposited. Its objectives are to take advantage of the land supply in the Jerusalem area in order to prevent sales to Israeli bodies through the construction of commercial and residential buildings. It has identified a number of properties, including a large plot of land opposite the U.S. consulate in East Jerusalem.[54] The main difficulty it has encountered in this respect has been delays of up to ten years in obtaining licensing and planning permission.[55] It has sought to come to a number of agreements with the Awqaf Administration over the financing of property development on *waqf* land. It would like, for example, to finance the development of the Suq al-Qattanin, an architecturally important market area in the Old City, but no agreement has yet been reached. In general, negotiations have been held up by the reluctance of the Awqaf Administration to consider any loss of control over its land and property. In addition, it is required by a new Jordanian law to restrict long leases to a maximum of twenty-nine years.

For its part, JEDICO requires leases to be at least fifty years for there to be a sufficient return on its investment. The Israeli tax on land is so high that in many cases it exceeds the initial down payment of rent. In addition, JEDICO cannot accept clauses in the lease that restrict the kinds of activities in the new development (such as the sale of alcohol).[56]

These are details that may in the end be negotiated away. But the general impression is that the Awqaf cannot freely cooperate with the private sector for two reasons. One, it has neither the management nor financial skills to think creatively about different forms of private sector involvement, such as joint-stock companies, or an "enterprise" arm that manages its property more commercially. Two, it is obliged to respond to initiatives such as the one from JEDICO with excessive caution in case the land or property so leased is somehow deemed as "less than *waqf*" by the Israelis and used as a pretext for acquisition.[57] Finally, the Awqaf does not have the resources to establish an inspectorate to monitor the use of its property in conformity to religious values, adding to its caution in dealing with commercial enterprises.[58]

It is clear that the parallel with the Jordanian period cannot be pushed too far. The Israeli government is not sympathetic to a revived role for the *waqf*, and a mistake on the part of the administration would open the door to major losses. However, the parallel with the Jordanian period survives to the extent that it highlights the potential of *waqf* property under more favorable political circumstances. At the same time, it must be stressed that these are early days and that the process of negotiations over leases may yet produce new ideas. As the political circumstances change, new opportunities for private sector–*waqf* cooperation may evolve.[59]

Turning to our other example drawn from the voluntary sector, we can see that the Palestinian voluntary, or NGO, sectors have always played an important role in East Jerusalem since 1967. As a result of the abolition of the Arab municipality by the Israeli government in 1967 and the Palestinian consensus to boycott Israeli municipal elections, NGOs as well as the Awqaf Administration sought to supply the services and representative functions of local government. As we have seen, at this particular political juncture the role of NGOs deserves attention. This section will look at the role of one Palestinian NGO, the Welfare Association, and its program in Jerusalem.

The Palestinian Welfare Association is registered in Geneva with offices in London, Ramallah, and Amman and draws its financial support from Palestinian supporters in exile. In the 1980s it was the recipient of funds from the Islamic Conference Organization's al-Quds Committee, and following the Oslo Accords it has participated in a number of programs with the World Bank. It is probably the largest Palestinian NGO operating in the land of former Palestine and the Arab world. Its operational offices in Jerusalem are registered as a trust (Hebrew, *amutah*) under Israeli law, which gives it a degree of latitude not available to most other Palestinian NGOs. Since 1997, it has embarked upon an ambitious program of renovation in the Old City of Jerusalem Revitalization Program (OCJRP). The program has a number of objectives, three of which concern this study:

1. To establish links with formal and informal organizations and public and religious institutions that are active and collaborative in the process of development.
2. To implement a preservation, management, and maintenance program for historical monuments and sites of special architectural, cultural, and historical significance.
3. To improve living conditions and standards for residents, and provide better, more secure properties and buildings.[60]

Clearly, implementing these objectives necessarily involves close coordination with the Awqaf Administration and with *waqf dhurri mutawallis*. This process of coordination illustrates the nature of *waqf*-NGO relations in Jerusalem during this transitional phase.

The OCJRP has focused on the rehabilitation of selected courtyards and monumental buildings. With regard to the first focus, consultations are held with owners and tenants in order to determine whether the provision of modern services should be prioritized over the need to preserve the architectural features of the sites. A recent review of the program recommended greater tenant participation in the rehabilitation as a means of securing their cooperation and commitment to the work being carried out. However, there is a possibility that this would create another problem: Tenant participation might strengthen the claims of the tenants over that of the owner to a particular property. Such an emphasis could perhaps lead to a tenant "buyout." It is certain that as the landlord the Awqaf Administration would resist such a move because it would be held responsible if during this period properties so disposed of would end up in the hands of Israeli settler groups. The second focus on monumental building is more indicative of the possible role of NGOs in developing *waqf* property. The OCJRP has selected two sites in the Old City for its activities: the Dar al-Aytam and the Suq al-Qattanin.

The Dar al-Aytam is the largest complex in the Old City and was built as a private residence in the fifteenth century, extended during the Ottoman period, and in 1922 became an orphanage and vocational training institute. By renovating the building and upgrading the training facilities, the OCJRP intends to draw in more students and give a boost to the local economy, thus revitalizing one of the poorest and more run-down areas of the Old City.[61] As mentioned previously, the owner of the Dar al-Aytam is the Awqaf Administration, and the process of renovation is complicated by the fact that while the Awqaf Administration is nominally in charge, the PNA also has an interest. The PNA has acknowledged that under the current political circumstances of Israeli occupation of the Old City, there cannot be a transfer of ownership of the property. Nonetheless, the organization has indicated through various intermediaries that it is the ultimate source of authority on programs of this kind. As a result, this project is a highly sensitive one. The Awqaf Administration retains ownership and is closely consulted on every step, but the OCJRP is responsible for the technical and rehabilitation program, for the financial provision, and for the restructuring of the educational activities. The arrangements with the Suq al-Qattanin are similar but at an earlier stage. The Awqaf Administration is the owner, and the nature of the rehabilitation work of the OCJRP will be decided in consultation with them. At this stage a feasibility report has been commissioned. The delaying factor here is the problem of multiple tenancies and a number of competing interests, including al-Quds University, which has set up a Centre for Jerusalem Studies in the Khan Otuzbir courtyard and the Hamam al-Ayn, which are all part of the Suq al-Qaltanin Complex.[62]

Neither of these examples provide an ideal model for relations between the Awqaf Administration and the private and voluntary sectors. This is partly due to the large number of unwritten and tacit agreements and to the uncertain legal and political framework prevailing. Nevertheless, it shows how in the current political climate mutual trust and coordination can work and be effective. The evidence suggests that the prospects for joint development projects are better between the Awqaf Administration and the voluntary sector than the administration and the private sector. To an extent, this is due to the more flexible and tacit nature of the cooperation and to the nature of the funds being made available that do not require a commercial return.

Conclusion

It is clear that the Muslim community's dominance in the Old City has been severely eroded since 1967. The loss of communal assets in the Magharib quarter and Jewish Quarter and the steady encroachments of Israeli settlers are undermining both the functioning of its principal institution, the Awqaf Administration, but also of the hold the community has through its religious leadership of its holy places. Indeed, one can go on to say that the Islamic ambience and way of life within the walls are also under threat. The great fear of the community is the fate that has befallen Hebron in the interim phase laid down by the Oslo Accords. Here the city is divided into two zones, one of which is controlled by the Israeli state giving free rein to the activities of the settlers. We shall examine this in greater detail in Chapter 6.

For the Awqaf Administration, the interim period has been a particularly difficult phase of its existence. Budgetary and political constraints have obliged it to pursue a holding operation that does not permit it to take advantage of its central role in the life of the Old City. Apart from a small handful of exceptional individuals, its bureaucracy and middle management lacks the training, expertise, and capacity to plan strategically for the future. Its deference to both the Jordanian and Palestinian political leadership restricts its ability to develop strategic relations with the wider Islamic world and with possible allies in the Jewish and Christian communities. However, despite these shortcomings, it is still a central actor in the life of the Old City. The range of its activities, the control over properties, and the proactive role taken by its leadership mean that any discussion of the future of the Old City that excludes consideration of the Awqaf Administration and the perspectives of its officials is unlikely to succeed.

Notes

1. For further details, see R. Friedland and R. Hecht, "The Politics of Sacred Place: Jerusalem's Temple Mount/*al-Haram al-Sharif*," in *Sacred Places and Profane Spaces: Essays in the Geographies of Judaism, Christianity, and Islam*, eds. J. Scott and P. Simpson-Housley (New York: Greenwood Press, 1991), 33.

2. *Report of the Commission by His Majesty's Government—with the Approval of the League of Nations to Determine the Rights and Claims of Moslems and Jews in Connection with the Western or Wailing Wall at Jerusalem* (London: Her Majesty's Stationery Office, 1931).

3. For further details, including excerpts of an interview with the Israeli major in charge of the operation, see T. Abowd, "The Moroccan Quarter: A History of the Present," *Jerusalem Quarterly File*, no. 7 (winter 2000): 9–12.

4. Friedland and Hecht, "The Politics of Sacred Place," 38.

5. A. L. Tibawi, *The Islamic Pious Foundations in Jerusalem: Origin, History, and Usurpation by Israel* (London: Iraqi Cultural Foundation, 1978), 35; R. Khatib, "The Judaization of Jerusalem and Its Demographic Transformation," in *Jerusalem: The Key to World Peace* (London: Council of Europe, 1980), 114. A survey carried out by George Dib and Fuad Jabber calculated that 290 rooms were demolished. See G. Dib and F. Jabber, *Israel's Violation of Human Rights in the Occupied Territories: A Documented Report* (Beirut: Institute of Palestine Studies, 1970), 217–227; M. Benvenisti, *Jerusalem: The Torn City* (Minneapolis: Israel Typeset, Ltd., and the University of Minneapolis, 1976), 306, gives a figure of 619 people evicted; David Hirst, "Rush to Annexation: Israel in Jerusalem," *Journal of Palestine Studies* 3, no. 4 (summer 1974): 3–31, mentions 1,000 people, or 129

families; and the *Jerusalem Post*, 19 June 1967, estimates the number of families evicted at 200.

6. Benvenisti, *Jerusalem: The Torn City*, 307.

7. Y. Schweid, "The Unification of Jerusalem: The Planning Aspect," *Kivunim*, no. 35 (1987). The quotation is from an unofficial translation from Hebrew.

8. N. Shepherd, *The Mayor and the Citadel: Teddy Kollek and Jerusalem* (London: Weidenfeld and Nicholson, 1987), 21; see also an interview in "Keeping the Balance," *Jerusalem Post International Edition*, 2 June 1990, 9.

9. See, for example, the description of the quarter made by the Muslim historian Mujir id-din, cited in F. E. Peters, *Jerusalem* (Princeton: Princeton University Press, 1985), 392.

10. See, for example, T. Tobler, *Denkblatter Aus Jerusalem*, 1853, 125–126, and J. T. Barclay, *The City of the Great King: Or Jerusalem as It Was, as It Is, as It Is to Be*, 1858, 432–444, as cited in Y. Ben Arieh, *Jerusalem in the 19th Century: The Old City* (New York: St. Martin's Press, 1984), 317–318.

11. Tibawi, *Pious Foundations*, 45–46; Arieh, *Jerusalem: The Old City*, 316.

12. See A. al-'Arif, *Mufassal tarikh al-quds* (Jerusalem: Ma'ari Printers, 1986), 431–432. See also C. Ritter, *The Comparative Geography of Palestine and the Sinaitic Peninsula* (Edinburgh, 1866), 191, cited in Tibawi, *Pious Foundations*, 44. Ben Arieh is quite explicit about this, too, in *Jerusalem: The Old City*, 327–328. Benvenisti estimates that no more than 20 percent of the quarter was Jewish-owned at the outbreak of the 1948 war in *Jerusalem: The Torn City*, 239.

13. Interview with Antony Bakrijian, historian, former UNRWA official, and resident of the Old City, 3 October 1989. See also S. Graham-Brown, "Jerusalem," *Middle East*, no. 136 (February 1986): 48; Benvenisti, *Jerusalem: The Torn City*, 44; Tibawi, *Pious Foundations*, 38. See also A. Plascov, *The Palestinian Refugees in Jordan, 1948–1957* (London: Frank Cass, 1981), 68, 109, 112.

14. Statement by R. Khatib, deported mayor of Jerusalem, published in Dib and Jabber, *Israel's Violation*, 176. Of the expropriated properties, twelve belonged to the Awqaf Administration (of which three belonged to the Mughareb Mosque *waqf*) and ninety-nine to the Abu Madyan al-Ghauth *waqf*. Figures for *waqf dhurri* are harder to ascertain, but from my own fieldwork, at least fifty-five *waqf* properties were expropriated, including sixteen from the Khalidi family, thirteen from the al-'Asali family, and eight from the Ja'ouni family. Other figures for *dhurri waqf* are Dajani, three; Hariri, one; Daqqaq, one; Abdo, one; Hallaq, one; Khatib, two; Husayni (one branch), one; and Quttayni, three.

15. Cited in Dib and Jabber, *Israel's Violation*, 178.

16. For further details, see M. Dumper, *The Politics of Jerusalem Since 1967* (New York: Columbia University Press, 1997), 176.

17. *Laws of the State of Israel*, 1966/67, vol. 21, 75–76.

18. It is frequently referred to, inaccurately, as the Supreme Muslim Council, in which case the Arabic would be *al-majlis al-islamiyya al-'ula*. Other terms include Awqaf Council, Waqf Council, and Islamic Trust.

19. For further details, see M. Dumper, *Islam and Israel: Muslim Religious Endowments and the Jewish State* (Washington, D.C.: Institute for Palestine Studies, 1994), 78–79.

20. Dumper, *The Politics of Jerusalem*, 173.

21. Dumper, *Islam and Israel*, 109–110.

22. For a summary of these issues, see "Temple Mount Faithful v. Attorney-General et al.," *Catholic University Law Review* 45, no. 3 (spring 1996): 861–941.

23. Yitzhak Ya'acovy, former director of the East Jerusalem Development Company (EJDC), a joint government-municipal company, claimed in an interview with me in Jerusalem on 3 February 1987 that the EJDC could not have better relations with the Awqaf Administration and gave several examples: (1) When militant Orthodox Jews tried to tunnel their way under the Haram area, Ya'acovy claimed the Awqaf Administration supplied building materials and that the EJDC's workmen went down wells to block off the tunneling; and (2) although the al-Ghazali Square beside St. Stephen's Gate and the Via Dolorosa is being developed by the Awqaf Administration, it is the EJDC that planned and designed the work. Indeed, Ya'acovy went on to claim that EJDC's consultations with the Awqaf Administration extend directly to the Jordanian government and that he has plans in his offices that are stamped and signed by the minister of occupied territories in Amman.

24. See *al-Fajr* (English-language weekly), 17 May 1987, 14.

25. All accounts originally reported anywhere between nineteen and twenty-one deaths. The Palestine Human Rights Information Center lowered the death toll to seventeen at a press conference on 15 October, and other organizations and reports followed. Of the deaths initially reported, one person had died of a heart attack, two who were thought to have died were only injured and survived, and one had been shot in another section of Jerusalem and died later.

26. See "The Haram Al-Sharif (Temple Mount) Killings, Special File," *Journal of Palestine Studies* 20, no. 2 (winter 1991): 136, 138.

27. See "Chronology," *Journal of Palestine Studies* 20, no. 2 (winter 1991): 219.

28. *Zamir Report*, Jerusalem, 26 October 1990, as translated from the Hebrew and summarized by the Israeli Government Press Office and reproduced in *Mideast Mirror,* 29 October 1990.

29. "Haram al-Sharif Killings," 141.

30. Conversely, the al-Awqaf shaikh could be heard calming the crowds with these words:

> Move inside the mosques. Al-Haram is a place for worship not for fighting. There are dead and wounded. Call the police to speak to us because a massacre is taking place in Al-Aqsa mosque. Do not stand before the soldiers. Do not confront the soldiers. Do not make your bodies subject to death in order to preserve your lives and the Holy Aqsa. Stay away from the walls of al-Aqsa and al-Makameh area and the Western Wall where the soldiers are stationed.

This announcement was recorded on tape at the time it was made. Al-Haq excerpted this quote from the simultaneous recording, which is available at al-Haq. It could also be heard on the videotape known as the Mount of Olives tape, filmed by a tourist from the Mount of Olives.

31. "Chronology" (winter 1991): 220–223. In addition, Israel informed the UN that it would be willing to give Secretary General Perez de Cuellar a copy of the findings of Israel's own inquiry into the Haram shootings in lieu of accepting a UN investigation team.

32. See "Chronology," *Journal of Palestine Studies* 26, no. 2 (winter 1997): 176.

33. Ibid., 176. Seven Palestinians were killed, and hundreds were wounded

(including two executive Awqaf Administration members and the mufti of Jerusalem). Eight Israeli soldiers were injured by rocks and bottles. Twelve Palestinians and two Israelis were injured after clashes in Bethlehem. *Palestine Report,* 2 October 1996, e-mail edition, 3.

34. "Chronology" (winter 1997): 176. President Yasser Arafat considered the tunnel opening to be a "major crime against our holy places" and the cause of a grave crisis in the relations with Israel. Other reactions: The United States demanded that Israel make a gesture concerning the tunnel and later demanded that Israel close the tunnel and withdraw from Hebron. It initiated meetings in Washington between Arafat, Netanyahu, King Hussein of Jordan, and President Mubarak of Egypt. Jordan condemned the tunnel opening as an act of provocation, and King Hussein was furious that he had not been informed in meeting with Dore Gold two days earlier. One thousand students demonstrated against the tunnel opening in Amman. The Arab League condemned Israel's tunnel digging in Jerusalem. Egypt's foreign minister warned Israel against taking provocative measures and violating the peace process. EU countries issued their strongest condemnation against Israel since 1980. The UN Security Council passed a resolution (14-0, with 1 abstention) calling for the "reversal of all acts which have resulted in the aggravation of the situation."

35. *SWB (Summary of World Broadcasts), BBC Monitoring, Middle East,* 26 September 1996, 5, 6; "Chronology" (winter 1997): 178; *SWB,* 27 September 1996, 19.

36. Indeed, the PNA Ministry opened an office in an Awqaf *madrasa* in the Old City close to the Haram, and the picture of Yasser Arafat hangs on the wall above the desk of the current director-general in the Awqaf Administration's main office.

37. Dumper, *Islam and Israel,* 106, note 20.

38. Ibid.

39. N. Shragai, "Solving the Puzzle in the Old City," *Ha'aretz* (Internet version), 18 June 2000.

40. Y. Reiter, *Islamic Institutions in Jerusalem: Palestinian Muslim Organization Under Jordanian and Israeli Rule* (The Hague: Kluwer Law International, 1997), 149. It is interesting to contrast the rate of *waqf* creation during the Jordanian period with that of the Israeli period until 1990, during which, according to Reiter, 90 *waqf*s were founded. This averages at four per year compared to the less than one per year under the Jordanians.

41. *Idara al-awqaf al-islamiyya al-'ama, bayan: Al-awqaf al-islamiyya fi al-daf al-gharbiyya, 1967–76* (Jerusalem: Da'ira al-awqaf al-islamiyya, no date), 20–25; *Idara al-awqaf al-islamiyya al-'ama, bayan: Al-awqaf al-islamiyya fi al-daf al-gharbiyya, 1977–82* (Jerusalem: Da'ira al-awqaf al-islamiyya, no date), 12, 14.

42. However, this figure can be misleading and requires explanation. In 1967 the Israeli Ministry of Education tried to impose its authority and curricula over all schools in the enlarged Jerusalem area. The then-director of education for these schools under the Jordanian government coordinated with the Awqaf Administration to reestablish the schools under the umbrella of the Awqaf Administration. The curriculum for these schools is devised by the Jordanian Ministry of Education and has no special religious significance because of its *waqf* associations. Its inclusion under the Awqaf Administration should be seen a political device and not a religious commitment, as in the case of the religious seminaries and colleges.

43. Dumper, *Islam and Israel,* 112.

44. D. Farhi, "ha-mo'atza ha-muslemit be-mizrah yerushalayim u-vi-yehuda

ve-shomron me'az milhemet sheshet ha-yamin" (The Muslim Council in East Jerusalem and in Judea and Samaria since the Six Day War), *Ha-mizrah He-hadash* (The New East) 28 (1979): 15.

45. Family endowments were also active in recreating a commercial center for East Jerusalem after the 1948 war. For example, the Shitayya *waqf* undertook "one of the largest building operations of waqf properties in Jerusalem" during the Jordanian period. See Reiter, *Islamic Institutions,* 71. Up to 19 shops were built and plans were approved for an additional 15 shops, 9 storerooms, 31 offices, a 147-room hotel, and 10 apartments.

46. Welfare Association, *Jerusalem Old City Revitalisation Programme: Souq al-Qattanin Study* (MMIS Management Consultants) (unpublished report, Jerusalem, November 1998).

47. These innovations are derived from Reiter, *Islamic Institutions,* 69–80.

48. Isam Anani, legal adviser to the Awqaf Administration. Interview by author, Ramallah, 9 February 1999.

49. Y. Reiter, *Waqf in Jerusalem 1948–1990* (Jerusalem: Jerusalem Institute for Israel Studies, 1991), 45.

50. Reiter, *Islamic Institutions,* 35.

51. The implications of this development require further research and discussion with lawyers, clerics, and charitable organization officials. It does appear, however, that it may allow a *waqf* to be categorized as an NGO and, therefore, eligible for a wider range of development assistance, such as World Bank loans, than hitherto available. I am grateful to Anis al-Qassim, Amman, for this observation made during a meeting of the Awqaf Discussion Group (supported by the International Development Research Centre, Canada), Cairo, 3–4 April 1997.

52. Washington Declaration, 1994, para. 3. Neither the declaration nor the subsequent Jordan-Israel Peace Treaty mention the Awqaf Administration, but it is implicit in paragraph 3: "Israel respects the present special role of the Hashemite Kingdom of Jordan in the Muslim Holy in Jerusalem. When negotiations on the permanent status will take place, Israel will give high priority to the Jordanian historic role in these shrines."

53. S. Musallem, *The Struggle for Jerusalem* (Jerusalem: PASSIA, 1996), 105.

54. Isam Anani interview.

55. Wa'el Kan'an, director-general, JEDICO. Interview by author, Jerusalem, 1 February 1999.

56. Ibid.

57. Adnan Husseini, director-general of the Awqaf Administration. Interview by author, Jerusalem, 6 February 1999.

58. Isam Anani interview.

59. Mazen Qupti, lawyer, specializing in *waqf* affairs. Interview by author, Jerusalem, 3 February 1999.

60. Welfare Association, *Jerusalem Old City Revitalisation Plan: Interim Summary Report,* Jerusalem, January 1999, 10.

61. *Tanmiya,* the quarterly newsletter of the Welfare Association on Palestinian development issues (October 1998): 1.

62. Ibid. and brochure supplied by the center following a personal visit in November 2000.

5

The Christian Community: The Growing Role of the Laity

There are two ways to characterize the position of the established Christian communities in the Old City since 1967. First, they are communities in crisis. Demographically declining, alienated from an increasingly unsympathetic Israeli body politic, and their paramount position gradually being usurped by new evangelical groups (particularly from the United States), their influence and role is being circumscribed in every direction. Second, they are communities in the process of consolidation, which, despite very difficult circumstances, are retaining an active presence in the Old City, expanding their international network connections and international support, and repositioning themselves to take into account the prospect of a Palestinian national presence in the Old City.

This chapter examines the accuracy of both these characterizations and comes to some conclusions about the role of the Christian communities in this post-Oslo period of transition. It should be made clear that the Christian presence in the Old City and the presence of its holy places vastly add to the complexity of the peace negotiations over the future of Jerusalem and the Old City. If the dispute over the city's future were restricted to a simple national one between Israelis and Palestinians, each with holy sites that belonged to the dominant religious community, Judaism and Islam, this would be complex enough. Rivalries over roles and responsibilities in the shared holy sites in the Old City appear intractable as it is. The Christian presence, however, ensures that negotiations are not merely bilateral. Not only do Palestinian Christians constitute an important and influential component of the Palestinian constituency with a direct interest in the holy places themselves, the Christian community itself is fragmented into a number of denominations, all of which have overlapping but specific interests. Furthermore, the hierarchies of the communities represent wider international communities and international concerns, and in this way external interests are also brought to bear upon the negotiations. Thus, when the Palestinian-Israeli peace negotiations begin to touch on religious issues in Jerusalem, and specifically on the future status and administration of the Old City, from the perspective of the Christian communities, they should become multilateral negotiations.

This chapter shows how the control and disputes over the Christian Holy Places in the Old City play a central role in these dynamics. It argues that not only does this role add to the complexity of the negotiations but that a bilateral agreement over the future of the Old City between the two main parties without the involvement of the Christian communities will neither work nor be acceptable to them. As a result, any such agreement is unlikely to be acceptable to the international community either, thus undermining the credibility and implementation of the agreement.

The chapter begins with an overview of the Christian Holy Places and the evolution of the Christian Status Quo arrangements. It will then outline the main political trends since 1967 that have affected the role of the Christian communities in the Old City, specifically discussing the impact of the "Arabization" of the clergy hierarchies and the growing salience of the PNA in the post-Oslo period. While doing so, it will also examine several key disputes that illustrate intradenominational, Muslim-Christian, church-state, and Christian-Jewish tensions in the Old City and, hence, the additional complexity of the peace negotiations. We will conclude by drawing together these themes in order to discuss the role of the Christian communities in the peace negotiations and the extent to which it will determine the future of the Old City.

Historical Background

The history and important role played by the Christian Holy Places in the Old City is the subject of much dispute and controversy. A British Mandate memorandum, "The Status Quo in the Holy Places," prepared by a former district governor of Jerusalem, L. G. A. Cust, introduced the Christian Holy Places in the following way:

> The history of the Holy Places is one long story of bitter animosities and contentions, in which outside influences take part in an increasing degree, until the scenes of Our Lord's life on earth become a political shuttlecock, and eventually the cause of international conflict. If the Holy Places and the rights pertaining thereto are an "expression of men's feelings about Him whose story hallowed those sites," they are also an index of the corruptions and intrigues of despots and chancelleries during eight hundred years. The logical results have been the spirit of distrust and suspicion, and the attitude of intractability in all matters, even if only of the most trivial importance, concerning the Holy Places.[1]

Much of the conflict over the Christian Holy Places occurred in the context of the struggle by the clergy of the three main communities in Jerusalem: the Greek Orthodox, the Roman Catholic (also known as the Latins), and the Armenian Orthodox. The struggle was primarily over access and custodianship, or the *praedominium*, over the different shrines in Jerusalem, particularly those in the Holy Sepulchre, where Christ was believed to have been crucified. It should be noted that while many of the disputes were of a theological nature, there were also strong economic reasons for retaining the *praedominium*. Apart from endowments and donations, pilgrimages were often the only source of income of the communities and the clergy. A dominant position in a holy site would increase the attraction to pilgrims from a certain denomination and, thus, the income generated to that community.

During the Crusader period, the Latins achieved primacy; during the Ayyubid and Mamluk periods, the Armenians were dominant. The Greek Orthodox attained their dominant position during the Ottoman period despite frequent challenges from the other two denominations. For example, in 1604, 1637, 1673, and 1757, the primacy in the Holy Sepulchre swung between the Latins and the Greek Orthodox communities, finally resting with the Greek Orthodox Patriarchate where it remains today, albeit fragilely.

The rivalry over access, the maintenance of building, of restoration and cleaning works, and over the conduct and timing of services and festivals often led to public disorder and the involvement of outside powers. This led the Ottoman authorities to adjudicate and recognize certain arrangements that became known as the "Status Quo Legislation of the Holy Places." These laws were codified in 1852 and 1853 and issued as Ottoman decrees (*firmans*). In codifying the Status Quo arrangements, the Ottoman authorities were also succumbing to the pressures of the European powers. Russian influence in the Ottoman Empire was frequently and successfully exerted on behalf of the Greek Orthodox. One of the causes of the Crimean War (1853–1856) was the attempt by France to wrest control over the Christian Holy Places from the Greek Orthodox in favor of the Roman Catholics. Western governments saw the Christian presence in Jerusalem and the historic ties to Christian Holy Places as providing them with a pretext for greater presence and involvement in Palestine and Jerusalem. Thus, the Status Quo arrangements were recognized in international treaties such as the Paris Peace Convention of 1856 after the Crimean War, the Congress of Berlin in 1878, and the Versailles Peace Treaty of 1919. All these treaties confirmed the primacy of the Greek Orthodox Patriarchate, which was accepted by the other denominations even though they were not regarded as permanent and immutable.[2]

This precedent of external political involvement in the relations among the different hierarchies and communities and between them and the state authorities continued toward the latter part of the nineteenth and during the twentieth century. The growth of Protestant missions increased the congestion of Christian denominations and intensified the tensions over Christian Holy Places. It also increased the number of denominations that could be sponsored or put under the protection of different governments.

In the post-1967 period of Israeli occupation, the precedent has resurfaced in the form of Israeli and U.S. support for fundamentalist right-wing evangelical groups and for the Church of the Latter Day Saints (Mormons). The construction of the Mormon Brigham Young University campus on the Mount of Olives, the largest Christian construction since 1967, is a concrete manifestation of this continued trend.

Evolution of the Term *Holy Places*

As briefly discussed in Chapter 2, the term *holy places* has both a popular and a technical use, which has caused some confusion. In addition, the legal and technical usage has evolved over the past hundred years so that its more recent definitions are much broader than the initial usages. In popular usage, it refers to all holy sites including cemeteries, shrines, mosques, synagogues, churches, seminaries, prayer rooms, convents, monasteries, and specific locations associated with particular events or people.

The technical and legal use of the term *Christian Holy Places* restricts the meaning to specific sites and refers to the practice of certain rites and proprietorship within them. The point of departure of most discussion over definitions is the 1852 *firman* of the Ottoman sultan Abdul Majid. The firman mainly addresses a number of disputes concerning the use and maintenance of the Holy Sepulchre and strongly declares that its decision is final. The 1852 *firman* refers to the following Christian Holy Places in Jerusalem: the Church of the Holy Sepulchre and its dependencies (Old City); the convent of Dayr al-Sultan (Old City); the Sanctuary of the Ascension (on the Mount of Olives); and, finally, the tomb of the Virgin Mary (in Gethsemane). However, the main thrust of the *firman* was to confirm the "status quo" without providing details of it. The absence of a detailed inventory of practices meant that the possibility for minor encroachments and misunderstandings was endless and the cause of much tension between the established churches. At the same time a written inventory was not welcome because it would have enshrined practices that, although they may have been the prevailing ones, were not consensual and may have been in place through force majeur. It also meant that the succeeding secular authority did not have a reference document and was often working in the dark.

The British Mandate authorities followed the Ottoman tradition by undertaking to preserve the Status Quo in these places. Article 13 of the League of Nations Mandate for Palestine stipulated, inter alia:

All responsibility in connection with the Holy Places and religious building or sites in Palestine, *including that of preserving existing rights and of securing free access to the Holy Places, religious buildings and sites and the free exercise of worship*, while ensuring the requirements of public order and decorum, is assumed by the Mandatory [emphasis added].[3]

Article 14 of the mandate also called on Britain to appoint a special commission to "study, define and determine the rights and claims in connection with the Holy Places and the rights and claims relating to the different religious communities in Palestine."[4]

From these official documents, it is clear that no written document of the various rights existed and that the Status Quo pertaining to the Christian Holy Places consisted of tacit and ad hoc decisions accumulated over the centuries. These were therefore subject to subtle shifts in the relative strengths of the different communities both on the ground and through their international supporters. It was in order to rectify this absence that Cust was asked to write his memorandum, "The Status Quo in the Holy Places." Cust's memorandum is an extraordinary document and well worth reading. It leaves a lasting and sobering impression of the intricacies of administering and maintaining a shared religious site. Every part of the Holy Sepulchre is subject to some regulation or understanding, and the fact that there is no agreed document that spells out the details lends itself to disputes. Changes in personnel, calendar clashes, the increase and decrease of congregations, and changes in the economic fortunes of the churches all lead to minor alterations that led to clashes. For example, Cust writes:

1. The Entrance Doorway and the Façade, the Stone of Unction, the Parvis of the rotunda, the great Dome and the Edicule are common property. The three rites consent to the partition of the costs of any work of repair between them in equal proportion. The Entrance Courtyard is in common use, but the Orthodox alone have the right to clean it.
2. The Dome of the Katholikon is claimed by the Orthodox as being under their exclusive jurisdiction. The other communities do not recognise this, maintaining that it is part of the general fabric of the Church, and demand a share in any costs of repair. The Orthodox, however, refuse to share payment with any other community. The same conditions apply *mutatis mutandis* to the Helena Chapel, claimed by the Armenians, and the Chapel of the Invention of the Cross claimed by the Latins.
3. The ownership of the Seven Arches of the Virgin is in dispute between the Latins and the Orthodox, of the chapel of St. Nicodemus between the Armenians and the Syrian Jacobites, and of the Deir al-Sultan

between the Copts and the Abyssinians. In these cases neither party will agree to the other doing any work of repair or to divide the costs.[5]

There are pages and pages of these notes that set out the main points of agreement and disagreement among the communities. However, three points need to be made regarding Cust's memorandum: First, as an account of "modern practice," it does not have the authority of consensual agreement of the different communities and served mainly as a guide to officials of the government of Palestine.[6] Second, while providing the detailed inventory hitherto lacking, its very existence was controversial. It implicitly converted a snapshot of practices into a benchmark or reference point when in reality they were part of ongoing disputes. Third, the government of Palestine, in its bureaucratic zeal to lay down procedures and understandings, added additional Christian (and Muslim and Jewish) holy sites to the Ottoman list and which by default and over time became also known as the holy places. Most of these were not inside the Old City itself, and the Status Quo arrangements derived from the Ottoman period did not apply to them. But it introduced the precedent of extending the term *holy place* to include other holy sites and thereby diluting the original use of the term. Hence the distinction made in this book between the Christian Holy Places and holy places and sites. The Holy Places Commission mentioned in Article 14 of the mandate was never set up. Protracted disputes between the various denominations and their outside supporters meant that no acceptable formula for appointing the members or defining their roles was reached. Consequently, the government of Palestine resolved that all decisions affecting all the holy places and Status Quo would be the prerogative of the high commissioner.

Further complexity was introduced when the United Nations debated and prepared reports on the subject. The UN Special Committee on Palestine (UNSCOP) and the Conciliation Commission on Palestine (CCP) both referred to the holy places, but their definition was more a list of recognized holy sites of interest and importance rather than sites to which the Status Quo arrangements were applied. Additional sites were the Church of St. Anne, the Church of St. James, and the Church of St. Mark, all in the Old City. Thus, a more general and popular definition came into being that did not differentiate between the status of the different sites.

Christianity in Jerusalem During the British and Jordanian Periods

Christian life in Jerusalem and the Old City flourished under the British Mandate. The employment opportunities offered by government service,

greater tourism, and the increased provision of schools and space for housing development outside the walls all added to an increase in numbers of
Christians coming to the city. Between 1922 and 1946 the Christian population of Jerusalem more than doubled, increasing from 14,700 to 31,300,
though relative to other religious groups its proportion went down from 23
to 19 percent.[7] Their rise in socioeconomic position as government administrators and teachers was reflected in their continued replacement in the
retail trade in the Christian quarters of the Old City by Muslims.

An important reform introduced by the government of Palestine was
the introduction of separate religious courts for the Christian communities.
While recognizing the primacy of the Muslim community in Palestine, the
government removed the Christian courts from the jurisdiction of the
Shari'a courts.

Another major dispute that occurred during the mandate period was the
struggle between the lay members of the Greek Orthodox community and
its clergy over the appointments to senior positions, the administration of
its institutions, and the allocation of the budget. This struggle has long
antecedents but came to the fore in the late nineteenth century when the
predominantly Arab laity came to voice their grievances against the almost
exclusively Greek and Cypriot clergy. The mandate period saw the growing
alignment of the Arab laity with the Palestinian national movement, and
sales of church lands to the Jewish National Fund for the purposes of
Zionist settlement only served to exacerbate the tensions.[8] As we shall see
later on, this struggle continues to have ramifications in the post-1967 period.

During the conflict over the establishment of the State of Israel in
1948, many Palestinians fled to Jerusalem for refuge. Many Christians
lived in the new suburbs in the western part of Jerusalem and had relatives
either in Ramallah, Jerusalem, or the Bethlehem area and were taken in by
them. Nevertheless, the Old City was inundated, and refugees packed the
narrow streets and alleys. An Israeli census in 1967 showed that even twenty years later as many as 37 percent of Palestinian Christians were still officially classed as refugees.[9] Where possible, Christian institutions also
responded. The Armenian Patriarchate, for example, opened the Monastery
of St. James to Armenian refugees and provided what were to become permanent residences.

With Jerusalem divided and controlled by two states, the church hierarchies were at pains to protect their position and receive assurances that the
Status Quo in the Christian Holy Places would be maintained. Clearly, the
poverty-struck Jordanian government was aware that it was not in a position compete with the wealth of the churches in providing educational
facilities. In addition, it was concerned that Western interests in Jerusalem
would take advantage of the weakened real estate market in order to

acquire large tracts of land in Jerusalem. In contrast to the picture painted by Daphne Tsimhoni, most of these safeguards were forthcoming from the Jordanian government.[10] Some restrictions were placed on the ability of churches to purchase land, though they could still continue to develop property. In the same way, interference in Christian educational activities was limited. Schools, such as the Anglican St. George's and the Coptic High School, which had a majority of students who were Muslim, were obliged to provide Islamic instruction.

Life in the Old City was difficult for the Christian communities. There was an economic decline that led to the departure of many Christian families to Amman, Beirut, Cairo, and further afield where they found employment opportunities more suitable for their experience and education. A Jordanian census in 1961 shows that the Christian population of Jerusalem, most of whom lived in the Old City, dropped by 62 percent from its 1946 figure, that is, to 11,000 people. By 1967, it was said to be about 15 percent of the total population of the city.[11] At the same time, religious life also suffered. The natural hinterland for the shrines of the Old City included congregations in Abu Ghosh, Jaffa, Haifa, Galilee, and all parts of former Palestine under Israeli rule. Ecclesiastical units were divided and senior clergy based in the Old City had to seek special permission to visit their coreligionists or their property and institutions in Israel. The numbers of pilgrims and visitors also declined.

Post-1967 Demography

Many factors impinge on the life of Christians in the Old City. Perhaps the most important one is the demographic one. While its absolute numbers are keeping steady, since 1967 the Christian population of the city has dramatically declined as a proportion of the total population including both Israeli and Palestinians. Table 5.1 shows that the population has remained at approximately 11,000, but the total population of the city has climbed from 267,000 to more than 600,000. This means that the proportion of Christians dropped from 4.4 percent to less than 3 percent. One should recall that in 1946, Christians constituted more than 19 percent of the population of the city. In 1998, Christians constituted 5.5 percent of the 200,000 Palestinians who inhabited East Jerusalem.

Of that 11,000, approximately 55 percent, or 6,000, live in the Old City itself. As in previous periods, Christians are to be found mainly in the Christian quarters and Armenian Quarter with some families living in the Muslim quarters (see Table 2.2). Most live close to the Christian Holy Places. Some found employment in the commercial and retail sectors, but most took up employment either in tourism or in the liberal professions such as teaching, law, health, and accounting.

Table 5.1   Christian Population of Jerusalem, 1967–1998 (by denomination)

	1967	1978	1990	1998	Percentage in 1998
Greek Orthodox	4,000	3,000	3,500	3,500	32.1
Armenian Orthodox	2,000	1,200	1,500	1,500	13.7
Armenian Catholic	100	210	150	n/a	n/a
Syrian Orthodox	300	165	200	250[a]	2.3
Syrian Catholic	40	60	50	n/a	n/a
Coptic Orthodox	370	185	40	250[a]	2.3
Coptic Catholic	30	35	32	n/a	n/a
Ethiopians	50	53	50	60	0.6
Maronites	50	38	35	100	0.9
Greek Catholic	300	335	35	500	4.6
Roman Catholic	3,900	4,210	480	3,900	35.7
Lutheran	300	400	40	410	3.8
Other Protestant	250	300	300	440	4.0

Source: Figures for 1967, 1978, and 1990 from D. Tsimhoni, *Christian Communities in Jerusalem and the West Bank Since 1948: An Historical, Social, and Political Study* (Westport, Conn.: Praeger, 1993), 26; figures for 1998 from B. Sabella, "Palestinian Christians: Realities and Hopes" (manuscript, 1998).

Note: a. Sabella does not distinguish between Syrian and Coptic Orthodox and Catholic, and does not provide figures for Armenian Catholics.

Main Policies of Israel

It is important to remind ourselves of the political context in which these developments occurred. Since 1967, Christian community matters were dealt with by the mayor and his advisers in the Israeli Jerusalem Municipality by the Christian Division of the Ministry of Religious Affairs, the Department of External Christian Relations in the Ministry of Foreign Affairs, and the district governor of Jerusalem. Representatives of these departments met regularly to coordinate approaches to the churches and to pursue the overall policy objectives of the Israeli government in the city. With regard to the Christian communities, this policy appeared to consist of three main goals.

1. There was the tactical and strategic goal of heading off any possibility of a Muslim-Christian religious coalition, which would strengthen and protect the Palestinian nationalist leadership. In this way, additional freedoms and privileges were given to the Christian clergy. This made their experience of Israeli rule significantly different from that of their Muslim counterparts, and a series of networks between clergy and Israeli officials was established. The aim was to make the possibility of coordinated Muslim-Christian activity and declarations difficult to achieve.

2. The government sought to discourage the creation of a united Christian front against Israeli policies in Jerusalem. One aspect of this poli-

cy was to court and co-opt senior clergy, most of whom, though local, were also non-Arab, to counter any sentiments of solidarity among the laity. By taking advantage of the age-old rivalries over the Status Quo and other intra-Christian matters, a state of perpetual suspicion and dissension could be achieved, from which Israel could secure some advantage.

3. Israeli government policy was also to acquire or lease as much church-owned land as possible. This policy had two advantages. It would provide additional space for construction of Israeli Jewish housing and thus increase the demographic dominance of Israeli Jews in the city. But it also had the added benefit of compromising the leadership of the churches in the eyes of their own laity and driving a wedge between the Palestinian Muslim and Christian populations.

Because of the control Israel had over planning issues, immigration, and tourism, Christian leaders often felt compelled to acquiesce or compromise with these policies, in order to secure consent on many of their administrative and cultural activities. This was particularly the case over building permits that church leaders saw as essential for the future provision for their communities. There is no doubt that over the years many good, cooperative relations were established between Israeli officials and church leaders. An example of this interplay can be seen in the Dayr al-Sultan incident, which contains the elements of both interchurch rivalry and government intervention.

The Dayr al-Sultan (Sultan's Monastery) comprises a courtyard on the roof of the Holy Sepulchre with some rudimentary dormitory accommodations and a passageway leading through two chapels down to the Parvis in front of the main door of the Holy Sepulchre. Early in the nineteenth century, the Dayr was owned by the Ethiopian Coptic Church while the Egyptian Coptic Orthodox Church had the right to process from its adjacent monastery of St. Antonius through the courtyard and the passageway on Christian feast days. Partly as a result of deaths through a plague in 1838 and partly through the support of Ibrahim Pasha, then later of the Ottoman authorities, the Egyptian Coptic Orthodox Church took possession of the courtyard, passageway, and chapels. By 1863, its possession over the Dayr was officially recognized. Although they were permitted to conduct their Easter services in the courtyard, the Ethiopians never accepted this new Status Quo arrangement.

Despite representations to them by the Ethiopians, the British Mandate authorities maintained the Status Quo. During the Jordanian period between 1949 and 1967, the Jordanian government initially ruled in favor of the Ethiopians but finally reversed its decision to keep the Status Quo. It is clear that Jordanian-Egyptian relations played its part in this reversal as Jordan sought to end its isolation in the Arab world.[12]

Tensions between the two communities continued into the Israeli period, flaring up each Easter as the Ethiopians conducted their ceremonies in the courtyard. In March 1970, while Coptic monks were conducting their Easter celebrations in the Holy Sepulchre, the Ethiopians changed the locks to the two chapels. When the Copts tried to reenter, they were prevented by Israeli police who claimed they did so on the grounds of maintaining public order. Thus, the Ethiopian Copts remained in possession but allowed the Copts the right to process from their monastery down to the Parvis. The Copts appealed to the Israeli Supreme Court, which ruled in 1971 that the Ethiopians were not entitled to evict the Copts. However, the Court also ruled that the decision as to who owned it was a government decision and, therefore, the government could leave the situation while it studied the argument.[13] A commission was set up, but no recommendations were made public. Further legal appeals to enforce the government to act took place in 1977, 1980, and 1982. In 1993, the government set up another interministerial commission, which ducked the main issue by recommending that until a settlement between the two communities could be reached, the Ethiopians should retain the keys of the two chapels but that the Coptic community would have free access to the Dayr.[14] The reason for this prevarication on the part of the Israeli government is clear: For most of the period under discussion, Israel sought to establish good relations with the Ethiopian government in an attempt to find allies in the Middle East. Even after the signing of the Camp David Accords with Egypt, the nature of the peace between Egypt and Israel was such that it did not see any advantage in alienating the Ethiopian government. As Tsimhoni observed: "Under Israeli rule, as under Jordanian rule, this conflict has become a diplomatic issue involving relations with Egypt and Ethiopia. Both are essential to Israeli interests and therefore the problem has remained unresolved."[15]

One result of the Dayr al-Sultan incident was to confirm to the leaders of the established churches their fears that the Status Quo arrangements were not safe in Israeli hands. Furthermore, the incident indicated that Israel was prepared to alter the arrangements to its advantage. Henceforward, this threat pervaded much of the relations between the established churches and the Israeli government. Finally, the Dayr al-Sultan incident led to the revival of the lapsed interchurch Holy Places Commission, which had been initiated in the mid-1960s to resolve internal disputes.[16] This embryonic institutional cooperation came into its own during the Palestinian intifada of 1987–1991/92 and the St. John's Hospice incident, which will be discussed later in this chapter.

Shifts in Israeli Policy

Following the Likud Party's election to government in 1977, the pattern and network of relations described above was interrupted. Militant Israeli nationalists, both secular and religious, were appointed to important positions in the Ministry of Justice, the Ministry of Religious Affairs, the Ministry of Housing, and in the Israel-Lands Administration. These were the key ministries and departments in the new government's strategic program of ensuring an Israeli Jewish dominance over East Jerusalem, and their priorities overrode the sensitivities and patterns of negotiations that had existed between the churches and the government hitherto. Even though the Likud Party fell from power in 1992, many officials sympathetic to its views remained in their positions. Indeed, this trend was only to accelerate following the election of a Likud mayor to Jerusalem, Ehud Olmert, who was committed to strengthening Israeli Jewish domination over the whole city and showed much less interest in protecting its religious pluralism. His arrival was accompanied by the departure of many officials who had developed good working relations with the churches.[17] In 1997, he controversially appointed Shmuel Evyatar, a militant settler who was involved in the takeover of St. John's Hospice, as his adviser on the Christian communities in Jerusalem.[18]

These Likud appointees showed much less sensitivity to maintaining good relations with the Christian communities. For example, in 1979 and 1980, there were a series of arson attacks and incidents of vandalism against church property carried out by Israeli militants and Jewish fundamentalists. The Dormition Abbey on Mount Zion, the Christian Information Centre near Jaffa Gate, and the Protestant Bible Bookshop were all damaged, and a Baptist church in West Jerusalem was burned to the ground. Although there was a police investigation and some people were charged, the impression church leaders received was of a government generally uninterested and unsympathetic. What confirmed this impression were two other developments: First was the covert support that the Likud government gave to the activities of Israeli settlers in the Old City and their attempts to penetrate the Christian quarters. This culminated with their occupation of St. John's Hospice, owned by the Greek Orthodox Patriarchate, which will be discussed in greater detail below. Second was the encouragement given to Christian fundamentalist supporters of Israel, particularly those operating under the umbrella of the International Christian Embassy in Jerusalem (ICEJ). The primary function of the ICEJ has been to coordinate pilgrim tours and educational projects sympathetic to Israel, but many of its supporters also channel funds to militant Israeli organizations such as the Temple Mount Foundation (see also Chapter 3). Relations between the ICEJ and the established churches is one of great hostility. One measure of the extent of official Israeli support for the ICEJ is that the president and prime minister usually address its annual Feast of the Tabernacle celebration in Jerusalem.

The First Intifada and the Peace Process

The first intifada (1987–1992) was a major change in the political context in which the Christian communities in Jerusalem and the Old City were living. From 1987 to the early 1990s, there were repeated strikes, curfews, and demonstrations leading to nearly 1,000 deaths as well as thousands being imprisoned and many thousands receiving injuries from beatings or tear gas or gunshot wounds. It was also a period that saw the rise of the militant Islamic movement Hamas, operating independently of the PLO, and the legal termination of Jordanian influence in the West Bank.

The Christian community was directly involved in the intifada in many ways. In 1988, the son of a prominent Christian family was killed in Gaza, and some months later the first Christian resident of the Old City died after being caught up with a clash with the Israeli Army. A tax revolt in the Christian village of Bayt Sahhur, just between Jerusalem and Bethlehem, led to the Israeli Army imposing a forty-six-day siege, finally leading to forty arrests and the confiscation of $3 million of goods. The siege received international media attention and demonstrated clearly the involvement of the laity of the Palestinian Christian community in the national movement.[19] As the deaths, detentions, and injuries mounted, Christian religious leaders came under increasing pressure to declare their positions regarding the intifada. In addition, the success of the intifada, not only of putting Israel on the defensive militarily, but also of causing the virtual collapse of its administrative control, demonstrated the long-term vulnerability of the Israeli state in the occupied Palestinian territories.

In 1991, Israel agreed to meet with Palestinian representatives at the Middle East Peace Conference in Madrid; two years later in the Oslo Accords, Israel recognized the PLO. These events set in train a new set of political conditions that affected the established Christian communities and their relations with Israel. The legalization of the PLO, the surfacing of banned political parties, the international credibility and support for Palestinian positions, and the arrival of the Palestinian quasi-state apparatus first in Gaza and Jericho, then in Ramallah and Bethlehem and areas adjacent to Jerusalem, marked a dramatic reconfiguring of the political landscape. It was no longer sufficient for the church leadership to have cooperative relations with just Israeli and Jordanian officials. The PNA was now the main interlocutor on the Arab side even though the Oslo Accords had only ushered in interim arrangements. Indeed, the status of Jerusalem had been deferred until the completion of the permanent status negotiations. However, the replacement of many hitherto Jordanian functions by the PNA meant that the PNA, to Israelis' dismay, would be heavily involved in many areas of life in Jerusalem. Today, it has de facto control over the education system in Palestinian schools in East Jerusalem, including the curricula, and it is gradually usurping Jordanian control over religious administration and the *waqf* system by setting up a Ministry of Religious Affairs.

What has been the response of the established churches to all these changes since the mid-1970s? Clearly there has been a mix of responses, prompted partly by external stimuli but also as a result of changes within the Christian communities themselves.

There are three main developments in the overall religious and political context that have affected the Christian community since the 1980s and have had a direct impact on its role in the Old City. These are: (1) social and political engagement of the clergy and laity, (2) greater coordination among the hierarchies as a result of the intifada, and (3) a repositioning in the wake of the Oslo Accords and the ongoing permanent status negotiations.

Engagement of the Clergy

Throughout the latter part of the twentieth century to the present, virtually all churches have felt the pressures for greater accountability and devolved administration. These pressure have arisen from a number of sources: the greater education of the laity; the loss of accumulated financial reserves from land reforms leading to a greater dependence upon lay donations; a global trend away from direct colonization; and, finally, the spread of democratic processes. They have all combined to introduce more transparent ecclesiastical structures in different churches. In Israel and the West Bank and Gaza Strip, the church hierarchies have experienced similar pressures. Indeed, as a result of the Arab-Israeli conflict, some of the pressures have been particularly acute. One result has been both the Arabization and Palestinianization and greater social and political engagement of the clergy, as the Palestinian laity demanded a greater involvement in the running of their respective churches and a greater scrutiny of their clergy's stance on social and political issues pertaining to the conflict. Similarly, there has been a growing sense that a Palestinian national identity has replaced a sectarian or religiously defined one. The high profile of Arab Episcopalians (Anglicans) such as Hanan Ashrawi, former spokesperson for the Palestinian negotiating team, and Jonathan Kuttab and Raja Shehadeh, prominent human rights lawyers, reflects this close identification by the laity with the Palestinian movement. The 1980s saw the appointment of outspoken bishops such as Samir Qafity for the Arab Episcopalians, Lutfi Laham for the Greek Catholics, and Michel Sabbah for the Roman Catholics. These were politically aware, articulate, and internationally connected Palestinians who at the same time closely reflected the concerns and aspirations of their community, and their appointments illustrated the deeper shift taking place within the churches. Church land, property, and administrative structures were increasingly perceived as belonging to the embryonic Palestinian nation.

Similar moves were attempted in the Greek Orthodox community but with much less success. The conflict between the Greek Orthodox Patriarchate with its Greek and Greek Cypriot clergy and the Arab and Palestinian lay members of the community is a long-running one that originated in the late nineteenth century. The main issues concerned questions of lay participation in the management of church property and financial assets and the appointment of Arab clergy to senior positions. No resolution was achieved despite the intervention at different times by the mandate authorities and by the Jordanian government. Despite reforms within the Greek Orthodox Church elsewhere in the world that permitted greater lay and indigenous involvement, the patriarchate in Jerusalem refused to alter its structures. The main reason given was that the Greek Orthodox Patriarchate existed to serve and support the monastic Brotherhood of the Holy Sepulchre, which acted in the interests of the worldwide Greek Orthodox community and could not be accountable to a small fraction of it, the Palestinian laity. In addition, the patriarchate was aware that by aligning itself with the nationalist demands of the Palestinian laity, it would jeopardize its relations with the Israeli government, which were essential if it was to retain its autonomy. The patriarchate also takes a long-term strategic view. To maintain its preeminent position in the Holy Sepulchre in the centuries to come, it must continue to respond cautiously to political change, making adjustments where necessary but ensuring that its political alliances will not lead to any undermining of its position. The political circumstances of the present day require deft footwork on its part. It has no imperial protector as in the nineteenth century, and any major shift will require careful planning and guarantees.

During the mid-1980s, in the circumstances of heightened political tension, the issue of land sales came to the fore. Due to a great shortage of funds, to the extent that the patriarchate received subsidies from the Greek government, the patriarchate began to enter into long-lease arrangements with Israeli developers, some extending up to ninety-nine years. To the native Palestinian orthodox laity, this was deemed, in effect, as a sale of church land by the patriarchate to the Israeli government and was deeply disturbing and offensive. Indeed, in the face of the constant construction of settlements for the arrival of new Jewish immigrants and the eroding Palestinian presence in Jerusalem, it was seen as also potentially dangerous to the community's coexistence with the Muslim majority. The Palestinian laity established the Arab Orthodox Initiative Committee, which pressed for reforms in the process of appointing bishops and for greater accountability in the financial affairs of the patriarchate. It also demanded greater

control over land sales. In October 1992, the committee convened a conference in East Jerusalem and passed the following resolution.

> The Executive Committee [of the Arab Orthodox Initiative Committee]
> will work to amend the Laws and Regulations which define the relation-
> ship between the Patriarchate and the Arab Orthodox sect, in order to
> redress the grievances and the injustices suffered by the members of the
> Arab Orthodox sect and to comply with the new developments at large. In
> this regard the Conference approves the amendments forwarded by the
> Arab Orthodox Initiative Committee, to the Laws of the Orthodox
> Patriarchate (No. 27 of 1958) that would secure the rights and the partici-
> pation of the Arab Orthodox community in handling the affairs of the
> Patriarchate and its supervision over the endowments, budgets and build-
> ings of schools.[20]

The land sales issue received particular prominence, and resolutions
were passed emphasizing that church lands were no longer seen as the
exclusive domain of the Greek and Greek Cypriot hierarchy but part of the
Palestinian patrimony. For example, another resolution declared:

> The conference will make sure to oversee and protect all church proper-
> ties in order to curb any attempts at selling religious and physical endow-
> ments. Efforts will be made in taking inventories of the properties to be
> invested for the benefit of the community, for *they are considered to be an
> integral part of the Palestinian land*, the tampering of which is considered
> to be national treason [emphasis added].[21]

Significantly, a follow-up conference held in Amman received the support and recognition of both the Jordanian government and the PLO, which
increased the pressure on the patriarchate to distance itself from the Israeli
government. It was in this political maelstrom of shifting allegiances and
conflicting pressures that the occupation of the Greek Orthodox Hospice of
St. John by militant Israeli settlers took place. This incident is a defining
incident and will be analyzed in greater detail below. At this point, it will
be sufficient to indicate that the patriarchate strategy of maintaining good
relations with the Israeli state did not seem to offer the rewards it used to.

In the remaining established churches, the situation is different. Most
are either very small and the laity very weak or they do not have an ethnic
divide between the hierarchy and the congregation. Only the Armenian
Patriarchate has been subjected to the same pressures.[22] However, the
Armenian community is close knit and based almost entirely inside the
Monastery of St. James or in the immediate vicinity of the Armenian
Quarter.[23] Despite the fact that the Jerusalem Patriarchate has been exempt-
ed from the democratizing reforms enacted in other parts of the Armenian
Orthodox Church, the close living conditions of the community have meant

that lay influence in the affairs of the patriarchate is strong. While the Brotherhood of St. James's Monastery is the owner of the monastery and all the property within the compound, many lay Armenians are employed by the Brotherhood and are thus involved in the day-to-day decisionmaking.

Interdenominational Coordination

The second major response of the churches to the changing political context was a distinct phase of closer and unprecedented coordination. As has been described, the Palestinian intifada between 1987 and 1993 changed the political landscape and resulted in the loosening of Israeli control and Jordanian influence in the West Bank, Gaza Strip, and Jerusalem. It also precipitated a crisis in Israeli-church relations with the engaged clergy and laity pressing their more conservative co-religionists to declare an outspoken position against the Israeli occupation and policies of suppression. There were a number of dynamics in play at this time. The Arabized hierarchies were anxious to declare their solidarity with the Palestinian national movement in light of the active participation of their members in the intifada, whereas the non-Arabized ones were aware that they could be left exposed to a nationalist wave, which, if the strength of the Israeli state and its hold over the occupied Palestinian territories faltered, would eventually engulf them. Both factions understood the importance of a united and coherent Christian position. What followed was a series of actions that marked a decisive shift in the attitude of the churches to Israeli rule and a change in their hitherto competitive and fragmented activities.

The most public aspect of this change was seen in the publication of a series of "Statements by the Heads of the Christian Communities in Jerusalem" between January 1988 and December 1992.[24] However, there were also actions involving participation in strikes and boycotts, the closing of churches and shrines, concerted bell-ringing to mark specific occasions, joint delegations to present their views to political and religious leaders and visiting dignitaries and politicians, and the coordinated suspension of major services and ceremonies. Following the seizure of the Greek Orthodox Hospice of St. John in 1990, the Holy Sepulchre was closed in protest for twenty-four hours—the first time this was to have occurred in 800 years. For three years running, between 1987 and 1989, Christmas celebrations were curtailed and public services suspended. These were significant steps not only in terms of expressing solidarity with the Palestinian national movement and the suffering of the people but also in demonstrating the degree of intrachurch cooperation. It should be noted that the Christmas period generates considerable income for those churches dependent upon pilgrim donations and tourist expenditure.

This greater coordination can be divided into three phases and is best reflected in an analysis of the statements referred to above. The three statements that appeared in 1988 were tentative and cautious in their support for the Palestinian intifada. Their support was couched in general terms:

> We, the Heads of the Christian Communities in Jerusalem, would like to express in all honesty and clarity that we take our stand with truth and justice against all forms of injustice and oppression. We stand with the suffering and oppressed, we stand with the refugees and the deported, with the distressed and the victims of injustice, we stand with those who mourn and are bereaved, with the hungry and the poor.[25]

What was particularly significant about these early statements was that they were signed by all the heads of the major communities:.

- His Beatitude (HB) Diadorus, Greek Orthodox Patriarch of Jerusalem
- HB Michel Sabbah, Latin Patriarch of Jerusalem
- HB Yeghishe Derderian, Armenian Orthodox Patriarch of Jerusalem
- Most Reverend Father Cechitelli (Order of the Franciscan Monks), Custos of the Holy Land
- Bishop Samir Qafity, President Bishop, Episcopal Church in Jerusalem and the Middle East
- Archbishop Lutfi Laham, Patriarchal Vicar, Greek Catholic Patriarchate of Jerusalem
- Bishop Naim Nassar, Evangelical Lutheran Church in Jordan
- His Grace Basilios, Coptic Orthodox Archbishop of Jerusalem
- Archbishop Dionysios Behnam Jijjawi, Syrian Orthodox Patriarchal Vicar of Jerusalem

The only signatories who did not sign this statement but signed later ones included the Ethiopian archbishop of Jerusalem and the Lutheran propst of Jerusalem. The signature of the former was unlikely, as the Ethiopian Coptic community was in serious dispute with the major established churches due to its takeover of the Dayr al-Sultan Monastery from the Coptic Orthodox community. The Lutheran propst would not be expected to sign, as he is a representative of the German Lutheran Church and not usually regarded as a member of a local church.

This response of the churches was a major blow to the Israeli government policy in Jerusalem. Hitherto, it had succeeded in establishing bilateral relations with all the churches and preventing this kind of united response to its occupation. It was, in addition, a further sign that the network of personal relations that had evolved since 1967 between church leaders and the municipality, and officials in the relevant government departments were being superseded by the new political forces on both the Palestinian and Israeli side.

The second phase took place between 1989 and 1991 and comprised the most explicit expressions of solidarity with the suffering and aspirations of the Palestinian people. For example, the Statement of 27 April 1989 declared:

> In Jerusalem, on the West Bank and in Gaza *our* people experience in their daily lives constant deprivation of their fundamental rights because of arbitrary actions deliberately taken by the authorities. *Our* people are often subjected to unprovoked harassment and hardship. . . . We protest against the frequent shooting incidents in the vicinity of the Holy Places. . . . We demand that the authorities respect the right of believers to enjoy free access to all places of worship on the Holy Days of all religions. . . . *We request the international community and the UN to give urgent attention to the plight of the Palestinian people, and to work for a speedy and just resolution of the Palestinian problem* [emphasis added].[26]

This open identification became more forceful and strident following the occupation of St. John's Hospice.

The final phase came in the wake of the Madrid Peace Conference of 1991. During this phase, there was a return to more general condemnations of injustice and violence and more specific references kept to strictly incidents of vandalism and theft against churches. To some extent this reflected optimism with the peace process and church leaders "retired in favour of the Palestinian delegation to the peace talks."[27] It was also a period of confusion in the direction of the Palestinian national movement and much discussion as to whether tactical gains, such as temporary autonomy, could be accepted without jeopardizing strategic objectives, such as full independence. However, despite this deference, the ongoing incidents of curfews and closures limiting access to holy places, of attacks against clergy and church property, and the damaging of Christian artifacts and archaeological sites, provoked great anger from church leaders leading them to threaten to call for international protection.

> We demand the authorities to provide protection against these depredations and take prompt action to forestall any further harassment in the future, and preserve the newly discovered relics of the early Christian Church in Jerusalem. If no appropriate and satisfactory measures are taken to protect Christian archaeological sites, we will consider seeking international protection to preserve our universal Christian heritage.[28]

Before moving on to the third response of the Christian churches to the new political conditions, that of its repositioning closer to the Palestinian position, it would be instructive to examine the St. John's Hospice incident in greater detail. There have been many references to this event in this chapter, and the incident can be seen as the defining moment in church-state relations after 1967.

St. John's Hospice Incident

The occupation of the property known as St. John's Hospice belonging to the Greek Orthodox Patriarchate by Israeli settlers in April 1990 can be seen as the defining moment in the relations between the Israeli government and the established churches of Jerusalem (see Map 3.1). As the former secretary to the Armenian patriarch, Kevork Hintlian, remarked: "The Christian Quarter of after April 11th is not the same Christian Quarter as before then."[29] As the incident was probably the most serious in church-state relations since 1967, with ramifications that are still being played out today, it demands an in-depth discussion.

The property was occupied on the eve of Good Friday, during the lead-up to the Easter celebrations, when Greek Orthodox pilgrims in large numbers come to Jerusalem. About 150 members of the Ateret Cohanim settler group entered the building claiming that they had bought it from a Panamanian-registered company, SBC, Ltd.[30] It later transpired that the original tenant, an Armenian Catholic, Mardiros Matossian, who had already been barred by the Armenian patriarch for misdemeanors in the mid-1980s, had sold it to the company for a sum variously estimated at between U.S.$3.5 million and U.S.$5 million. The Greek Orthodox Patriarchate insisted that the lessee had no right to sell the property and that the occupation was entirely without legal foundation. Despite appeals to the Israeli High Court, the settlers were permitted to stay pending a full hearing. On Maundy Thursday itself, 13 April, following the annual foot-washing ceremony in the Holy Sepulchre, Patriarch Diodorus I led a demonstration to the hospice. A monk tried to remove the Star of David that had been attached to the doorway, and in the ensuing scuffle, the Israeli police sprayed the crowd with tear gas and the patriarch was sent sprawling to the ground.[31] On 27 April, the Israeli High Court ruled that pending the outcome of legal proceedings in the magistrates and district courts over the legal title to the property, the company could keep twenty people in the building for security and maintenance purposes. To date the building is still the subject of litigation.

What this incident revealed is the degree of support the settler movement in the Old City was receiving from official government sources. The minister of commerce and industry, Ariel Sharon, and the speaker of the Knesset, Dov Shilansky, spoke openly in support of the occupation. The veteran Israeli observer of the settler movement in the Old City, *Ha'aretz* journalist Nadav Shragai, also reported that Prime Minister Shamir intervened to delay an eviction order to give the settlers time to appeal.[32] It later turned out that the Ministry of Housing had funded up to 40 percent of the purchase, possibly illegally, which gave impetus for the setting up of the Klugman inquiry under the succeeding government mentioned in Chapter 3. However, the incident can also be seen as a grave miscalculation on the part of both Ateret Cohanim and the Israeli government. It precipitated a very strong reaction not only from the Christian communities but also from the Muslim community, from within Israel, and from Western governments. Furthermore, it exposed the activities of the settlers to an unprecedented extent. After the St. John's incident, everyone following the Palestinian-Israeli conflict knew about Ateret Cohanim, and henceforth their covert operations received widespread media attention.

In the first place, the occupation of the hospice took place during Holy Week, when the patriarchate, the Brotherhood of the Holy Sepulchre, and the Arab Orthodox lay community in general are in the fullest glare of their wider international community, receiving visitors, hosting pilgrims, and meeting with church leaders and dignitaries from around the world. The humiliation of having a large property very close to the Holy Sepulchre taken away from under their noses was coupled with the very public humiliation of the patriarch being tear gassed and knocked to the ground by a gang of squatters. The situation was intolerable and marked the deepest crisis in the patriarch's relations with the Israeli government. From his perspective, he had cooperated with the government over the leasing and sales of land at the risk of alienating himself and his brethren from their lay community; he had refused for many years to participate with the other established churches in concerted attempts to oppose the Israeli occupation, and he had allowed himself to be paraded by municipal and government officials at official receptions and ceremonies as a token of Christian acceptance of Israeli rule. At the very least, the quid pro quo was that the patriarchate's property would not be acquired by nefarious means with the connivance of the government that the patriarch had cooperated with, particularly in the humiliating manner it was. The occupation of St. John's Hospice signaled that this government was not interested in cooperative relations with the patriarchate at the expense of its wider goals of securing a Jewish dominance in the Old City. The result was a complete breakdown in relations. There was a bitter exchange of letters between the patriarch and the president of Israel.[33] The dispute also spilled over into the diplomatic domain when the patriarch went as far as calling upon the Greek government to suspend attempts to improve Greek-Israeli relations.[34]

The incident was a key factor in binding the Christian communities together to a much greater extent. For the churches, the prospect of a settler movement out of control in the Christian quarters with the overt support of a right-wing government was a nightmare scenario. Where would they strike next? Which community would suffer in the future? The statement that followed this incident was the strongest yet authored by the established church leadership.

> This government-backed action continues to provoke almost daily incidents in and around the area containing the Holy Sepulchre and the centres of church governance, and has occasioned the provocative presence of numerous armed men in the same restricted area. Consequently, freedom of access to the Holy Sepulchre and freedom of worship within it have been threatened.
>
> This act of armed settlement seriously jeopardises the integrity, and cultural and religious autonomy of the Christian, Armenian and Muslim Quarters, in violation of the centuries-old status and character of these quarters of the Holy City, honoured by all the previous rulers of Jerusalem, and the international community (and which the Israeli authorities have repeatedly pledged themselves to uphold).
>
> This action further endangers the survival of all Christian communities in the Holy City.
>
> We, the heads of Jerusalem's Christian Churches and Communities unreservedly condemn the actions of the settlers.
>
> We deplore the open support and encouragement it has received from Israeli government quarters.
>
> We demand that the Israeli authorities effect the immediate removal of these settlers and secure the property for its legitimate owners, the Greek Orthodox Patriarchate.
>
> We appeal to the International community, to all churches and religious leaders, and to all people of goodwill throughout the world to give their support to our call.[35]

In addition to the usual signatories, the Ethiopian archbishop, who had close links with the Israeli government, and the Lutheran propst also signed it. The statement announced the closure of Christian Holy Places in Jerusalem, Nazareth, and Bethlehem, a funeral bell toll and a special day of prayer. These steps were unprecedented and marked the nadir of church-Israeli government relations. The tone and terminology of this statement would have been inconceivable five years previously and illustrated the extent to which the churches were moving out of the Israeli orbit. Whatever misgivings the church leadership may have had at the prospect of a Muslim-dominated Palestinian state, the St. John's Hospice incident suggested that it would be no worse than the current state of affairs. Indeed, they were more likely to have more influence over the policy of a bicommunal Palestinian government toward religious minorities than an exclusive Jewish one.

Another aspect of the incident was to strengthen the hands of Christians outside the Holy Land who were pushing for a greater identification with Palestinian aspirations. The World Council of Churches, the worldwide ecumenical organization representing Protestant and Orthodox churches, expressed its support for the "national aspiration of the Palestinian people on the basis of equality which is the only guarantee for peace in the Holy Land."[36] The Vatican continued to express its sympathy for the Palestinian position, and the views of Patriarch Sabbah over Vatican-Israeli relations were given greater weight. Similarly, in the United States, leading Catholics condemned the occupation of the hospice, and the National Council of Churches began to lobby actively in support of Palestinian positions.

Finally, the incident also caused divisions within the Israeli body politic. In addition to denunciations by the Israeli peace movements Peace Now and Oz ve Shalom, the citizen rights movement member of the Knesset, Yossi Sarid, led a vociferous campaign against the covert financing of the occupation.[37] Furthermore, the mayor of Jerusalem at the time, Teddy Kollek, despite his criticism of the strong reaction of the Greek Orthodox patriarch, was also highly critical of the settlers' action. In an interview with the Israeli daily *Ha'aretz,* he said:

> The work of years has been ruined, perhaps irreparably. For years we have struggled towards the goal of getting the world to recognize Jerusalem as the capital of Israel . . . and every episode of this sort sets us back years. The Greek church, of which we are speaking, has leased us more land in Jerusalem than any other church. The whole belt of land around the Old City is from them. Also the Sultan's Pool, Liberty Bell Garden, 'Omariah [school]. Clearly it will be hard for them to continue to do things like these.[38]

He concluded his interview with the statement, "I think this action in the Old City is really traitorous."[39] Indeed, even leading pro-Israel groups in the United States, such as the American Israel Public Affairs Committee and the Anti-Discrimination League of B'nai B'rith, attacked the government for undermining its work in support of Israel in Congress.[40]

Repositioning of the Church Leadership

The third and final major response to the changing political context brings us up to the immediate contemporary period. Following the mutual recognition of the PLO and Israel in the Oslo Accords in September 1993, the Christian communities shared the same euphoria experienced by most of the Palestinian people. In the wake of the staged limited withdrawals by the Israeli Army in the Gaza Strip and the West Bank, the PLO leader, Chairman Yasser Arafat, received a tumultuous welcome in Bethlehem. Bishop Samir Qafity likened his arrival to the arrival of the Caliph 'Umar, the most just and far-sighted of the four early caliphs, and who respected the position of Christians in Jerusalem. The PNA was quick to demonstrate its long-term intentions for Jerusalem and the Old City, in spite of the restrictions placed on it by the interim agreements. It established a Ministry for Religious Affairs whose first moves were the appointment of a new mufti of Jerusalem and the opening of an office in the Old City. It also appointed the veteran lawyer and Arab Orthodox lay person, Ibrahim Qandalaft, as the deputy minister for Christian affairs.

At the same time, Israel took few steps to repair the damage of the intifada years and to reestablish good relations with church leaders. The Ethiopian Coptics remained in control over Dayr al-Sultan, despite court rulings that said it should be returned to the Coptic Orthodox; Ateret Cohanim remained in possession of St. John's Hospice; the appointment of the settler Shmuel Evyatar as the mayor's adviser on Christian affairs led to a virtual boycott of relations with the municipality; and the provision of residency permits and visas to foreign clergy and volunteers continued to be problematic.[41] Another indication of the low priority being accorded to the Christian community at this time was the lack of progress in resolving differences between the Vatican and Israel despite their agreement in December 1993. It was reported that during an audience with the pope the prime minister of Israel, Benjamin Netanyahu, denied knowledge of promises to create special legal status for church personnel and for its property. In addition, Uri Mor, director of the Division of Christian Communities in the Israeli Ministry of Religious Affairs, was denied an office for more than a year and forced to meet with religious dignitaries in cafés.[42] It should be noted that the Israeli plans for the millennium celebrations made only two references to events organized by the established churches though its official program contains many announcements of activities by the International Christian Embassy in Jerusalem.

It is clear that the Israeli policy of attempting to co-opt the Christian leadership has been suspended during the post-Oslo period. The main reason is not likely to be its lack of strategic worth; rather the suspension is more likely to be the result of the dominance of the narrow exclusive vision for the city exhibited by the right wing in Israeli politics and its settler supporters. As a recommendation by the influential Israeli research center, the Jerusalem Institute for Israel Studies, states:

> Israel should allow international Christian bodies to operate in Jerusalem and should assist in transforming the city into a spiritual centre forming a focus for large-scale pilgrimage and tourism while enjoying the economic advantages deriving from this status. However, Israel must not encourage the participation of the Vatican in the political negotiations on the Jerusalem question. Its inclusion might bring about a Muslim-Christian coalition likely to cause additional difficulties for Israel. Nevertheless, efforts should be made to promote negotiations with non-Arab Christian

elements, such as the Greek Orthodox, the Armenian community and Armenia, Georgia, Ethiopia. A stable coalition of interests might be created between these elements and the State of Israel which will be beneficial for all parties.[43]

However, the implementation of such a policy has little chance of success in light of Israeli coalition politics that obliges the government to seek the support of Zionist parties intent on promoting Jewish settlement in the city.

Despite the strong identification of the local Roman Catholic community with the Palestinian national movement and the outspoken statements by Patriarch Michel Sabbah, the Vatican took the opportunity offered by the Oslo Accords to come to a preliminary agreement with the Israeli state and to establish diplomatic relations. The "Fundamental Agreement Between the Holy See and the State of Israel" of 30 December 1993 contained a range of understandings on the administration of the Christian Holy Places, pilgrimage, education, welfare, and media issues. It is significant that the Vatican affirmed its "continuing commitment to respect the aforementioned 'Status Quo' and the said rights" and did not seem to be keeping open the possibility of extracting some advantage from the Israeli government.[44] The agreement also provided for the establishment of subcommissions to examine the Vatican's request for a special legal personality to be given to its personnel and the disputes concerning property and fiscal matters. It is also significant that the Vatican did not recognize either Israeli or Palestinian claims to Jerusalem as their capital. The issue of sovereignty was simply not mentioned.[45] It has also been reported that an unpublished annex contains a guarantee that the Vatican would be accorded an equal place on any council of Christians set up to manage the Holy Places.[46]

It is clear that by this agreement, the Vatican sought to reestablish its influence and present itself as an interlocutor in the discussion over the future of the city, particularly of the Old City. While it was content to accept the Status Quo arrangements, it wished to ensure that it was well-positioned to have a say in the future administrative arrangements. Having been marginalized during the Madrid Conference in 1991, it did not wish to be excluded from further discussions by being more pro-Palestinian than the PLO. Nevertheless, the failure to include any declaration of support for Palestinian rights over the city dismayed many Christian activists who felt the agreement sent the wrong message to both the Israelis and the wider Palestinian national movement. In addition, the agreement itself and the rumors of secret annexes alarmed the other church leaders who suspected the Vatican of obtaining some reward for their recognition of Israel. Anxieties about the future of the Status Quo arrangements threatened to unravel the coordination that had been achieved during the intifada years. The Greek Orthodox are clearly very concerned about any preference being given to the Vatican.[47]

Despite this uncertainty, or perhaps because of it, extra efforts were made to construct a Christian position on Jerusalem. The Oslo Accords had made Jerusalem one of the six Permanent Status Issues that would be negotiated between Israel and the PLO not earlier than 1996. Church leaders agreed that it was important that a unified Christian position, however general, should be formulated and used as a basis for interventions to the negotiations. On 14 November 1994, a memorandum on the significance of Jerusalem for Christians was published. The memorandum is of huge importance for four reasons. First, it is the definitive reference point for the position of the established churches on the nature, status, and future of Jerusalem. All the main heads of communities including, significantly, the Ethiopian archbishop who normally avoids signing any joint statements, signed it. As such, it is the official Christian contribution to the negotiations over the future of the city irrespective of the positions taken by the ICEJ. Second, the memorandum is explicit in its recognition of the sanctity of the city for both Judaism and Islam and makes no exclusive claims. This is an important signal to both the Jewish and Muslim communities of the Christian recognition of the need to share the holiness of the city. Third, it affirms the centrality of the Status Quo arrangements and makes no allusions for alteration or reform.

> Those rights of property ownership, custody and worship which the different churches have acquired throughout history *should continue to be retained by the same communities. These rights which are already protected in the Status Quo of the Holy Places according to historical "firmans" and other documents, should continue to be recognised and respected* [emphasis in the original].[48]

To some extent this may serve as an assurance by the Roman Catholic leadership to the Armenian and Greek Orthodox Patriarchates. Whatever the outcome of the discussions between the Vatican and the Israeli government, stemming from their Fundamental Agreement, the Catholic leadership would not be seeking to reverse the *praedominium*.[49]

The fourth and final reason for the memorandum's importance lay in its call for a special statute for the city to be guaranteed by the international community. While not entering into specifics, the memorandum calls for the representatives of the three religions and "local political powers," presumably Israel, Jordan, and the PNA, to draw up and apply the proposed statute. An essential feature of the statute would be the involvement of the international community.

> Because of the universal significance of Jerusalem, the international community ought to be engaged in the stability and permanence of this statute. Jerusalem is too precious to be dependent solely on municipal or national political authorities, whoever they may be. Experience shows that an international guarantee is necessary.[50]

The term guarantees were understood to cover exemption from taxes on religious property, protection against confiscation, and the issuing of building permits.

The call for a special statute with international guarantees is the final nail in the coffin for the supporters of the internationalization of Jerusalem. The churches were the last bastion of support for this aspect of UN Resolution 181. However, the failure to delineate the geographical area to which the statute is to be applied is interesting. It implies that it is a much greater area than the holy places themselves—Christian, Muslim, and Jewish—and even a greater area than the Old City. Indeed, while applying the statute to the Old City would have been the most obvious application of the statute, this was an option not adopted by the church leaders. Neither is the memorandum explicit over the issue of Jerusalem as a capital city for both Israelis and Palestinians. The issue is side-stepped leaving open the possibility of a dual capital. Clearly, the statute would not appeal to the Israeli government, as it would result in a loss of its sovereign powers over the whole of the city. However, the church leaders were hoping that the prospect of international recognition of Jewish religious rights and the possibility of international recognition of part of the city as the Israeli capital would make the statute proposal sufficiently attractive to the Israeli government. Despite these hopes, the official Israeli line remained that Jerusalem would continue to be the undivided eternal capital of Israel.

On the Palestinian side there was disappointment that the memorandum did not call for East Jerusalem to be the Palestinian capital. In addition, there were strong misgivings at the prospect of involving non-Palestinian Muslims and Christians in formulating a statute. Despite the rhetoric of diplomacy, Palestinians did not wish to encourage Jordanian, Saudi Arabian, Moroccan or, for that matter, Iranian involvement in the running of the city. Nevertheless, the statute proposal received a cautious welcome partly because the PNA was able to seize the moral high ground but also because with the limited leverage at its disposal, a special statute with international guarantees would help to prize away the Israeli grip over the city.[51]

During the years following the publication of the 1994 memorandum, a closer alignment between the church leadership and the Palestinian position can be discerned. For example, in 2000 a "Basic Agreement" was signed between the Vatican and the PLO, and it reveals an evolution in the position of a major church during this period. The Basic Agreement calls for a solution of the Arab-Israeli conflict based upon UN resolutions, which has been a central Palestinian demand for many years. To some extent the change was forced upon the Vatican by the strong reaction of the churches to the Fundamental Agreement (with Israel) that was perceived as a dangerous breaking of ranks so soon after the first intifada. To some extent the change also reflected a reassertion of the influence of the local church and the authority of the Latin patriarch Michel Sabbah over Vatican diplomacy toward Israel and the PLO.

Muslim-Christian Relations

An important element in the repositioning of the churches was a gradual shift in the relations between Muslims and Christians in the Old City. As we have already discussed, lay Christian participation in the wider Palestinian political scene was quite extensive, with many leading politicians and spokespersons being Christian. However, their participation has been less as representatives of their communities per se but as members of a particular political faction or supporters of a particular ideology. The participation of church leadership has been more tentative and only more visible since the intifada.[52]

There has been an absence of coordination between the two religious communities at the leadership level. Both the Muslim and Christian clergy have been conservative as well as suspicious of interfaith links. Theological differences over the deity of Jesus Christ and the primacy of the Prophet Muhammad, together with cultural differences—the Christian clergy tend to be more cosmopolitan than their Muslim counterparts—conspire to make effective cooperation difficult. To be sure, there have long been regular exchanges of visits on respective feast days and frequent public messages of support and congratulation to mark official occasions. However, these have been largely cosmetic and have not produced a consistent framework for consultation and joint planning.

In the mid-1980s, the Al-Liqa' Centre was set up in Bayt Sahhur. The Al-Liqa' Centre is run and supported by a number of clergy and prominent Palestinian lay people who wished to look more deeply into the relevance of their faith to contemporary social and political issues.[53] The center ran a series of conferences and seminars under the title of "Arab-Christian and Muslim Heritage in the Holy Land." It brought together clerical leaders and theologians of both faiths to explore points of agreement and disagreement. Although major differences were not resolved, the dialogue itself eased theological tensions and created both a channel for further communication and, more important, cross-cutting personal networks that hitherto had been lacking. More recently, the theological and intellectual foundations of the trend to situate the church within its social and political environment have been underpinned by the formulation of a "Palestinian theology of liberation" led by Reverend Dr. Na'im Ateek and the work of the Sabeel Ecumenical Liberation Theology Centre.[54]

During the intifada, these networks came to fruition and a number of joint activities took place. For example, during the St. John's Hospice incident, the Higher Council for Islamic Waqf Affairs and Holy Sites, headed by the mufti of Jerusalem, Shaykh Sa'ad al-Din Alami, denounced the Israeli action in the following way:

> The Higher Council for Islamic Waqf Affairs and Holy Sites is following with profound anxiety and pain the dangerous Israeli aggressions taken up by settler groups supported by the Israeli government upon the Christian holy places and properties in the heart of the historic Christian Quarter in the Holy City of Jerusalem. After studying the statement and decisions published by the Patriarchs and heads of the Christian churches and denominations, and to declare its unlimited solidarity with what was said in the statement, [the Higher Council] considers that this aggression is aimed at the holy places and rights of all Palestinian Muslims and Christians in the Holy Land, as it is an attack on the Christian world in its entirety and its undisputed right to worship in the Holy Land and the rest of Palestine.[55]

More significantly, the Higher Islamic Council synchronized its protest with the established churches and closed the doors of the Haram ash-Sharif for twenty-four hours. This was on the same day as the churches in the Holy Land closed theirs, 27 April 1990, which was, to add to the significance of the gesture, a Friday, the day when the Haram is at its busiest. In addition, a few days later, Shaykh Muhammed al-Jamal, inspector of the Shari'a courts, paid a visit to the Greek Orthodox patriarch, Diodorus I.[56] These were major steps in displaying a newfound cooperation and unity of purpose and revealed the extent to which clergy from both communities were prepared to put aside their differences in order to combat what they perceived to be a serious threat to their existence in the Old City.

The following year, in 1991, a Palestinian Muslim-Christian delegation met the pope in Rome and presented him with a letter from the mufti of Jerusalem. These joint activities led to the creation in 1992 of a Muslim-Christian committee comprising the church leaders Sabbah, Laham, and Qafity, and the mufti of Jerusalem to express the views of the religious leadership concerning the current political issues. One of the early steps taken by this committee was to send a message to the pope expressing their concern that the improvement in Vatican-Israel relations should not be at the expense of other religious communities and denominations.[57] To a certain extent, the formation of this committee was the most dramatic expression of the shift in the allegiances of the church away from a passive neutral position to an overtly pro-Palestinian stand, certainly for the churches whose clergy and congregations were predominantly Palestinian and Arab. In addition, it was a way in which the churches could reposition themselves and pave their way for participation in a Palestinian state under Muslim domination.[58]

One example of the tangible benefits of the improved relations is the resolution of the dispute concerning the Khanqah Salahiyya. The Khanqah Salahiyya, an Ayubid structure, lies to the west of the Holy Sepulchre in the Christian quarters. Originally a Sufi center, it is now a mosque. During renovations and extensions to the ablutions area in 1997, workers discovered two small rooms buried in the wall separating the mosque form the Holy Sepulchre. The Greek Orthodox Patriarchate claimed the rooms as Greek Orthodox property and, indeed, had access to them from the Holy Sepulchre side. The Awqaf engineers argued that they were within the fabric of the mosque and, therefore, belonged to the mosque.

The dispute threatened to become inflammatory when Patriarch Diodorus I approached the Israeli government for support. Prime Minister Netanyahu publicly intervened by calling for a meeting with the church leaders.[59] In response, the PNA quickly set up a joint committee to resolve the issue, making Diodorus I and the Palestinian minister of religious affairs, Shaykh Hassan Tahbub, co-chairs.[60] Furthermore, the Jordanian government offered to mediate. It was able to suggest a compromise whereby the two rooms went to the mosque and in return, the Greek Orthodox Patriarchate was restored a church in al-Karak, Jordan, which had been converted into a mosque.[61] The compromise was accepted.

This incident reveals a number of points. There is evidence to suggest that the Israeli government was anxious to mend its bridges with the Greek Orthodox Patriarchate after the St. John's Hospice incident by intervening on its side. By doing so, it hoped to both reestablish its influence over the established churches and to undermine the new era of Muslim-Christian cooperation at the leadership level. The actions by the PNA and the Jordanian government were both interventions to exclude Israel, thereby encouraging the repositioning trend discussed earlier and also to establish their own claims to be the adjudicating and, therefore, the legitimate authority regarding the holy places in the Old City.

Conclusion

The political future of Jerusalem is, at the point of publication, still the subject of intense negotiations. The impasse over the fate of the city has been credited for the failure of the Camp David summit in July 2000 and the postponement of a final settlement between Israelis and Palestinians. Clearly, it is not possible to predict with any certainty the extent to which the Palestinians will be obliged to accept Israeli and U.S. demands for Israeli sovereignty over the city. However, what is clear is that those demands are not supported by the Christian churches of Jerusalem, either by the laity or by the clergy. The Camp David summit confirmed both the failure and the abandonment of the Israeli approach to co-opt the church leadership in its drive to gain international recognition for control over the city.

In the midst of the Camp David summit, the three patriarchs of the Greek Orthodox, Armenian Orthodox, and Catholic communities dispatched a vigorous and public plea to President Bill Clinton, Prime Minister Ehud Barak, and President Yasser Arafat to take into account their views and long historical association with the city. News had leaked out of Israeli proposals to divide the Old City administratively so that the Jewish and Armenian Quarters would be incorporated into the Israeli state. The open letter declared:

> We regard the Christian and Armenian quarters of the Old City as inseparable and contiguous entities that are firmly united by the same faith. . . . Furthermore we trust that your negotiations . . . will ensure that the fundamental freedoms of worship and access by all Christians to their holy sanctuaries and to their headquarters within the Old City are not impeded in any way whatsoever.[62]

The letter also asked for an invitation to send representatives to the summit or any other forums concerned with the future of the city. While couched in polite and diplomatic terms, the letter indicated categorical opposition to the Israeli and U.S. proposals. It also revealed the extent to which Israeli views on the Holy City and its preceding thirty years of policy-making had yielded no results. Prior to the St. John's Hospice incident, there had been a possibility that the non-Palestinian elements of the churches could have been enticed into accepting Israeli sovereignty. But after that point, all the evidence has shown a clear move by the established churches that, in order to protect their interests, they need to distance themselves from the Israeli position. Whatever attempts were made to rectify the post-incident relations between Israel and the churches, the fact that the separation of the Armenian Quarter could have been made without consultation with any of the church leaders, let alone the Armenian patriarch, only served to confirm the fears of the Christian community that it was an exclusive vision of Jerusalem that the Israeli government had promoted at Camp David. And it was a vision in which the churches had little part to play.

Notes

1. L.G.A. Cust, *The Status Quo and the Holy Places* (facsimile version, Jerusalem: Ariel Publishing House, 1980), 3.

2. See S. P. Colbi, "The Christian Establishment in Jerusalem," in *Jerusalem: Problems and Prospects,* ed. J. L. Kraemer (New York: Praeger, 1980), 162–170.

3. "Terms of the British Mandate for Palestine," Article 13, cited in R. Lapidot and M. Hirsch, *The Arab-Israeli Conflict and Its Resolution: Selected Documents* (Dordrecht, Netherlands: Kluwer Academic Publishers, 1992), 28.

4. Ibid., Article 14.

5. Cust, *The Status Quo,* 14.

6. Ibid., Introductory Note by H. C. Luke. See also A. Rock, *The Status Quo in the Holy Places* (Jerusalem: Franciscan Printing Press, 1989), 17–18.

7. See M. Dumper, *The Politics of Jerusalem Since 1967* (New York: Columbia University Press, 1997), 62.

8. See D. Tsimhoni, *Christian Communities in Jerusalem and the West Bank Since 1948: An Historical, Social, and Political Study* (Westport, Conn.: Praeger, 1993), 35–36; S. Roussos, "The Greek Orthodox Patriarchate and Community of Jerusalem," in *The Christian Heritage in the Holy Land,* eds. A. O'Mahoney, G. Gunner, and K. Hintlian (London: Scorpion Cavendish, 1995), 219–222.

9. Cited in M. Benvenisti, *Jerusalem: The Torn City* (Minneapolis: Israel Typeset, Ltd., and the University of Minneapolis, 1976), 53.

10. For further details, see Tsimhoni, *Christian Communities in Jerusalem,* 1–9.

11. See M. Dumper, *The Politics of Jerusalem,* 69.

12. Tsimhoni, *Christian Communities in Jerusalem,* 96.

13. *The Orthodox Coptic Motaran of the Holy See in Jerusalem and the Near East v Minister of Police,* Israel Supreme Court sitting as a High Court of Justice, 16 March 1971 (extracts), in R. Lapidot and M. Hirsch, *The Jerusalem Question and Its Resolution: Selected Documents* (Dordrecht, Netherlands: Kluwer Academic Publishers, 1994), 507–515.

14. O. Meinardus, "The Copts in Jerusalem and the Question of the Holy Places," in *The Christian Heritage in the Holy Land,* O'Mahoney, et al., eds., 127.

15. Tsimhoni, *Christian Communities in Jerusalem,* 96.

16. K. Hintlian, "Pathways to Christian Unity I," in *Jerusalem: What Makes for Peace?* eds. N. Ateek, C. Duaybis, and M. Schrader (London: Melisende, 1997), 25.

17. The most noteworthy departure was Amir Cheshin, former adviser to the mayor on Arab affairs, whose brief covered all of East Jerusalem. See also A. Cheshin et al., eds., *Separate and Unequal: The Inside Story of Israeli Rule in East Jerusalem* (Cambridge, Mass.: Harvard University Press, 1999).

18. Y. K. Halevi, "Squeezed Out," *Jerusalem Report,* 10 July 1997, 5.

19. Tsimhoni, *Christian Communities in Jerusalem,* 167–168, 175.

20. Recommendations and resolutions of the Arab Orthodox conference held in Jerusalem 23 October 1992. English translation in author's possession.

21. Ibid., Resolution No. 16.

22. Because the Armenian community is reputed to be the largest landowner in the Old City and one of the largest in Jerusalem, government interest, be it Jordanian or Israeli, in the community's affairs is also strong. An example of this occurred during the Jordanian period when the intervention of the Jordanian government ensured the appointment of Patriarch Yeghishe Derderian. See Tsimhoni,

Christian Communities in Jerusalem, 68–71. The Armenian Orthodox Patriarchate's acceptance of Israeli pressure to lease land and property to the Israel-Lands Administration prompted the same disquiet within the community and led to a public rupture between the patriarchate and the Israeli government.

23. See chapters 4 and 5 of V. Azarya, *The Armenian Quarter of Jerusalem* (Berkeley and London: University of California Press, 1984). See also K. Hintlian, *History of the Armenians in the Holy Land* (Jerusalem: Armenian Patriarchate Printing Press, 1989), 46–50.

24. I am indebted to Gunilla Linden for some of the ideas contained in this section. See G. Linden, *Church Leadership in a Political Crisis: Joint Statements from the Jerusalem Heads of Churches, 1988–1992* (Uppsala: Swedish Institute of Missionary Research, 1994).

25. "Statements by the Heads of the Christian Communities in Jerusalem," 22 January 1988. Full citation in Middle East Council of Churches, *Perspectives,* no. 8 (July 1990): 76.

26. "Statements by the Heads of the Christian Communities in Jerusalem," 27 April 1989. Full citation in Middle East Council of Churches, *Perspectives,* no. 8 (July 1990): 75–76.

27. Linden, *Church Leadership,* 136.

28. In addition to the seizure of St. John's Hospice, the specific incidents mentioned are anti-Christian and racist demonstrations and the burning of the Vatican flag outside St. Saviour's Monastery; an assault on the Syrian Catholic convent; the slashing of car tires in the Armenian Quarter; the daubing of anti-Christian and racist slogans on a gate in the Armenian Quarter; the vandalism against a rare sixth-century Byzantine mosaic; the immolation of a sixth-century Armenian monastery; and the obliteration by roadworks of two monastic complexes beside the Jaffa and Damascus Gates. Taken from "Statement by the Heads of the Christian Communities in Jerusalem," 30 May 1991, and 14 January 1992, cited in Linden, *Church Leadership,* 107, 120–121.

29. Cited in "A Provocation with Massive Support from the Government," *News from Within,* 2 May 1990, 11.

30. Newspaper reports cite SBC, Ltd., as the name of the company. Tsimhoni cites it as FDC. See her *Christian Communities in Jerusalem,* 176.

31. "Riot Erupts in Old City," *Jerusalem Post,* 13 April 1990.

32. *Ha'aretz,* 20 April 1990, cited in *News from Within,* 2 May 1990, 10.

33. An open letter from the president to the patriarch was published in the *Jerusalem Post,* 18 May 1990. The patriarch's reply was issued in a press release 28 May 1990 but not published.

34. "Greek Patriarch Campaigns to Stop Improvement in Greek-Israel Ties," *Jerusalem Post,* 16 May 1990.

35. "Statements by the Heads of the Christian Communities in Jerusalem," 23 April 1990. Full citation in Middle East Council of Churches, *Perspectives,* no. 8 (July 1990): 71.

36. Tsimhoni, *Christian Communities in Jerusalem,* 181.

37. "Old City Settlers Funded by Ministry," *Jerusalem Post,* 23 April 1990.

38. *Ha'aretz,* 20 April 1990, cited in "A Provocation with Massive Support from the Government," *News from Within,* 2 May 1990, 12.

39. Ibid.

40. "US Jewish Leaders Furious over Alleged Covert Funding," *Jerusalem Post,* 25 April 1990.

41. Y. K. Halevi, "Squeezed Out," *Jerusalem Report,* 10 July 1997, 15–16.

42. Ibid., 15

43. A. Ramon, "The Christian Element and the Jerusalem Question," Background Papers for Policy Papers, No. 4 (unofficially translated by the Society of St. Ives (The Jerusalem Institute for Israel Affairs: Jerusalem, 1997), 17.

44. Article 4, para. 1, cited in Palestinian Academic Society for the Study of International Affairs, *Documents on Jerusalem* (PASSIA: Jerusalem, 1996), 26.

45. Article 11, para. 2, states that the Vatican is "solemnly committed to remaining a stranger to all merely temporal conflicts, which principle applies specifically to disputed territories and unsettled borders."

46. See R. Friedland and R. Hecht, *To Rule Jerusalem* (Cambridge: Cambridge University Press, 1996), 478.

47. C. K. Papastathis, "A New Status for Jerusalem: An Eastern Orthodox Viewpoint," *Catholic University Law Review* 45, no. 3 (spring 1996): 730–731.

48. "Memorandum of Their Beatitudes the Patriarchs and of the Heads of the Christian Communities in Jerusalem on the Significance of Jerusalem for Christians," para. 11, cited in Palestinian Academic Society for the Study of International Affairs, *Documents on Jerusalem* (PASSIA: Jerusalem, 1996), 29.

49. I have not ascertained to what extent the memorandum was approved by the Vatican itself, but it does contain not only the signature of Latin patriarch Michel Sabbah but the Franciscan custos of the Holy Land.

50. "Memorandum of Their Beatitudes," 30.

51. In February 2000, the PLO signed a "Fundamental Agreement" with the Vatican, containing clauses that mirrored the Israel-Vatican Agreement.

52. See the interview with the former Anglican bishop in Jerusalem, Samir Qafity, *Jerusalem Times*, 4 August 1998.

53. The director of the center is Jiryis Khoury, a Greek Catholic. Sponsors include Greek Catholic archbishop Lutfi Laham and Latin patriarch Michel Sabbah. Other active members are Canon Naim Ateek (Evangelical Episcopal-Anglican), Father Rafiq Khoury (Roman Catholic), and Bernard Sabella (Greek Catholic).

54. See, for example, "The Jerusalem Sabeel Document: Principles for a Just Peace in Palestine-Israel," *Corner Stone* (Sabeel Ecumenical Liberation Theology Centre) 19 (summer 2000): 4–7.

55. "Statement of Solidarity with the Christian Churches in Jerusalem by the Higher Council for Islamic Waqf Affairs and Holy Sites," April 1990, cited in Palestinian Academic Society for the Study of International Affairs, *Documents on Jerusalem* (PASSIA: Jerusalem, 1996), 15.

56. Tsimhoni, *Christian Communities in Jerusalem,* 177.

57. Ibid., 181–182.

58. Ibid., 182.

59. "Dispute Grows over Khaniqah [sic] Mosque Renovation," *Jerusalem Times,* 2 May 1997, 2.

60. "Committee for al-Khanqah," *Jerusalem Times,* 6 June 1997, 2.

61. "Khanqah Mosque Dispute Resolved," *Jerusalem Times,* 27 June 1997, 2.

62. "Patriarchs Demand Old City Stay United," *Ha'aretz,* 20 July 2000.

6

The Old City
and the Peace Process

The argument of this book has been that since 1967 the issue of the Old City has become a more complex subject to resolve in the discussions over the future of the city of Jerusalem. Contrary to the impression given by numerous peace proposals, the Old City has a number of features and has undergone a number of transformations since 1967 that have increased the difficulties in creating an equitable solution. From the previous chapters it should be clear that the Israeli government has created a new political status quo. In absolute terms, the number of Israeli Jews living in the Old City, let alone in the areas outside of the Jewish Quarter, does not amount to more than 10 percent of the population of the Old City. The Muslim and Christian Palestinian majority is overwhelming. Yet the destruction of the Magharib quarter, the expansion and renovation of the Jewish Quarter, the penetration of the Muslim and Christian quarters by the Israeli settler movement, and the undermining of key religious institutions have all combined to introduce concrete physical factors, as well as political ones, to obstruct the return to the state of affairs that existed before 1967.

It is quite apparent that, however successful the Palestinians may be in achieving sovereignty over much of East Jerusalem, given the current balance of power, parts of the Old City are likely to remain under Israeli sovereignty. The question is, how much? There is an Israeli consensus over the Western Wall and the Jewish Quarter. But have the settlers succeeded in building up a sufficient attachment to Jewish sites in other parts of the Old City to make them "goods" to be negotiated away or exchanged for other goods? As we have seen, there is certainly institutional support for them, and there is no doubt that their activities have entered the political mainstream. Nevertheless, the evidence provided in this book is that this support is not hegemonic in the sense that it is open to reversal in the same way as many of the settlements in the West Bank and Gaza Strip will also be goods that are negotiated away.[1] One cannot compare the status of the Diskin

139

Orphanage or Bet Galicia or Moshe Wittenburg's House in the Muslim and Christian quarters of the Old City to the status of the Jewish Quarter and the Western Wall in Israeli culture.[2] They are in a completely different league.

All the same, the nature of Israeli electoral politics is such that a government can only be formed through a coalition with many smaller parties. The influence of the settler movement is much greater in government formation than it is in consolidating Israeli attachments to Jewish sites in the Muslim quarters in the national consensus. One can argue that in the peace negotiations, the Israeli public is unlikely to jeopardize an overall agreement for the sake of newly and possibly illegally acquired sites in the Muslim quarters. However, the government may need to provide incentives to the political representatives of the settlers in order to retain power. The question, then, is which sites will the settlers insist on keeping as a condition for their support for the government on other issues? These considerations are likely to play an important part in determining the nature of the future regime in the Old City.

The second complicating factor is the multilateral nature of the discussions over the Old City. It is in the Old City where the religious communities most reflect the concerns of their international diasporic connections. This is most visible within the Christian churches, with their cosmopolitan staff, their huge numbers of pilgrims, and their externally funded institutions. But it is also the case within the Muslim community where Saudi Arabia, Morocco, Iran, and Jordan have a strong interest in the political and administrative structures that are set up in the Old City insofar as they affect the Islamic holy places. Similarly, the Israeli government is to some extent tied to what its supporters in both the secular and Orthodox Jewish Diaspora would accept for the Old City. Thus, the negotiations over the Old City will need to take into account the aspirations of a much wider circle of interested parties than those involved in either the rest of Jerusalem or in the other Permanent Status Issues.

The third and final complicating factor is peace in itself. All political agreements have both a retrospective and prospective element. They attempt to resolve outstanding issues of contention, but they also need to preempt further contentions arising from the new relationship by introducing mutually acceptable frameworks and procedures. A permanent status agreement will bring a host of new problems to Jerusalem, mostly to do with landownership issues and resource allocation, but there will also be issues that are specifically related to the holiness of the city, which will be most intensively felt in the Old City. For example, issues of freedom of access to and worship in the holy sites will require significant coordination and planning between the three communities to avoid sectarian confrontations that arise from greater local, regional, and international access to the holy places of the Old City.

This chapter aims to elucidate these issues by focusing on three areas. First, it will briefly examine a range of peace proposals in order to determine whether the current models available sufficiently reflect the transformations in the Old City and take into account the complexity of the issues involved. Second, it will examine the peace process itself, paying particular attention to possible precedents. The case of the Ibrahimi Mosque in Hebron and the Oslo framework of disaggregating areas and functions into Areas A, B, and C seem to exemplify some of the problems and may reveal lessons to be learned. Third, it will study some of the problems posed by the geography of the place and the location and size of the holy places. A comparison with the logistical problems faced by the administrators of the *haj* (pilgrimage) to Mecca will be drawn. Finally, the chapter will delineate what appears to be the basic requirements of an arrangement over the future of the Old City that is both equitable and has a chance of working in practice.

Old City Peace Plans

Proposals concerning the future of the Old City are invariably entwined with those concerning the holy places of Jerusalem. There is no doubt that any future disposition regarding the Old City will be strongly influenced by the arrangements required to establish a regime for the holy places that will satisfy not only the states of Palestine and Israel but also the leadership of the different religious communities. Nevertheless, it is also important to recognize that the proposals for the holy places are not necessarily congruent with those for the Old City as a whole. This section will briefly review a number of proposals for the holy places before turning to the more general ones for the Old City.[3]

Most of the proposals share either explicitly or implicitly the concern for guarantees for freedom of worship and freedom of access to the holy places. Where they differ is the mechanisms and regime structures suggested to provide such guarantees. These range from internationalization through shared administrative committees to extraterritorialization. There are two kinds of internationalization proposed: territorial and functional. Territorial internationalization of the holy places was proposed in UN Security Council Resolution 181 and the draft statute for Jerusalem prepared by the UN Trusteeship Council in 1950. Subsumed into the overall internationalization of the city of Jerusalem, it contained the following provisions pertaining to the holy places:

- A governor of Jerusalem appointed by the UN Trusteeship Council would be responsible for protecting the holy places.
- S/he would decide which sites should be granted that status and be the final arbiter in disputes between the religious communities.
- The governor would ensure respect for the property rights of churches, missions, and other religious or charitable agencies.
- Subject to the requirements of public order, the governor would guarantee free access to and freedom of worship in the holy places.

This proposal was supported by most Western countries, including the Vatican, and eventually by most of the Arab states, notably excluding Jordan. Functional internationalization is essentially a variant of the above in that it reduces the area to be internationalized to the holy place only, leaving the rest of the city under either single or divided sovereignty.[4]

The holy places were dealt with in other ways. Some proposals suggested that certain functions of the holy places, particularly those concerned with access, freedom of worship, and protection, be allocated to either an international committee or a UN supervisory board.[5] Some proposals include elements of the above but go further by suggesting that an interreligious supervisory committee be established comprising representatives of each of the three faiths.

There are, in addition, a number of proposals based on the concept of extraterritorialization—the removal of the site in question from the sovereignty of the state in which it is located. A mild or weak version of this concept is to enhance the diplomatic immunities and privileges to the holy places and the personnel who run them but stopping short of transferring sovereignty. It is a kind of de facto extraterritorialization. The stronger version would be granting full extraterritorial status to those sites, thereby giving them an independent status in relation to the state that had sovereignty over that part of the city. Thus, if Israeli sovereignty was recognized over the Old City, the Muslim and Christian holy places would be extraterritorialized and, conversely, if Palestinian sovereignty was recognized, the Jewish holy places would be extraterritorialized.[6]

There are almost no proposals that deal with the Old City specifically as a single geographical unit. Most of the proposals that identify the Old City as a separate unit do so in the context of dividing the city into a number of boroughs or municipal subunits, of which the Old City is simply one. The Old City is not granted a special regime for itself. During the Camp David summit in July 2000, it was revealed that the Israeli government proposed separating the Jewish and Armenian Quarters out from the Old City and placing them under Israeli sovereignty, with the Muslim and Christian quarters being given devolved municipal autonomy under the Israeli state.[7] The only published proposal that views the Old City as a single unit with a special regime and which has received wide publicity is that drawn up by the former Permanent Representative of Jordan to the United Nations, Ambassador Adnan Abu Odeh. Without elaborating his ideas in great depth, Abu Odeh's proposal amounts to an extraterritorialization of the whole of the Old City, which would be governed by a council representing "the highest Muslim, Christian and Jewish religious authorities."[8]

A final proposal requires consideration: the "nonpaper" agreement between the Israeli justice minister Yossi Beilin and PLO general secretary Mahmud Abbas (Abu Mazen), known as the Abu Mazen–Beilin Plan. The plan was never officially published, and it always remained a document for discussion, but the detail and wide-ranging nature of the plan has made it a reference point and starting point for serious negotiation. It was widely seen as the basis for Israeli and U.S. proposals during the Camp David summit in July 2000. Within a framework of the Joint Higher Municipal Council and an Israeli and Palestinian submunicipality, the plan also proposes a special regime for the Old City.[9] The submunicipalities shall be responsible for the municipal concerns of their respective citizens and their property in the Old City. The resolution of disputes and the "preservation of the unique character of the Old City" shall be referred to a joint parity committee appointed by the two submunicipalities.[10] Finally, Palestinians will be granted extraterritorial sovereignty over the Haram ash-Sharif. The significance of this point is that in exchange for accepting that the Palestinian submunicipal areas are not close to the 1967 borders, thus detaching the Old City from a Palestinian hinterland, the Israelis were prepared to concede sovereignty over the Haram compound. A separate paragraph deals with guarantees of freedom of worship and access to the holy places.

Following the collapse of the Camp David talks in July 2000 and the start of the second Palestinian intifada, informal discussions between the two sides have centered on notions of an "open city" and a "holy basin." These would encompass both the Old City and holy places in and around it. While they suggest new approaches to an apparently intractable issue, these notions also bring with them difficulties. Palestinians fear that they could be a vehicle for an extension of Israeli sovereignty into East Jerusalem, while Israelis are reluctant to lose exclusive control over their holy sites.

Precedents for Sharing Holy Places in the Old City

In negotiating a framework for the Old City, this book has indicated that there are enormous difficulties in attempting to accommodate the range of interests involved. Even prior to 1967, the lack of coordination and sympathy between and within the different religious communities made effective cooperation on practical issues difficult. Since 1967, the extension of

Jewish rights and presence in the Old City has been met by revived Muslim and Christian activities in order to redress their diminishing role under Israeli rule. Indeed, when one considers the precedents presented by the experience of Israeli rule, it is understandable that the prospect of continued Israeli control over non-Jewish holy places is not acceptable to the Palestinians in general and to the Muslim and Christian religious leadership in particular. Before taking this discussion any further, it would be useful to examine some of the available precedents for the resolution of the problem of the holy places and the Old City. This section will make a detailed examination of the Ibrahimi Mosque as a case study of a shared site under Israeli rule.

Since 1948, the government of Israel has demonstrated an ambiguous policy on non-Jewish holy sites. On the one hand, the government has sought to demonstrate that, by representing a minority religion itself, it is respectful of other religious practices and places of worship, particularly in view of the support it wished to receive from Western countries. Most of this took place on the formal and rhetorical level through the promulgation of laws to protect religious property, such as the Holy Places Law of 1967, and through participation in interfaith dialogues and international conferences. On the other hand, the drive to consolidate the Jewish nature of the new Israel led to the widespread confiscation of religious property and land. In addition, the administrative structure of the state was constructed largely to serve the Jewish population, leading to gross neglect and marginalization of many Christian and Muslim sites.[11] Following the occupation of the West Bank and Gaza Strip, there was little change in this ambiguity.

The situation with regard to the Ibrahimi Mosque is of particular interest because the changes that have taken place there are potentially very applicable to the situation in Jerusalem. The mosque is the site of the tomb of Abraham, Sarah, Joseph, Rebecca, Jacob, and Isaac and has constituted an integral part of the Muslim concept of the Holy Land. Together with the Haram ash-Sharif, it forms the "Haramayn," and Muslim pilgrims to Jerusalem usually continued on their way to Hebron to pay their respects to the prophets buried there. The mosque is also supported by the Tamimi al-Dari *waqf,* the earliest recorded *waqf* in Islam. As the site of the tomb of Abraham, arguably the founder of Judaism, it is one of the most revered places in Judaism. Known as the Cave of Machpela, or the Tomb of the Patriarchs, it has been the focus of Jewish pilgrimage and study for millennia.

The arrangements concerning access to worship have evolved over a thirty-year period through a series of incremental steps, which have led to the loss of control over the mosque by the Muslim population of Hebron. In addition, the Palestinian-Israeli Hebron Agreement of 1997 and its provisions for Jewish access to the mosque has created a possible model that may be imposed on Jerusalem. Furthermore, while the controversy was mainly over access to and control over a shared Jewish and Muslim holy place, there were at the same time a number of subthemes that added to the intensity and passion of the situation and that have strong parallels in the Old City of Jerusalem. In the first place, there is the issue of access, which is symbolic of the Judaic versus the Islamic nature of the site and indeed of the whole of Hebron. Second, it is also a reflection of the political strength of the Israeli settler communities inside Hebron and on the outskirts in Kiryat Arba and their influence on the Israeli government as well as to the Palestinian community. Finally, the Ibrahimi Mosque case highlights the deficiencies in the dual role played by the Israeli military as both protectors of the existing religious arrangements and as guardians of the settlers.

In examining the developments that took place during the first decade of the occupation, one can see how the mutually agreed arrangements established for access and times of worship were gradually eroded in favor of Israeli settlers as the tensions between the settlers and the Muslim religious community were heightened.

As early as October 1967, the minister of defense, Moshe Dayan, made arrangements with the Awqaf Administration for the joint use of the building. Jewish visitors were admitted between 7:00 and 11:00 A.M. and 1:30 and 5:00 P.M., and these hours were enforced by guards provided by the Israeli Army chaplaincy. In addition, a Yom Kippur service could be held in the evening. The rest of the time the mosque would remain a Muslim place of worship. During Ramadan, the building would be closed to Jewish worshippers for the afternoon period.[12] However, over time incremental changes were made that gave Israeli settlers greater and greater access.

In October 1968, a special Yom Kippur service was extended by Jewish worshippers in the mosque beyond the agreed hours. This led to tension in the town, culminating in a grenade attack on Jewish worshippers. In retaliation, the military government demolished an eighth-century stairway leading to the mosque, which led to widespread objections against Israeli policies, although Israeli officials claim the demolition was unrelated to the grenade attack but in accordance with a town landscaping program.[13] The following year, no Yom Kippur service was permitted by the army in an attempt to defuse the conflict. However, in 1971 Israeli settlers were permitted to bring Torah scrolls into the chamber containing the tombs of Abraham and Sarah. This action was to give the chamber the feature of a synagogue. By 1972 the Israeli settlement of Kiryat Arba had considerably expanded, and many more worshippers were attending the mosque, particularly on Sabbath eves and feast days. To cater to this increased use, the Israeli government unilaterally enlarged the praying area allocated to Jews and extended the permissible hours for prayers.

The following year clashes led to several people receiving wounds.

Consequently, the Israeli government banned Jews from the Arab part of the mosque.[14] Then again in 1975, as a result of pressure from Orthodox Jews and militant settlers, the government introduced new arrangements to allow Jewish prayers inside the mosque, which again led to widespread protests by Palestinian Muslims and disturbances in Hebron. Jewish worshippers also appropriated the Tomb of Jacob. The increased tension culminated in fights that broke out inside the mosque and tomb area, with a number of religious paraphernalia (Muslim and Jewish) being seriously damaged and finally with settlers setting fire to part of the mosque. The army made a number of arrests of leading Israeli settlers and Palestinians and, in an attempt to regain control over the situation, clamped a two-week curfew on the Old City of Hebron while allowing settlers to attend services.[15]

During this period it had become clear that while the Israeli government was anxious not to antagonize the Awqaf Administration and the Hebronite community over the question of Jewish access to the Tomb of the Patriarchs, it would not countenance any lessening of its control over Hebron. To this end it was only prepared to deny *unlimited access* to the tomb for the Israeli settlers as a means of assuaging Muslim claims over the mosque and tomb. As a consequence of the Likud Party's victory in the 1977 elections, the settlers in Hebron began to receive much greater political, economic, and military assistance. By 1979 it appeared that the Israeli government had decided that the interests of the settlers overrode any fears about antagonizing the local community or concerns to adhere to the existing religious arrangements laid down by international law. In the same year, hundreds of the settlers marched into the mosque and drove out the Muslims at prayer and even clashed with Israeli soldiers. Rather than issuing any punishment, the government gave in to their demands and permitted Jews to have access to the mosque on Saturdays.[16] These arrangements remained in force until the establishment of the interim phase of the Oslo Accords. The potential threat to Jewish access to the tombs, which was integral to the Oslo Accords, precipitated the massacre of more than fifty Muslim worshippers by an Israeli settler, Baruch Goldstein, on 26 February 1994. This resulted in even greater security measures, thus deterring Muslim worshippers even more.

As we have seen during the interim phase of the Oslo Accords, the Israeli government agreed to a withdrawal from the Palestinian urban areas in the West Bank. As a result, however, of the large numbers of Jews inside the Old City of Hebron and the political strength of the settlers, the city of Hebron was made an exception. The Hebron Protocol signed between Israel and the PLO in January 1997 divided the city into two parts: H1—the municipal area transferred to the PNA, and H2—the municipal area remaining under Israeli rule but comprising approximately 400 settlers and 40,000 Palestinians. The Ibrahimi Mosque/Tomb of the Patriarchs was located in H2. The Hebron Protocol contains references to holy sites in Hebron, initially by referring to the 1995 interim agreement that states, "Both sides shall respect and protect the religious rights of Jews, Christians, Muslims and Samaritans concerning the protection and free access to the Holy sites as well as freedom of worship and practice."[17] The protocol goes on to list a number of Jewish holy sites in the Palestinian area of H1 and establishes the right of access and use to worshippers by stipulating that they are to be accompanied by joint Palestinian-Israeli units. A similar right is not conferred to worshippers wishing to attend the Ibrahimi Mosque. Indeed, the arrangements concerning access to the mosque existing prior to the Hebron Protocol remained in place pending a permanent agreement. Thus, irrespective of the peace process and the Oslo Accords, Israeli guards control the gates to the mosque and subject all worshippers to security checks.

The lessons Palestinian and religious leaders of the churches learned from the Ibrahimi example are that incremental steps taken by the Israeli government over a protracted period of time significantly eroded the Palestinian control over the mosque. Minor infringements of agreements add up to significant alterations in the nature and use of a site. In addition, the Israeli Ministry of Defense is not a neutral arbiter in disputes between the Muslim religious hierarchy and Israeli settlers. An international or joint Israeli Palestinian body would be much more preferable. Moreover, the current situation freezes the arrangements that are unfavorable to Palestinians and Muslim worshippers, and, finally, Israel is not prepared to concede Palestinian security control over areas in which shared holy sites are located, even if the physical access of worshippers is subjected to Israeli security checks.

If one also considers other holy sites affected by Israeli rule in the West Bank and Gaza Strip, similar examples can be seen of disputes over access and control. This has occurred in the tomb of Nabi Samwil on the outskirts of Jerusalem, the tomb of Nabi Musa just off the road from Jerusalem to Jericho, and Rachel's Tomb, on the road to Bethlehem. All these disputes resulted in the gradual usurpation of the Awqaf Administration's jurisdiction of these sites. Since 1995, the tomb of Nabi Musa has been allocated to the PNA while Rachel's Tomb, which is not in Area C, has been taken over completely by the Israeli Ministry of Religious Affairs.[18]

Challenges Posed by Peace:
Logistics of Pilgrimage in the Old City

Before examining what elements are required for a long-term and stable agreement for the Old City, it is important to peer into the future to see what challenges lie ahead. A simple return to the 1967 borders may not be in the interests of either the Israelis or Palestinians; once peace is achieved, a whole series of new problems will need to be resolved. An agreement that provides a framework and modus operandi for the current situation, its balance of power, and its demographic configurations without providing space for development, change, and flexibility will simply be to fashion a straitjacket that will burst at the seams in the coming years. Peace will bring many changes to Jerusalem and the Old City, and it would be an unwise negotiator who ignores them. The changes are both general and specific. This section will discuss the challenges that the future poses for the Old City and how a peace agreement would not be sustainable if these challenges were not addressed. The first part of this section discusses some of the general trends; the second looks at two specific examples arising from the greater accessibility to the city following a peace agreement.

Jerusalem is a relatively minor city with limited resources and infrastructure but is at the center of global attention for both political and religious reasons. Already it is a magnet for pilgrimage and tourism. The possibility of a peace agreement that brings stability and freedom of movement to people hitherto denied access to the city opens up the possibility of huge movements of people to the city, particularly at peak periods during festivities. What has been repeated many times in this book, but in this context needs to be emphasized, is that Jerusalem is a city holy to three faiths, not just one, as in the case of most holy cities. Thus, there are three communities to whom it is a center for pilgrimage, thereby increasing the reservoir of potential and actual pilgrims quite considerably. This brings additional pressures for accommodation, servicing, and transportation links. It also increases the likelihood of disagreement and conflict over the proper administration of both the sites and the pilgrimages among followers of the different religions, if not even within the faiths themselves.

Past and current trends indicate that Jerusalem will continue to act as a magnet for religious communities well into the future. The role that the holy sites of Jerusalem have played in their liturgy and rituals of organization of religious communities has had an important impact upon political developments in the city. Changes in religious organization will change the form and nature of those impacts. In planning for the future of the holy places and therefore the Old City, it is important first to consider the impact that the presence of holy places has had on the city and their attendant communities. There are four main effects: First, there is the creation of a religious bureaucracy. The administration and guardianship of sites have created a bureaucracy and religious leadership whose positions depend upon the continued control over those sites. Second, holy sites have created annual cycles of pilgrimage and its modernized version, tourism. This has resulted in the importation of wealth and revenue and has strengthened and created international affiliations and solidarities. Third, the presence of holy sites has led to an extensive program of construction to provide places of worship, places for accommodation (hotels, hostels, monastic dormitories, and residence for religious personnel), and places of education (seminaries, theological colleges, law and jurisprudential schools). In turn, this has affected land use, property ownership, and income levels in the city. Fourth, external funding such as donations and *waqfs* are channeled into the city to support all these religious activities. The city and religious organizations are not reliant upon the wealth derived from local sources. One result of this availability of external finance is that internal sectional affiliations are consolidated, namely, small religious groups need not cooperate extensively with the state authorities or with other similar religious groups, as they are financially independent.

Taken together, these four factors have resulted in a degree of extraterritorialization of property, personnel, and finance in the city. The authority of the state is weakened. It provides security and educational and welfare services but it has limited ability to extract revenue, to control property use, or to exert direct influence over the residents. In this situation, semiautonomous enclaves are established, and the state is forced into accepting religious hierarchies as mediators between itself and the members of the religious group. This is not simply the result of the legal ambiguity over the Israeli occupation of the city. It is a feature of cities dominated by holy sites.

It is also important to recognize the transformations that religious organization had undergone in the twentieth century. Religious organization throughout the world has been greatly affected by advances in technology. Since 1948, two have affected Jerusalem in particular: The first advance is faster and more convenient transportation; the second is that of rapid communication. Quicker postal services, telegraph, telephone, telex, facsimile, and now e-mail have all transformed the way religious organizations communicate and organize their activities.

The impact of these changes has been extensive. The opportunity for greater mobility, due to the advent of mass air transportation in the mid-1960s, has led to ever larger numbers of pilgrims and religious officials visiting the city. One should recall the impact that the mandate period offered to Zionist Jews and their access to the Wailing Wall (see Chapter 2). In addition, despite their dispersal, there is greater interaction within religious sects as a result of quicker transportation and communication advances. This has led to a number of other relevant developments such as intrasect solidarity and a greater ease in transferring funds between different sections of the religious community. There is a greater participation in the decision-making processes by the local communities but a greater central intervention in appointments of senior clergy. Finally, there is a greater accountability of the local structures to the parent community. These developments have contributed to the transformation of the archaic organizational structures of the religious communities. For example, many of the Christian ecclesiastical provinces, or patriarchates, evolved largely because of problems related to inaccessibility and revenue capacity. New technologies are creating a much more centralized, rationalized, and consultative structure.

A further result of these developments lies in the relationships between the religious communities themselves. As finance is more readily available from abroad and as decisionmaking becomes more centralized, the need for cooperation at a local level diminishes. On one hand, there is less dependency upon the host government for support and protection and consequently less need to respond to and accommodate state pressures. On the other hand, there is also greater potential for external intervention by other state powers by using religious organizations.

During this transition phase toward a permanent status settlement, a number of the above global trends can be discerned taking place in Jerusalem. For instance, the growth in Christian and Jewish pilgrimages to Jerusalem has to a large extent already occurred. Following a permanent status agreement, the main rise in numbers will be from the Islamic world, particularly from Southeast Asia, West Africa, and Central Asia. In addition, there will be a growing interest in the city from other religious groups around the world. This will extend beyond the three Abrahamic traditions to include Buddhism, Hinduism, and other New Age religions. There will be a demand for space for religious institutes, places of worship, branch offices, and accommodation. In the face of these developments, the indigenous base to host and absorb this influx will be proportionately reduced. If current population growth projections are correct, Jerusalemites will not only feel swamped but there will also be competition over land and property. The incoming groups will have—as a result of the technological advances already outlined—stronger links with their parent communities than has been the case, and they will be less concerned to accommodate their social and religious behaviors to the local communities. In addition, the regulation and monitoring of their activities will require greater administrative and financial resources on the part of the Israeli and Palestinian governments. However, the point to be emphasized that is running through all of these trends is that the power of the state will be weakened. This will occur particularly if the permanent status agreement leads to some form of shared administration that will allow religious groups to play off the different secular authorities against each other.

Probably the most important challenge facing the Old City following a permanent status agreement is dealing with the huge projected increase in pilgrims. As already mentioned, the increase is most likely to be from

Muslim countries of Southeast and Central Asia and West Africa because most of the Jewish and Christian increase has already taken place. But even in the latter case, there is likely to be an increase as the region stabilizes and more pilgrims finally make their pilgrimage. Preparing and organizing for this increase will require interreligious coordination and intergovernment cooperation on a scale hitherto lacking.

Before looking at the question of pilgrimage to the Old City, it would be useful to examine the case of pilgrimage, or *haj,* to Mecca to gain an insight to the logistical stresses and challenges that are being addressed there. Clearly, Mecca is a very different pilgrimage site. It is dedicated to only one faith, whereas Jerusalem is a holy site for three religions, not just one. In addition, pilgrims to Jerusalem visit throughout the year, not mainly over the pilgrimage period. Finally, the holy places of Jerusalem are concentrated into a very small area in and around the Old City, while in Mecca they are spread out over a wider area. Nevertheless, there are two main reasons why a brief examination of the development of pilgrimage in Mecca is useful to this study. First, the *haj* authorities have had to deal with a steady but enormous increase in pilgrims over the past thirty years. The difficulties encountered and the solutions put forward may be relevant to the situation in Jerusalem after a permanent status agreement. Second, following a permanent status agreement, which permits Muslim pilgrims to visit Jerusalem, a large number of pilgrims to Mecca will extend their pilgrimage to take in a visit to Jerusalem as well.

The open topography of the surrounding countryside in terms of the transportation and accommodation of large numbers of people has made the management of the *haj* to Mecca easier. Furthermore, sites and rituals are concentrated over a relatively small area. The distance from Mecca to the Plain of Arafat, a secondary but obligatory holy site, is not greater than twenty-five kilometers, which is close enough for simple mass transit arrangements but far enough to allow for the dispersal of large crowds. The main disadvantage of the *haj* in terms of logistical management is the short period of time during which the bulk of the pilgrims are present. Huge numbers have to be catered to, accommodated, and transported over a two-week period.

However, the growth in pilgrim numbers to Mecca has increased exponentially since the 1960s, causing severe problems in managing large flows of people (see Table 6.1). The projected growth in pilgrim numbers for 2005 range as high as 3.7 million. Clearly, growth rates of this sort put a huge strain on the infrastructure and servicing capacity of the host country. The provision of accommodations, food, water, emergency services, crowd security, and more all need to be well planned in advance. The frequent incidences of fire and crowd stampedes leading to many deaths have underlined this point. The introduction of quotas for pilgrims from different countries is one attempt to control and manage the great pressures on the *haj* authorities.

The increase in numbers, particularly since 1971, has occurred partly as a result of technological advances in transportation that have been discussed. This has combined to create serious and unpleasant traffic congestion in and around Mecca during the *haj*. Table 6.2 illustrates the growth in vehicular traffic.

Table 6.1   Growth in Numbers of Foreign Pilgrims to Mecca, 1960–1995 (excluding Saudi nationals)

Year	Growth in Millions
1960	0.29
1965	0.28
1970	0.41
1975	0.61
1980	0.87
1985	0.91
1990	1.30*
1995	1.70*

Source: A. al-Yafi, *Management of Hajj Mobility Systems: A Logistical Perspective.* (Amsterdam: Johannes Enschede, 1993).
Note: * Estimates.

Table 6.2   Number of Vehicles Used by Pilgrims to Mecca, 1970–1984

Year	Total Vehicles	Total Pilgrims
1970	50,044	1,079,760
1971	54,071	1,042,027
1972	60,756	1,216,951
1973	68,283	1,122,545
1974	81,522	1,484,975
1975	89,735	1,557,867
1976	111,809	1,456,432
1977	115,038	1,627,589
1978	139,001	1,899,420
1979	113,690	2,079,689
1980	86,691	1,949,634
1981	95,837	1,943,180
1982	103,449	2,011,555
1983	126,615	2,502,855
1984	113,068	1,664,478

Source: A. al-Yafi, *Management of Hajj Mobility Systems: A Logistical Perspective.* (Amsterdam: Johannes Enschede, 1993).

The first response to this increase was the construction of motorways and parking lots to accommodate the sudden increase. Projected increases in vehicular volumes pointed to the prospect of virtually all of the twenty-five kilometers between Mecca and the Plain of Arafat falling under tarmac. This would have an adverse impact on the environment and erode the spirituality of the experience. To avoid this, strategies to reduce the number of vehicles were introduced, including the introduction of vehicle permits for Saudi nationals, limiting access for small vehicles, and providing inducements for the hiring of vans and minibuses.

The result of these strategies was to see a small fall in the numbers of vehicles per pilgrim, as shown in Table 6.3.

Table 6.3   Vehicles per Pilgrim to Mecca, 1970–1984

Year	Number of Vehicles
1970	.046
1971	.052
1972	.050
1973	.061
1974	.055
1975	.058
1976	.077
1977	.071
1978	.073
1979	.055
1980	.044
1981	.049
1982	.051
1983	.051
1984	.068

Source: A. al-Yafi, *Management of Hajj Mobility Systems: A Logistical Perspective.* (Amsterdam: Johannes Enschede, 1993).

From a peak in the mid- to late 1970s, the number appeared to be stabilizing between .050 and .070 vehicles per person.

One result of both the problem of vehicle increase and the responses by the *haj* authorities to it has been a certain stylization of the rituals associated with the *haj*.[19] The fact that this has occurred without any great reaction on the part of the pilgrims suggests that pragmatic developments of this sort can also be introduced in Jerusalem.

The example of Mecca illustrates both the problems and the possible responses associated with rapidly rising pilgrim flows. The congestion, environmental pollution, and erosion of the religious ambience are problems that will be faced by Jerusalem following a permanent status agreement. The solutions introduced by the Mecca authorities, such as quotas, restrictions on small vehicles, and the alteration of traditional rituals, may be relevant to the planning of a coordinated system in Jerusalem.

If we now turn back to Jerusalem, we can see a similar pattern of rapid growth developing, if not in a more acute version. One methodological drawback in dealing with the Jerusalem case is that, unlike Mecca, where most visitors are pilgrims, in Jerusalem it is virtually impossible to distinguish statistics relating to general tourist traffic from that of pilgrim traffic. The figures for tourist traffic up to 1999 can be seen in Table 6.4.

**Table 6.4   Guests and Overnight Stays in Tourist Hotels in Jerusalem,
1980–1999**

| Year | Guests (thousands) | | | Overnight Stays (thousands) | | |
	Total	Tourists	Israelis	Total	Tourists	Israelis
1980	629.8	542.6	87.2	2,302.0	2,113.8	188.2
1984	629.0	509.3	119.7	2,317.2	2,050.5	266.7
1985	715.5	575.2	140.3	2,631.4	2,332.7	298.7
1986	663.1	434.0	229.1	2,183.7	1,719.0	464.7
1987	852.3	625.3	227.0	2,922.7	2,460.0	462.7
1988	655.2	450.9	204.3	2,304.5	1,819.3	485.2
1989	661.9	456.8	205.1	2,310.0	1,825.9	484.1
1990	650.4	429.6	220.8	2,209.1	1,700.0	509.1
1991	566.6	314.6	252.0	1,873.2	1,298.6	574.6
1992	860.0	645.0	215.0	2,899.5	2,471.6	427.9
1993	883.5	671.1	212.4	2,916.0	2,538.5	377.5
1994	938.6	701.9	236.7	2,898.2	2,476.9	421.3
1995	1,057.0	810.6	246.4	3,300.2	2,875.7	424.5
1996	969.4	716.4	253.0	3,011.6	2,559.3	452.2
1997	910.6	620.7	289.9	2,701.6	2,204.6	497.1
1998	969.6	631.4	338.2	2,779.0	2,203.9	575.1
1999	1,200.3	841.6	358.6	3,281.2	2,707.7	573.5

Source: M. Choshen and N. Shahar, eds., *Statistical Yearbook of Jerusalem* (Jerusalem: Jerusalem Institute for Israel Studies, 1999), 316.

Projections as to future growth are entirely speculative, dependent both on local and regional developments. It is safe to say that the greater the peace and stability, the greater will be the tourist flows. There are three scenarios over the next ten years to consider (see Table 6.5). One would be a situation of continued political stalemate. In this situation the current trends indicate visiting rates hovering around the 1 million guests per annum mark. Overnight stays would be at around 3 million to 3.2 million per annum. A second scenario is one of greater regional cooperation in tourism (with Jordan and Egypt) but short of a permanent status agreement or a

Table 6.5   Projected Total Guests and Overnight Stays by Scenario (in millions)

	Total Guests	Overnight Stays
Scenario 1 (stalemate)	1	3–3.2
Scenario 2 (regional cooperation)	1.3	4
Scenario 3 (permanent status agreement)	1.75–2	5

comprehensive peace that would allow guests from Arab and Islamic countries to visit. In this scenario, visiting rates would be around 1.3 million guests per annum and up to 4 million overnight stays per annum. A third scenario is one in which there is a permanent status agreement and comprehensive peace settlement with all parties. Here rates would be around 1.75 million to 2 million guests per annum with up to 5 million overnight stays per annum.

Preparation for the effects of this kind of influx on the Old City and the holy places is a complex, multilayered process. There are two sets of important issues that will need to be addressed in an interrelated fashion. The first set deals with questions of a more religious nature. Unlike the Bethlehem 2000 festivities, preparation and planning have to take into account not just one religion but three religions. Clearly, this will have a bearing on numbers, as already highlighted previously. But, as important, there are a diversity of practices, rituals, and sensitivities to cater to. The provision of services, such as accommodations, food, and access times, will need to be differentiated to take into account the different requirements of the religious groups. Moreover, while there are clearly peak periods such as Id al-Fitr, Easter, and Yom Kippur in the religious year, there is also a constant flow and requirement for access throughout the year. This pattern not only creates congestion at peak periods, it makes maintenance, repairs and infrastructural development difficult, as there are no extended quiet periods. Finally, some festivities follow a lunar calendar whereas others a solar one, with the result that there are frequent occasions where festivities clash and overlap. This already causes congestion, dramatic swings in employment opportunities, and strains on service provision. Following a permanent status agreement (Scenario 3 above) with much greater numbers to deal with, the overlapping of festivities is quite likely to lead to shortages of accommodations, water, food, medical attention, public space for congregating, and thus lead to interfaith disturbances.

The second set of issues constitute broader planning issues. First, an influx of visitors to Jerusalem of this size and duration is not for a single event, such as those made for Bethlehem 2000. It is an ongoing, cumulative process that requires great investment in training, infrastructure, and public relations. The period of time under consideration is indefinite. The phenomenon of congestion already exists under current circumstances and can only get worse if no steps are taken to avoid it. The main cause of congestion, clearly, is the large number of visitors. But congestion is made worse by the concentration of holy sites into a very small area, mostly in the Old City or its immediate surroundings. Indeed, the structure of the Old City—with its narrow winding streets—makes it unsuitable for vehicular traffic. This makes the transportation and mobility of pilgrims slow and cumbersome. Coach and car parks are required in the vicinity of the Old City, using up valuable commercial and recreational land. The topography of the area also renders it unsuitable for mass transport systems such as trams and trains. Hence, there is a reliance on cars, taxis, and coaches to access the holy sites, creating a greater need for roads and car parks.

One needs to bear in mind that Jerusalem is a relatively small city by Middle Eastern and global standards, less than 1 million people, in contrast to Cairo (more than 10 million), Damascus (more than 2.5 million), Istanbul (more than 5 million), and Tehran (more than 10 million). The capacity to absorb fluctuations in pilgrims on the scale projected is limited. The possibility of dispersal throughout the city is also limited, and the impact of 1 million visitors per annum on a city of less than 1 million will have great social costs. The alternative will be to construct tourist villages and zones that may diminish the attractiveness of the city as a pilgrim center. These planning considerations have political implications. An example of what those might be can be seen in the debate around the management of visitors to the Holy Sepulchre for the millennium celebrations and the discussions over the absorptive capacity of the Haram ash-Sharif.

The Holy Sepulchre is a good example of how pragmatic considerations can create a viable working system. Without denying the existence of bitter, long-standing disputes between the various Christian sects that share the holy place, as outlined in Chapter 5, their agreement to abide by the Status Quo arrangements has allowed the continued access to the building to all Christian denominations and to non-Christians. As a result, it plays a central part in any Christian pilgrims' tour to the Holy Land.

Media reports and the interests of political groupings and states often play up the outstanding disagreements, but taken as a whole and in the context of historical rivalries dating back more than 1,000 years, the cooperation is quite remarkable. For example, there is agreement on the times of religious services, the use of areas of the buildings, the procedure by which repairs are identified and action taken, and on the payment of routine maintenance. Disputes center on issues of status, precedence, and the payment of ad hoc repair work. To a very great extent, as we have seen in Chapter 5, such disputes are fueled by the insecurities of the religious hierarchies of the different churches in a political environment of great instability and change. The fact that a cooperative framework is possible despite the unsettled nature of power relations in the region suggests that in a post–permanent status agreement period, the prospects of reasoned dialogue and coordination over the supervision of the holy places and of access to them is good.

The planned celebrations leading up to and after the year 2000 brought, as one might expect, many tensions to the surface. The chief one that, on one hand, exacerbated church divisions, and, on the other hand, ultimately brought unity to the three main patriarchates, was the Israeli government's proposal to open a new door in the Holy Sepulchre. In preparing for the expected influx of pilgrims for the millennium year, estimated to be between 4 million and 6 million, the Israeli government wished to open an alternative exit to ease the flow of pilgrims to, inside, and away from the Holy Sepulchre.[20] The existing two-way system where pilgrims entered via the main door, circumambulated the interior, and exited by the same door as they entered may be, they argued, sufficient for current flows. But for the estimated flows for the millennium year, this arrangement would cause serious congestion at the entrance and in the streets leading to the Holy Sepulchre during the peak periods of the celebrations. The Israeli Ministry of Tourism concluded that the Holy Sepulchre did not have the capacity to absorb the numbers expected to come. If it would be open twelve hours a day and each person spent between three and four minutes only in the interior, only 600,000 to 800,000 pilgrims could enter over the course of a year.[21] In addition, the Israeli government sought to avoid any disturbance. As self-appointed guardians of public order in the Old City, it wished to ensure that there would be no causes for panic and crowd stampedes, as the political repercussions would be serious and diminish its status in the eyes of its Western supporters. For the Israeli government, therefore, the stakes were high and a second exit was of critical importance.

From the perspective of the church leaders, there were other considerations. While they agreed that a second exit would address the issue of congestion and public order, their concerns centered on three aspects of the proposal.

The first concern was the location of the exit. The Holy Sepulchre is closely demarcated with specified areas under the oversight of a given denomination. No denomination would be interested in losing a part of their holding in the building for a general purpose. In addition, the most suitable route would be through the Dayr al-Sultan chapel belonging to the Coptic Orthodox Archbishopric, whose status would be enhanced as a result, upsetting the delicate balance of the Christian Status Quo arrangements.

The second concern was the duration of time when the exit would be opened. The churches sought assurances that the exit would be a temporary exit and not be permanently available. Their view was that the year 2000 was an exceptional period that merited exceptional measures but that the Holy Sepulchre's religious and spiritual ambience would be diminished if the exit allowed it to be a thoroughfare or shortcut across the Old City.

The third concern involved the control over the exit itself. There was a great suspicion that for security and public order purposes the Israeli government would insist on controlling the exit. The churches were aware that this would remove their monopoly over control over the entrance to the Holy Sepulchre. The loss of this control would subject the Holy Sepulchre to the same security operations currently in place in the Haram ash-Sharif. Neither were the churches blind to the precedents set in the Ibrahimi Mosque discussed above.

A compromise was put forward by the Israeli government. The compromise proposed that the exit be supervised by the Coptic Orthodox Archbishop and that a contract would be signed stating that the door would close again in 2001 and only be opened once a year for the Festival of the Holy Fire.[22] However, this was also seen as too risky. Church leaders feared that it would destabilize the Status Quo balance between the churches by giving a very minor sect (3 percent of Jerusalem Christians, 400 people) greater say than in the past. As a minor sect with very few members, it would be open to the possibility of pressure by the Israeli government. Additionally, the compromise proposed that the Israeli government would retain the keys of the exit. This was completely unacceptable to all the churches. With the disclosures of the extent of Israeli government involvement in the St. John's Hospice incident, the prospect of allowing it a foothold in the Christian primary shrine in the Old City was unthinkable. Moreover, there was a political angle. Traditionally the keys of the Holy Sepulchre are held by two venerable Jerusalem Muslim families. In the current political circumstances, this has the symbolism of including the Holy Sepulchre in the areas seen by Palestinians as their patrimony. To surrender the Palestinian monopoly of the site to the Israeli government in the period leading up to the permanent status negotiations would be seen as a great betrayal and fatally undermine the role of Christians in Palestinian society.

Failing to come to an agreement with the churches over a second entrance, the Israeli government decided to impose its own solution by controlling the numbers allowed into the Holy Sepulchre.[23] What this debate and dispute shows, then, is that Israel was not trusted to act in the wider public interest or to be the final arbitrator of disagreements over the management of the Christian Holy Places. A permanent status agreement that imposes this will be unacceptable to virtually all the non-Jewish parties and is very unlikely to work even in the short term.

Turning to the Haram ash-Sharif, one can see that a central problem facing its administration following a permanent status agreement is similar to that of the Holy Sepulchre: the logistics of managing pilgrim flows. It is clear that the main new influx of pilgrims will be from the Islamic world as well as from the Middle East. Therefore, there will be a great increase in visitors to the compound over the course of each year. There are no available projections of exact numbers, but unofficial estimates run at double the current rates.

Clearly, at some peak periods there will be a much greater number of pilgrims than at others, such as Layla al-Qadr and Id al-Fitr. The greatest number is expected after the *haj* in Mecca, when pilgrims will want to take the opportunity of being in the region to visit the al-Aqsa Mosque at the same time. This will particularly be the case in the first ten years after a permanent status agreement due to the curiosity factor of a Muslim holy place being under occupation for thirty years. With the opening of Gaza International Airport and the possibility of unimpeded tourist traffic to Jerusalem, the journey from Jeddah and Mecca to Jerusalem will take half a day at the most.

As already mentioned, projections for the *haj* pilgrimage in 2005 are in the region of 3.7 million pilgrims. If only 10 percent decide to visit Jerusalem after the *haj*, which is a conservative estimate, this will mean an increase of 370,000 pilgrims per annum, at least. This figure translates into approximately 30 percent of the projected annual total arriving in Jerusalem but, in this case, over a very short period. Indeed, it is also approximately 20 percent of the total projected population of Jerusalem. There are clearly serious challenges here in the general terms of providing sufficient accommodations, transportation, food and water, and emergency and health services. Yet what concerns us in this chapter is how this impinges upon the use of sacred space and the impact it will have on the other religious communities and the life of the Old City.

The overriding problem will clearly be that of space. The courtyard of the Haram ash-Sharif and the recently refurbished Solomon's Stables underneath the courtyard, now known as the al-Marwani Mosque, can accommodate approximately 300,000 pilgrims.[24] The occasions of full capacity are mainly at the Friday prayers during Ramadan and at Layla al-Qadr, and entry and exit can take up to two hours. It is fortunate that the Haram courtyard has many gates that ease the congestion, but this was not the case with the al-Marwani Mosque below the courtyard. Here there was only one entrance and exit—up a narrow single-file staircase. There were no other means of exit, and the public safety risks of a large number of people in this confined space were too terrible to contemplate. Therefore, a new entrance was constructed, and it was this work that led to the visit of Israeli politician Ariel Sharon to the Haram courtyard and, which in turn, provoked the second Palestinian intifada in October 2000.

To accommodate a greater number of pilgrims at more regular intervals increases the risks not only of panic and stampedes in holy sites like the al-Marwani Mosque and in the Haram courtyard but also of conflict with other religious communities in the surrounding streets of the Old City. Such risks are accentuated, for example, by the Muslim ritual of prayer that permits a worshipper to delineate a space as holy, normally through the use of a prayer rug. So long as the person is facing in the right *qibla* (direction of prayer), he or she is permitted to participate in the collective prayer. It is not an unusual sight even now in Jerusalem to see groups of worshippers in parks beside the Old City walls lined up facing Mecca and joining in the prayer conducted in the Haram, the service being available on the radio. In addition, Muslims believe the whole of Jerusalem is holy (in classical Arabic it is referred to as the House of Holiness, *bayt al-maqdis*) and not just the Haram area. Muslims feel entitled to pray anywhere in the city.

With the likelihood of between 250,000 and 370,000 extra Muslim pilgrims coming to the city, one can envisage a situation where the streets around the Old City are clogged with worshippers praying. These kinds of numbers raise the possibility of intercommunal strife, particularly on days when there is an overlap with the festivities of other religions. One can refer to the Western Wall incident of 1929 (see Chapter 4). Here the increase in use of the alleyway beside the wall by Jewish worshippers interfered with the traditions of the local residents, leading to mutual provocations and finally rioting. A comparable situation could arise at the end of the *haj* when a sudden influx of Muslim pilgrims forces prayers to be conducted in the streets around the city. Visitors may not be aware of the sensitivities or practices of Jewish or Christian worshippers, or the latter may become disturbed by the interruption of their normal routes through the Old City and clashes ensue.

What both these case studies indicate is that, following a permanent status agreement, there will a great need for close cooperation between the religious leadership of the three faiths and those who will be given planning responsibilities in the wake of the agreement. It is clear that some kind of holy place management body will need to be set up and that it should consider at least four issues to meet the challenges highlighted by the case studies. The first is the introduction of quotas. This is an increasingly common formula for sites under people pressure. A good example would be the limits placed on access to a city such as Venice where visitors have to book well in advance their intended days of sightseeing. Because Jerusalem is a holy city, restrictions would have to be dealt with sensitively and there are political implications involved in setting quotas. However, Mecca serves as a useful precedent. Here quotas for residents and nonresidents alike have been imposed, and countries are allocated quotas in relation to their total population. In Jerusalem, limits will also have to be made on the frequency of visits at peak festival occasions. A second issue concerns the need to allocate access times to the Old City to different religious communities and pilgrim groups due to the close proximity of holy sites to each other. For example, Christian tour groups could be given priority to the Old City on Sunday, Jews on Saturday, and Muslims on Friday. The remaining days of the week should be distributed according to a timetable reflecting pilgrim numbers and the occurrence of festivities. The organization of this is complex and politically highly charged, but it seems unavoidable if a harmonious ambience is to be achieved.

A third issue relates to the staging and timing of festivities. As a city for three religions, the possibility of increased congestion at times when festivities coincide points to the need for negotiation over timing and location of festivities. Where possible, festivities would need to be staged to allow for a moderate flow of pilgrims over a longer period. A fourth issue would be to consider the creation of alternative sites. Due to the concentration of holy sites in and around the Old City, it will be important to disperse the pilgrim flows and redirect them to alternative sites further afield in order to carry out religious activity. This can be done either by enhancing the status of minor sites or by constructing prayer gardens and parks in and around the city for devotional activities.[25]

Before embarking on a discussion of what elements are needed to construct a workable framework of administration in the Holy City, we should consider the kinds of issues that are of concern to the religious communities. The most important seem to be those having to do with access to shared sites such as the Western Wall/al-Buraq, and the Haram ash-Sharif/Temple Mount. Questions that need to be addressed would include:

- How does one provide access to other faiths without infringing upon the practice and rituals of one's own?
- How are the parties concerned to deal with claims for restitution and reparation, such as the destruction of the mosques and *zawiya* in the Magharib quarter in 1967, or the Hurva synagogue between 1948 and 1967?
- What will be the relationship between the religious structures administering the holy places and the state authorities put into place after a permanent status agreement?
- Which buildings and institutions are liable for taxation?
- Who is responsible for public order? What health and safety regulations can be applied?

Toward a Negotiating Framework for the Old City

In light of the above considerations, what would a sustainable agreement for the Old City look like? My preferred outcome of the permanent status negotiations is one that would largely be based upon international legality: the adoption of UN Security Council Resolution 242 and the withdrawal of Israeli forces to the 1967 borders with minor modifications. This would entail the Old City becoming part of the new Palestinian state with Jerusalem as its capital. However, this is not a realistic outcome for the foreseeable future. It would be, in the first place, totally unacceptable at present to the vast majority of the Israeli population because it would not take into account their attachment to the Jewish holy places and the historic Jewish Quarter. Second, but more important, in terms of our previous discussion, it would also not recognize some of the irrevocable changes that have taken place since 1967 or be concomitant with the need to establish a sustainable framework that recognized the challenges of the future. Resolution 242 in itself was essentially a return to the cease-fire lines of 1949 that were not by any means the ideal division of the city. Reifying those lines and divisions in a permanent status agreement would not necessarily create a harmonious environment for the Holy City nor serve the best interests of the religious communities and the inhabitants of the city. A fixation on past borders will not help to establish a long-term agreement. Thus, a framework based upon international legitimacy and a sustainable future would need to not only recognize legitimate Palestinian demands for sovereignty in East Jerusalem and the Old City but also accommodate a changed and changing situation.

Despite its final collapse and the revocation of the Israeli government proposals by the incumbent Israeli prime minister, Ariel Sharon, the Camp David summit may yet prove to be an important breakthrough. Detailed discussion on the most difficult issue was conducted for the first time by Israeli prime minister Ehud Barak: the repatriation of Palestinian refugees, the Israeli withdrawal from all settlements in the Gaza Strip and some from the West Bank, the exchange of territory and, finally, the sharing of Jerusalem. As the former Israeli deputy mayor of Jerusalem, Meron Benvenisti, writing in the centrist Tel Aviv daily *Ha'aretz* put it: "A taboo has been broken and Israel has participated in talks on Jerusalem that were focused on a partition of the city, even if the word 'partition' was not explicitly used. These two facts have created an irreversible situation."[26]

All analyses after the event of the summit agree that, together with the refugee issue, the issue of Jerusalem was the final stumbling block in the negotiations between Israeli and Palestinian teams. While the gap had been narrowed on most of the other issues, there was little movement on either the refugee issue or the Jerusalem issue. The Israeli proposals comprised two main elements. The Israelis would relinquish control over the Palestinian-dominated suburbs of the city to the PNA and devolve administration in the central areas of East Jerusalem to Palestinian bodies. In exchange, Israel would retain overall sovereignty and security control over East Jerusalem including the Old City.

From the Israeli perspective, this should have been enough to entice Arafat to sign an agreement. The Israelis had never conceded so much. However, for the Palestinians what was being offered was not much more than what the Palestinians already have. It was certainly not enough for them to countenance the surrender of their claims to sovereignty over part of the city. Since 1967, when Israel occupied East Jerusalem, the neglect of the Palestinian residential areas by both the Israeli Jerusalem Municipality of and the central government led to the virtual absence of basic services, infrastructure development, and welfare programs.[27] Palestinian and foreign charitable associations, religious organizations, the PLO, and the Jordanian government attempted to fill the vacuum left by the Israeli state. In these areas, the only element of the Israeli state that is visible is the restrictive planning laws and the security forces. The rest of what has been termed the "partial annexation" of East Jerusalem by Israel continues.[28]

For example, Israeli concessions did not take into account that Palestinians already had extensive autonomy in many aspects of life in Jerusalem. As we have seen in previous chapters, the Muslim and Christian holy places and significant parts of the Old City are owned and administered by the churches or an Islamic foundation, the Awqaf Administration; the education system and curricula in Palestinian schools in Jerusalem is almost identical to that in the rest of the areas under Palestinian jurisdiction; the water supplied to the northern suburbs is piped by the Palestinian Ramallah Water Undertaking; power in all Palestinian areas is supplied by the Palestinian-owned East Jerusalem Electricity Company; and informally, but with the connivance of the Israeli Army, Palestinian security and policing services operate widely in Palestinian areas.

Israeli nationality was not imposed upon Palestinian Jerusalemites as it was in other annexed areas in the Galilee and the Little Triangle; the persistent boycott of Israeli institutions and municipal elections have led to a network of representative bodies such as the PLO-run Orient House, professional organizations such as the Jerusalem Chamber of Commerce and the Awqaf Administration and church leadership, and a myriad of smaller research and social institutions bypassing the Israeli Knesset and municipal council. Finally, East Jerusalem has been exempted from a whole raft of Israeli laws, ranging from health and safety regulations to labor laws to those concerned with the registration of businesses.

From the Palestinian perspective, therefore, Israeli concessions were based on the illusion and rhetoric of a full and complete Israeli sovereignty over East Jerusalem when that sovereignty did not exist in reality. On top of these considerations was the question of international legality. The Oslo Accords, signed in September 1993, upon which the Camp David summit was based, contain contradictions over the legal basis of the negotiations over Jerusalem. On the one hand, the agreements are derived from UN Security Council Resolution 242, which states that Israel should withdraw from territories occupied in 1967, that is, East Jerusalem. While on the other hand, the Permanent Status Issues identified by the accords refer to Jerusalem, and not simply East Jerusalem, implying that Palestinian claims to West Jerusalem were also open for discussion. From this perspective, the Palestinian position of relinquishing territorial claims to West Jerusalem—considering a special status to Israeli settlements in East Jerusalem and providing safe passage to the Western (Wailing) Wall and the Jewish Quarter in the Old City—was not asking the Israelis to do much more than accept UN resolutions and to go a bit beyond the existing situation.

A particular sticking point in the Camp David summit seems to have been the fate of the Old City. The Israeli proposal to partition the Old City, at least administratively, caused great dismay, not only in Palestinian Arab circles but also in the Christian communities. Such a partition would have legitimized the steady encroachments by Israel in the Old City and detached the Armenian Quarter from its religious and cultural hinterland.[29] The Camp David summit collapsed partly because it did not take into account these nuances in the Old City. The high-level horse-trading on such issues as land exchanges and the role of internal security forces could not deal with the details and sensitivities of control and authority in the narrow twisting streets of the Old City. The Israeli and U.S. tactic of offering Arafat more than he had anticipated on settlements, refugees, and border issues in order to entice him to accept overall Israeli sovereignty in Jerusalem, therefore, failed. Israeli prime minister Barak may have moved a great deal further on Jerusalem than his predecessors, but the shift was much less than it first appeared when measured against the reality on the ground.

In light of the above points, it is important to stress, however, that an Israeli objective of securing its position in Jerusalem within a framework of international legality and sustainability has considerable gains for Israel. Negotiating Jerusalem is not a zero-sum game, where Palestinian gains equal Israeli losses. The return to the 1967 borders would be the basis from which Israeli religious and some territorial claims can be recognized and accommodated. Basing its claims to Jerusalem within this framework would bring three clear and important gains.

First, Israel would no longer be responsible for the lives of the Palestinian Arab population in Jerusalem, amounting to almost one-third of the population, and increasing.[30] Once the details of this are fleshed out, it should appeal to a broad section of the Israeli Jewish population because it makes the creation of a Jewish Jerusalem a realistic goal, when under the current objectives it clearly is not.

Second, an agreement with Palestinians that takes into account the international legal position on Jerusalem would cement the whole package of agreements. In addition, by agreeing to a withdrawal from East Jerusalem in principle, Israel would strengthen its position on other issues such as water, security, refugees, and settlements.

Third, an agreement on Jerusalem based upon international legality would also finally give Israel the international recognition of its part of Jerusalem as being the capital city of Israel. More than any other issue it would reconcile Israel's neighbors to its presence and open the doors of recognition in the Islamic and Arab world.

The question to ask in the aftermath of the Camp David summit and the second Palestinian intifada is whether the Palestinians have sufficient room for maneuvering to allow them to reengage realistically with the Israelis in the peace negotiations and simultaneously to retain the Palestinian national consensus on Jerusalem. A national Palestinian consensus on Jerusalem has crystallized around the following components:

1. Jerusalem will be the capital for both Palestinian and Israeli sovereign states within the pre-1967 internationally recognized borders and to be administered by two municipal bodies, one Palestinian and the other Israeli.
2. The two municipalities will cooperate with regard to decisionmaking, provision of municipal services, and infrastructure projects.
3. There will be an equitable allocation of land use and respect for property rights, freedom of worship, and access to Jewish, Islamic, and Christian holy sites and geographic contiguity of Palestinian-held areas of Jerusalem with the north and south West Bank.
4. Jerusalem will be one city, open to all to circulate, live, and work.

A Palestinian negotiating agenda designed to achieve these goals and to obtain Israeli acceptance needs to be framed by two overarching principles: compatibility and reciprocity. Compatibility is straightforward and should not meet too many Israeli objections. It refers to the importance of ensuring that, whatever is agreed on, the status of Jerusalem should be both consistent and compatible with positions adopted in the other permanent status negotiations. Border permeability, employment and residency rights, economic and fiscal arrangements, and security and policing cooperation should all be compatible with other arrangements negotiated between Israel and the rest of Palestine. It would be both pointless and unworkable, for example, to agree to "hard," or impermeable, borders between most of the West Bank and Israel but have "soft," or permeable, borders for the areas between East Jerusalem and Israel. Irredentists on both sides could simply enter each other's territory via Jerusalem. This requirement for compatibility, however, need not exclude some special arrangements for Jerusalem as a result of its unique status of the site of holy places for three religions and the site of two national capitals. Thus, questions over access to holy places, taxation on religious property, and the operations of embassies will need to reflect this status.

The issue of reciprocity is more contentious but provides greater flexibility than it initially appears. The ceding of land, restitution claims, access, and jurisdiction to either side should all be in exchange for other "goods," though not necessarily the same goods. Hence, each meter of the border, each house and garden within a settlement, each municipal service and legal jurisdiction obtained, say, by the Israeli side, would be accompanied by a quid pro quo for Palestinians and vice versa. In this way the Palestinian position outlined above, which implies the acceptance of Israeli sovereignty over West Jerusalem, needs to be met by a reciprocal concession by Israel on de jure recognition of Arab East Jerusalem as the Palestinian capital. In the current political circumstances, this possibility seems remote, yet from the detailed surveys of Israeli opinion carried out by Professor Jerome Segal and his team and from recent Israeli opinion polls, such a prospect cannot be ruled out completely in the future.[31] Indeed, the degree to which the idea of a Palestinian state was formerly an anathema to Israeli public opinion and now is broadly accepted, suggests a flexibility that should not be overlooked amidst the rhetoric of politicians.

Once these principles are established, one is able to proceed to the employment of a negotiating device: that of *disaggregation*—the separating out of difficult issues or territories into smaller parts. This was used by the architects of the Oslo process. However, adopting the Oslo framework, particularly as applied to Hebron as a model for the implementation of an agreement on Jerusalem, would be detrimental to the integrity of the Old City and would not be appropriate. The introduction of zones, reflecting degrees of Israeli or Palestinian jurisdiction, such as Area A, B, and C and Hebron 1 and 2, were designed to meet Israeli security concerns. The same security imperatives do not pertain in Jerusalem. In addition, to agree to the introduction of zones such as East Jerusalem 1, 2, and 3 or Old City 1, 2, and 3 would essentially be a deferral of the issue of whose sovereignty in East Jerusalem when it is exactly that which is being negotiated. In fact, such a model would transform Jerusalem from a Permanent Status Issue into yet another stage in the interim phase.

While the Hebron model may not be the appropriate framework for Jerusalem, the device of disaggregation can still be put to good use. The negotiable goods of Jerusalem need to be broken up into their constituent parts both in terms of both geography and functions or responsibilities. The analogy here is a multilayered cake. The horizontal represents the geographic spread of the subareas of East Jerusalem; the vertical denotes the different layers or degrees of jurisdiction and control over political functions and responsibilities. The degrees of jurisdiction can be grouped around a number of core functions ranging from cultural and social affairs, at one end of the spectrum, through the provision of municipal services (such as local planning, road maintenance, waste disposal, tourist management), to the provision of central government services (including housing, public works, fiscal and trade regulation). During the negotiations, the Palestinian objective would be to create as many areas within Jerusalem where the jurisdictions are similar so that at some point a vertical slice can be made and a distinct Palestinian area delineated.

An essential element in the feasibility of this device is to incorporate a second negotiating device, that of phasing. This would make the whole process of withdrawal to the 1967 borders more acceptable to the Israeli side. The device of phasing has precedents, not only in the Oslo process but also in the 1994 Israel-Jordan Peace Treaty. It can take two forms: simple phasing and leaseback. Simple phasing is an agreement that sovereignty or jurisdictions will be ceded in stages to one party over an agreed period of time. Leaseback is the ceding of sovereignty and jurisdiction from the outset, but the land is retained by lease for a given period.[32] Thus, certain areas, such as the settlements, would be under Palestinian sovereignty but leased by the Israeli government for a given period, during which time Palestinian responsibilities would be highly limited.

How would this work out in practice for the Old City? There are two possible scenarios depending upon the extent to which the principle of reciprocity has been employed. The first scenario is one where the principle is accepted and widely employed. In this scenario, the Palestinian side would be happy to cede sovereignty over to the Jewish Quarter in exchange for some other territorial or political goods. One can envisage the possibility of a corridor skirting from the Jewish Quarter around the Old City walls to the Jaffa Gate or even to a bridge across the valley to the Hebron Road. In addition, this scenario would include guarantees of freedom of worship at the Western Wall, joint ownership of the wall itself, and compensation for expropriated properties in the extended Jewish Quarter. Finally, Jewish representatives would sit on an Old City administrative council whose remit would include the coordination of religious festivities, pilgrimage, and a number of submunicipal functions. With respect to the concerns of the Vatican and the Christian patriarchates, the Status Quo would be upheld, and a standing forum for the arbitration of disputes would be established under international supervision. Representatives from the denominations would sit on the Old City administrative council on a rotating basis.

In the second scenario, the principle of reciprocity is not fully employed, and the final agreement both closely resembles the division of the city in 1967 yet is only acceptable to the Israeli side if there is a strong measure of extraterritorialization of the Jewish Quarter. Here the territorial extent will be much the same as in the first scenario with the introduction of safe passages, but the relationship to the rest of the Old City will be much more that of an enclave than that of a neighboring district. Participation in general Old City issues would be more piecemeal and ad hoc, and representation on an Old City administrative council would be contingent upon other bilateral arrangements established between the Israeli and Palestinian states in other areas. Failing the acceptance of the principle of reciprocity, it is impossible to envisage a sustainable agreement for the Old City other than that which requires some form of internationalization of either the holy places or of the whole Old City.

Conclusion

Due to the complexity of the intercommunal and political dynamics of the Old City, the negotiations over the future of Jerusalem will be equally complex. The changes that have taken place since 1967 have led to a completely new city so that a return to the status quo ante is neither likely nor possible. To some extent the Oslo Accords are an indication of a softening of the Israeli position of Jerusalem as the "eternal, undivided capital" of Israel. This does not mean that the Jewish presence has weakened. This book has illustrated many ways in which it has become much stronger in the Old City. Nevertheless, the Palestinian Muslim community, although much diminished from its heyday in the nineteenth-century period, has begun to show signs of revival and self-assertion. Similarly the church leadership has passed through a long period of torn loyalties and fragmentation and has more recently made clear its disaffection with the Israeli vision of Jerusalem.

There is no doubt that peace will occur only when tough decisions concerning military security and issues of resource control are resolved. Yet as the Camp David summit in July 2000 showed, even when most of these were almost in place, the passions aroused by the issue of sovereignty over the Old City led to the collapse of the totality of all the agreements. A negotiated Israeli-Palestinian peace will need to involve the religious and historical concerns surrounding the holy sites. This, in turn, will mean involving the religious leaderships of all the communities. Although it has been tried and failed in the past, an interreligious council of some kind that can have input into the negotiating process may be the sine qua non for peace in Jerusalem.

Notes

1. See a detailed discussion of the use of the term *hegemony* as an analytical tool in I. Lustick, *Unsettled States and Disputed Lands: Britain and Ireland, France and Algeria, Israel and the West Bank–Gaza* (Ithaca, N.Y.: Cornell University Press, 1993), 26–51. See the application of this framework to Jerusalem in his "Reinventing Jerusalem," *Foreign Policy*, no. 93 (winter 1993–1994).

2. For a study of contemporary Israeli attachment to the Old City, see J. Segal et al., eds., *Negotiating Jerusalem* (Albany: State University of New York Press, 2000), 26–30. Although the majority of Israelis oppose any Palestinian sovereignty over the Old City, the attachment to the Jewish Quarter and the Temple Mount/Haram ash-Sharif is still stronger than over other areas in the Old City. The surveys of Segal and his colleagues do not deal with the Jewish settlements in the Muslim and Christian quarters specifically.

3. Useful references for this section can be found in R. Lapidot and M. Hirsch, *The Jerusalem Question and Its Resolution: Selected Documents* (Dordrecht, Netherlands: Kluwer Academic Publishers, 1994); and M. Hirsch, B. Housen-Couriel, and R. Lapidot, *Whither Jerusalem: Proposals and Positions Concerning the Future of Jerusalem* (The Hague: Martinus Nijhoff Publishers, 1995).

4. Israel supported this approach and made a formal proposal in May 1950. See Lapidot and Hirsch, *The Jerusalem Question*, 135–144.

5. See, for example, proposals by Professor Walid Khalidi, Dr. Shmuel Bercovitz, and Lord Hugh Caradon, cited in Hirsch, Housen-Couriel, and Lapidot, *Whither Jerusalem*, 74, 81, 98. The full version of Khalidi's proposal can be found in W. Khalidi, "Thinking the Unthinkable: A Sovereign Palestinian State," *Foreign Affairs*, no. 56 (1978).

6. See proposals by Dr. Raphael Benkler, Ya'aov Hazan, Professor Saul Cohen, and Professor Walid Khalidi, cited in Hirsch, Housen-Couriel, and Lapidot, *Whither Jerusalem*, 65, 82, 88, 98.

7. This was much opposed by the Palestinian side, particularly by the Armenian Patriarchate. See Chapter 4 and also "Patriarchs Demand Old City Stay United," *Ha'aretz*, 20 July 2000.

8. A. Abu Odeh, "Two Capitals in an Undivided Jerusalem," *Foreign Affairs* (spring 1992).

9. Para. 11 of the plan states: "In recognition of the special status and significance of the Old City area (see maps) or members of the Christian, Jewish and Muslim faiths, the parties agree to grant this area a special status."

10. Para. 12 of the plan.

11. For details on these policies, see M. Dumper, *Islam and Israel, Muslim Religious Endowments and the Jewish* State (Washington, D.C.: Institute for Palestine Studies, 1994), chapters 2 and 3. See also A. R. Peled, "The Crystallization of an Israeli Policy Towards Muslim and Christian Holy Places, 1948–1955," *Muslim World* 84, nos. 1–2 (January–April 1994): 108–109.

12. *Jerusalem Post,* 28 November 1967, and 1 October 1968, cited in A. Lesch, *Israel's Occupation of the West Bank: The First Two Years* (Santa Monica, Calif.: RAND Advanced Research Project Agency, 1970), 39. See also E. Cohen, *Human Rights in the Israeli-Occupied Territories, 1967–1982* (Manchester, England: Manchester University Press, 1985), 215.

13. *Jerusalem Post,* 13 October 1968, cited in A. Lesch, *Israel's Occupation of the West Bank,* 44. See also Cohen, *Human Rights,* 215.

14. Cohen, *Human Rights,* 215.

15. A. Lesch, *Political Perceptions of the Palestinians on the West Bank and Gaza Strip* (Washington D.C.: The Middle East Institute, 1980), Special Study No. 3, 80. See also Cohen, *Human Rights,* 215–216.

16. Lesch, *Political Perceptions,* 16.

17. "Protocol Concerning the Redeployment in Hebron," 15 January 1997, para. 6a.

18. During the second Palestinian intifada beginning in 2000, Rachel's Tomb was transformed into a military bunker and has become a focal point for clashes between Palestinians and Israelis.

19. For example, the individualized slaughter of a sheep and its consumption on the Id al-Adha has been replaced by state-regulated abattoirs and a canning factory for the distribution of products to the Muslim poor.

20. Figures taken from G. Gorenberg, "Warning! Millennium Ahead," *Jerusalem Report,* 19 February 1998, 18.

21. Ibid.

22. Interview by the author with Uri Mor, director, Ministry of Religious Affairs, Christian Division, Jerusalem, 7 February 1999.

23. R. Arnaout, "Israel to Limit Visitors in Holy Sepulchre," *Jerusalem Times,* 17 December 1999, 1; see also *Jerusalem Post,* 24 December1999, 6.

24. Issam Awad, chief architect, al-Aqsa Restoration Committee. Interview by author, Jerusalem, 4 February 1999.

25. Possible sites for enhancement include those in Azariyya (Bethany), on A-Tur, and the tombs of Nabi Daoud, Nabi Samwil, and Nabi Musa.

26. M. Benvenisti, *Ha'aretz* (Internet version), 28 July 2000.

27. This has been broadly accepted in Israeli circles and is well documented in A. Cheshin et al., eds., *Separate and Unequal: The Inside Story of Israeli Rule in East Jerusalem* (Cambridge: Harvard University Press, 1999). The authors argue that Israel has already lost the battle for Jerusalem through this official and ideologically inspired neglect. Cheshin and Melamed are former advisers on Arab affairs to the Israeli mayor of Jerusalem.

28. L. T. Rempel, "The Significance of Israel's Partial Annexation of East Jerusalem," *Middle East Journal* 51, no. 4 (autumn 1977).

29. See discussion in Chapter 5.

30. For further details of the politics of the demography of Jerusalem, see M. Dumper, *The Politics of Jerusalem Since 1967* (New York: Columbia University Press, 1997), 72–85.

31. Segal et al., eds., *Negotiating Jerusalem.*

32. See the annexes in the 1994 Israel-Jordan Peace Treaty relating to al-Baqura and al-Ghamr areas.

Bibliography

Abowd, T. "The Moroccan Quarter: A History of the Present." *Jerusalem Quarterly File*, no. 7 (winter 2000).

Abu Odeh, A. "Two Capitals in an Undivided Jerusalem." *Foreign Affairs* (spring 1992): 41.

Abu Shamseyeh, H. "Settling the Old City: The Policies of Labour and Likud." *Jerusalem Quarterly File*, no. 6 (autumn 1999).

al-Fajr (English-language weekly), 17 May 1987, 14.

Anani, Isam. Interview by author. Jerusalem, 9 February 1999.

"A Provocation with Massive Support from the Government." *News from Within*, 2 May 1990, 11.

al-'Arif, A. *Mufassal tarikh al-quds.* Jerusalem: Ma'ari Printers, 1986.

Arnaout, R. "Israel to Limit Visitors in Holy Sepulchre." *Jerusalem Times*, 17 December 1999.

al-'Asali, K., ed. *Jerusalem in History.* London: Scorpion, 1989.

Awad, Issam. Interview by author. Jerusalem, 4 February 1999.

Azarya, V. *The Armenian Quarter of Jerusalem.* Berkeley and London: University of California Press, 1984.

Bakrijian, Antony. Interview by the author. Jerusalem, 3 October 1989.

Ben Arieh, Y. *Jerusalem in the 19th Century: Emergence of the New City.* Jerusalem: New York: St. Martin's Press, 1989.

———. *Jerusalem in the 19th Century: The Old City.* New York: St. Martin's Press, 1984.

Benvenisti, M. *Jerusalem: The Torn City.* Minneapolis: Israel Typeset, Ltd., and the University of Minneapolis, 1976.

Burgoyne, M. *Mamluk Jerusalem: An Architectural Study.* London: World of Islam Festival Trust, 1987.

Cheshin, A., et al., eds. *Separate and Unequal: The Inside Story of Israeli Rule in East Jerusalem.* Cambridge, Mass.: Harvard University Press, 1999.

Choshen, M., and N. Shahar, eds. *Statistical Yearbook of Jerusalem* (Jerusalem: Jerusalem Institute for Israel Studies, 1999).

"Chronology." *Journal of Palestine Studies* 22, no. 2 (winter 1991): 219.

"Chronology." *Journal of Palestine Studies* 26, no. 2 (winter 1997): 176.

Cohen, E. *Human Rights in the Israeli-Occupied Territories, 1967–1982.* Manchester: Manchester University Press, 1985.

Cohen, S. *The Politics of Planting: Israeli-Palestinian Competition for Control of Land in the Jerusalem Periphery.* Chicago: University of Chicago Press, 1993.

Colbi, S. P. "The Christian Establishment in Jerusalem." In *Jerusalem: Problems and Prospects.* Edited by J. L. Kraemer. New York: Praeger, 1980.

"Committee for al-Khanqah." *Jerusalem Times,* 6 June 1997, 2.

Cust, L G.A. *The Status Quo and the Holy Places.* Facsimile version. Jerusalem: Ariel Publishing House, 1980.

Dib, G., and F. Jabber. *Israel's Violation of Human Rights in the Occupied Territories: A Documented Report.* Beirut: Institute of Palestine Studies, 1970.

"Dispute Grows over Khaniqah [sic] Mosque Renovation." *Jerusalem Times,* 2 May 1997, 2.

Dumper, M. *Islam and Israel: Muslim Religious Endowments and the Jewish State.* Washington, D.C.: Institute for Palestine Studies, 1994.

———. "Israeli Settlement in the Old City of Jerusalem." *Journal of Palestine Studies* 21, no. 4 (summer 1992): 32–53.

———. *The Politics of Jerusalem Since 1967.* New York: Columbia University Press, 1997.

Farhi, D. "Ha-mo'atza ha-muslemit be-mizrah yerushalayim u-vi-yehuda ve-shom-ron me'az milhemet sheshet ha-yamin" (The Muslim Council in East Jerusalem and in Judea and Samaria Since the Six Day War), *Ha-mizrah He-hadash* (The New East), no. 28 (1979).

Friedland, R., and R. Hecht. "The Politics of Sacred Place: Jerusalem's Temple Mount/al-Haram al-Sharif." In *Sacred Places and Profane Spaces: Essays in the Geographics of Judaism, Christianity, and Islam.* Edited by J. Scott and P. Simpson-Housley. New York: Greenwood Press, 1991.

———. *To Rule Jerusalem.* Cambridge, England: Cambridge University Press, 1996.

Gershon, A. *Israel, the West Bank, and International Law.* London: Frank Cass, 1978.

Gold, D. *Jerusalem.* Tel Aviv: Jaffee Centre for Strategic Studies, 1995.

Gorenberg, G. "Warning! Millennium Ahead." *Jerusalem Report,* 19 February 1998.

Graham-Brown, S. "Jerusalem." *Middle East,* no. 136 (February 1986): 48.

"Greek Patriarch Campaigns to Stop Improvement in Greek-Israel Ties." *Jerusalem Post,* 16 May 1990.

Ha'aretz, 20 April 1990. Cited in *News from Within,* 2 May 1990, 2.

Halevi, Y. K. "Squeezed Out." *Jerusalem Report,* 10 July 1997, 15–16.

Halper, J. "Jewish Ethnicity in Jerusalem." In *Jerusalem: City of the Ages.* Edited by A. L. Eckhardt. New York: University Press of America, 1987.

"Haram Al-Sharif (Temple Mount) Killings, Special File, The." *Journal of Palestine Studies* 22, no. 2 (winter 1991).

Hintlian, K. *History of the Armenians in the Holy Land.* Jerusalem: Armenian Patriarchate Printing Press, 1989.

Hirsch, M., B. Housen-Couriel, and R. Lapidot, eds. *Whither Jerusalem: Proposals and Positions Concerning the Future of Jerusalem.* The Hague: Martinus Nijhoff Publishers, 1995.

Husseini, Adnan. Interview by author. Jerusalem, 6 February 1999.

Idara al-awqaf al-islamiyya al-'ama, bayan: al-awqaf al-islamiyya fi al-daf al-gharbiyya, 1967–76. Jerusalem: Da'ira al-awqaf al-islamiyya, no date.

Idara al-awqaf al-islamiyya al-'ama, bayan: Al-awqaf al-islamiyya fi al-daf al-gharbiyya, 1977–82. Jerusalem: Da'ira al-awqaf al-islamiyya, no date.

Jerusalem Post. An open letter from the president to the patriarch was published on 25 April 1990.

Kan'an, Wa'el. Interview by the author. Jerusalem, 1 February 1999.

Kark, R. *Jerusalem Neighbourhoods: Planning and By-Laws (1855–1930).* Jerusalem: Magnes Press, 1991.

Karmi, G., ed. *Jerusalem Today: What Future for the Peace Process.* Reading, England: Ithaca, 1996.

"Keeping the Balance." *Jerusalem Post.* International ed. 2 June 1990, 9.

Khalidi, W. "Thinking the Unthinkable: A Sovereign Palestinian State." *Foreign Affairs,* no. 56 (1978).

"Khanqah Mosque Dispute Resolved." *Jerusalem Times,* 27 June 1997, 2.

Khatib, R. "The Judaization of Jerusalem and Its Demographic Transformation." In *Jerusalem: The Key to World Peace.* London: Council of Europe, 1980.

Klein, M. "The Islamic Holy Places as a Political Bargaining Card (1993–1995)." *Catholic University Law Review* 45, no. 3 (spring 1996): 747, 749–750.

Lapidot, R., and M. Hirsch. *The Arab-Israeli Conflict and Its Resolution: Selected Documents.* Dordrecht, Netherlands: Kluwer Academic Publishers, 1992.

———. *The Jerusalem Question and Its Resolution: Selected Documents.* Dordrecht, Netherlands: Kluwer Academic Publishers, 1994.

Latendresse, A. *Jerusalem: Palestinian Dynamics, Resistance and Urban Change, 1967–1994.* Jerusalem: PASSIA, 1995.

Laws of the State of Israel. Vol. 21. 1966–1967.

Layish, A. "Qadis and the Shari'a Law in Israel." *Asian and African Studies* (Journal of the Israel Oriental Society) 7 (1977): 237–272.

Lesch, A. *Israel's Occupation of the West Bank: The First Two Years.* Santa Monica, Calif.: RAND Advanced Research Project Agency, 1970.

———. *Political Perceptions of the Palestinians on the West Bank and Gaza Strip.* Washington D.C.: The Middle East Institute, 1980.

Linden, G. *Church Leadership in a Political Crisis: Joint Statements from the Jerusalem Heads of Churches, 1988–1992.* Uppsala: Swedish Institute for Missionary Research, 1994.

Lustick, I. "Has Israel Annexed Jerusalem?" *Middle East Policy* 5, no. 1 (January 1997).

———. "Reinventing Jerusalem." *Foreign Policy,* no. 93 (winter 1993–1994).

———. *Unsettled States and Disputed Lands: Britain and Ireland, France and Algeria, Israel and the West Bank–Gaza.* Ithaca, N.Y.: Cornell University Press, 1993.

Meinardus, O. "The Copts in Jerusalem and the Question of the Holy Places." In *The Christian Heritage in the Holy Land.* Edited by A. O'Mahoney, G. Gunner, and K. Hintlian. London: Scorpion Cavendish, 1995.

"Memorandum of Their Beatitudes the Patriarchs and of the Heads of the Christian Communities in Jerusalem on the Significance of Jerusalem for Christians." In Palestinian Academic Society for the Study of International Affairs, *Documents on Jerusalem.* Jerusalem: PASSIA, 1996.

Mor, Uri. Interview by author. Jerusalem, 7 February 1999.

Musallem, S. *The Struggle for Jerusalem.* Jerusalem: PASSIA, 1996.

Nyrop, R. *Israel: A Country Study.* Washington, D.C.: The American University, 1979.

"Old City Settlers Funded by Ministry." *Jerusalem Post,* 23 April 1990.

Offenbacher, E. "Prayer on the Temple Mount." *Jerusalem Quarterly File,* no. 36 (summer 1985).

O'Mahoney, A. "Church, State, and the Christian Communities and the Holy Places of Palestine." In *Christians in the Holy Land.* Edited by M. Prior and W. Taylor. London: World of Islam Festival Trust, 1994.

Palestine Report. E-mail ed., 2 October 1996, 6.

Papastathis, C. K. "A New Status for Jerusalem: An Eastern Orthodox Viewpoint." *Catholic University Law Review* 45, no. 3 (spring 1996): 730–731.

"Patriarchs Demand Old City Stay United." *Ha'aretz,* 20 July 2000.

Peled, A. R. "The Crystallization of an Israeli Policy Towards Muslim and Christian Holy Places, 1948–1955." *Muslim World* 84, nos. 1–2 (January–April 1994): 108–109.

Peters, F. E. *Jerusalem.* Princeton: Princeton University Press, 1985.

———. *Jerusalem and Mecca: A Typology of Holy City in the Near East.* New York: New York University Press, 1986.

Plascov, A. *The Palestinian Refugees in Jordan, 1948–1957.* London: Frank Cass, 1981.

Prior, M., and W. Taylor, eds. *Christians in the Holy Land.* London: World of Islam Festival Trust, 1994.

Qafity, S. Interviewed in the *Jerusalem Times,* 4 August 1998.

Qupti, Mazen. Interview by the author. Jerusalem, 3 February 1999.

Ramon, A. "The Christian Element and the Jerusalem Question." *Background Papers for Policy Papers,* No. 4. Unofficially translated by the Society of St. Ives. The Jerusalem Institute for Israel Affairs, 1996.

Recommendations and Resolutions of the Arab Orthodox Conference. Jerusalem, 23 October 1992.

Reiter, Y. *Islamic Institutions in Jerusalem: Palestinian Muslim Organization Under Jordanian and Israeli Rule.* The Hague: Kluwer Law International, 1997.

———. *Waqf in Jerusalem, 1948–1990* (in Hebrew). Jerusalem: Jerusalem Institute for Israel Studies, 1991.

Rempel, L. T. "The Significance of Israel's Partial Annexation of East Jerusalem." *Middle East Journal* 51, no. 4 (autumn 1977).

Report of the Commission by His Majesty's Government—with the Approval of the League of Nations to Determine the Rights and Claims of Moslems and Jews in Connection with the Western or Wailing Wall at Jerusalem. London: Her Majesty's Stationery Office, 1931.

"Riots Erupt in Old City." *Jerusalem Post,* 13 April 1990.

Ritter, C. *The Comparative Geography of Palestine and the Sinaitic Peninsula.* Edinburgh: 1866. Cited in A. L. Tibawi, *The Islamic Pious Foundations in Jerusalem: Origin, History, and Usurpation by Israel.* London: Iraqi Cultural Foundation, 1978.

Rock, A. *The Status Quo in the Holy Places.* Jerusalem: Franciscan Printing Press, 1989.

Romann, M. "The Economic Development of Jerusalem in Recent Times." In *Urban Geography of Jerusalem.* Edited by D. Amiran, A. Shachar, and I. Kimhi. Berlin: De Gruyter, 1973.

Romann, M., and A. Weingrod. *Living Together Separately: Arabs and Jews in Contemporary Jerusalem.* Princeton: Princeton University Press, 1991.

Roussos, S. "The Greek Orthodox Patriarchate and Community of Jerusalem." In *The Christian Heritage in the Holy Land.* Edited by A. O'Mahoney, G. Gunner, and K. Hintlian. London: Scorpion Cavendish, 1995.

Sabella, B. "Palestinian Christians: Realities and Hopes." Manuscript, 1998.

Safdie, M. *The Harvard Jerusalem Studio: Urban Designs for the Holy City.* London: Massachusetts Institute of Technology Press, 1986.

Schweid, Y. "The Unification of Jerusalem: The Planning Aspect." *Kivunim*, no. 35 (1987). Unofficially translated from Hebrew.

Segal, J., et al., eds. *Negotiating Jerusalem*. Albany: State University of New York Press, 2000.

Shehadi, R. *The West Bank and the Rule of Law*. New York: International Commission of Jurists and Law in the Service of Man, 1980.

Shepherd, N. *The Mayor and the Citadel: Teddy Kollek and Jerusalem*. London: Weidenfeld and Nicholson, 1987.

Shragai, N. "One House After the Other." *Ha'aretz*, 25 April 1986.

———. "Solving the Puzzle in the Old City." *Ha'aretz* (Internet version), 18 June 2000.

———. "Who Will Buy: Who Will Buy Me a House?" *Ha'aretz*, 23 April 1986. Translated from the Hebrew by Professor Israel Shahak.

Sprinzak, E. *The Ascendance of Israel's Radical Right*. Oxford: Oxford University Press, 1991.

"Statement by the Heads of Christian Communities in Jerusalem," 22 January 1988. In Middle East Council of Churches, *Perspectives*, no. 8 (July 1990).

"Statement of Solidarity with the Christian Churches in Jerusalem by the Higher Council for Islamic Waqf Affairs and Holy Sites," April 1990. In Palestinian Academic Society for the Study of International Affairs, *Documents on Jerusalem*. Jerusalem: PASSIA, 1996.

SWB (Summary of World Broadcasts), *BBC Monitoring, Middle East*, 26 September 1996, 5–6; 27 September 1996, 19.

Tahbub, Hasan. Interview by author. Jerusalem, 4 October 1988.

Tamari, S. "Jerusalem's Ottoman Modernity: The Times and Lives of Wasif Jawhariyyeh." *Jerusalem Quarterly File*, no. 9 (summer 2000): 5–27.

Tanmiya (the quarterly newsletter of the Welfare Association on Palestinian development issues) (October 1998): 1.

"Temple Mount Faithful v. Attorney-General et al." In *Catholic University Law Review* 45, no. 3 (spring 1996): 861–941.

Tibawi, A. L. *The Islamic Pious Foundations in Jerusalem: Origin, History, and Usurpation by Israel*. London: Iraqi Cultural Foundation, 1978.

Tobler, T. *Denkblatter Aus Jerusalem*. Contance: Germany, 1853.

Tsimhoni, D. *Christian Communities in Jerusalem and the West Bank Since 1948: An Historical, Social, and Political Study*. Westport, Conn.: Praeger, 1993.

Usher, G. "Fifteen Centuries and Still Counting: The Old City Armenians." *Jerusalem Quarterly File*, no. 9 (summer 2000): 37.

———. "Israel's Jerusalem Pyromania." *Middle East International*, 5 June 1998, 3–5.

"US Leaders Furious over Alleged Covert Funding." *Jerusalem Post*, 25 April 1990.

Welfare Association. *Jerusalem Old City Revitalisation Plan: Interim Summary Report*. Jerusalem, January 1999.

———. *Jerusalem Old City Revitalisation Programme: Souq al-Qattanin Study* (MMIS Management Consultants). Unpublished report. Jerusalem, November 1998.

al-Yafi, A. *Management of Hajj Mobility Systems: A Logistical Perspective*. Amsterdam: Johannes Enschede, 1993.

"Zamir Reports, The." Translated by the Israeli Government Press Office. In *Mideast Mirror*, 29 October 1990.

Zander, W. *Israel and the Holy Places of Christendom*. London: Weidenfeld and Nicolson, 1971.

Index

177

About the Book

Sacred to three traditions, the Old City of Jerusalem is the Gordian knot at the center of the Middle East conflict. This book explores how religious and political interests compete for control of this sacred space and how that competition affects the Middle East peace process.

Michael Dumper analyzes the religious dynamics in the Old City in political terms, investigating rivalries and tensions at three interrelated levels: among regional and international interests; among the Christian, Islamic, and Jewish establishments; and among sects and factions within the religions. A revealing portrait emerges of an ancient city in the context of contemporary change, central to the attainment of a lasting peace in the region.

Michael Dumper is senior lecturer in Middle East politics and director of the Graduate School of Historical, Political, and Sociological Studies, University of Exeter. His publications include *Islam and Israel: Muslim Religious Endowments and the Israeli State* and *The Politics of Jerusalem Since 1967*.